W9-ATP-657

Balzac: Fiction and Melodrama

Balzac
Fiction and Melodrama

Christopher Prendergast

Holmes and Meier Publishers, Inc
New York

First published in the United States of America 1978 by
HOLMES & MEIER PUBLISHERS, INC.
30 Irving Place, New York, N.Y. 10003

Copyright © 1978 Christopher Prendergast

ALL RIGHTS RESERVED

Prendergast, Christopher.
  Balzac: Fiction and Melodrama.
  Bibliography: P.
  Includes Index.
  1. Balzac, Honore De, 1799–1850—Criticism and interpretation.
  2. Melodrama. 1. Title. PQ2181.P68 1979 843'.7 78–11267

ISBN 0–8419–0457–X

PRINTED IN GREAT BRITAIN

Contents

Note

All references to *La Comédie humaine* are to the Pléiade edition, edited by Marcel Bouteron (11 volumes, Bibliothèque de la Pléiade, Paris 1951–65 © Editions Gallimard). Volume and page number are indicated in brackets immediately after the quotation.

Texts chiefly discussed are *La Fille aux yeux d'or, La Femme de trente ans, Béatrix, Le Père Goriot, Splendeurs et misères des courtisanes* and *La Cousine Bette.*

Acknowledgments

Parts of this book have appeared, in somewhat different forms, in the following journals: *Essays in French Literature, Modern Language Review, NOVEL: A Forum on Fiction, Forum for Modern Language Studies.* I am grateful to the respective editors for permission to reprint here. I should also like to express my thanks to all those friends and colleagues who, in a variety of ways and on a variety of matters, have helped me with information, advice and encouragement. In particular I should like to thank Will Moore, Alison Fairlie, Stephen Heath, Leslie Hill, Geoffrey Lloyd, Jonathan Nash and Tony Tanner. Their help and advice have been invaluable; naturally any misuse to which their advice may have been put is entirely my own responsibility. I should also like to thank Cerri Price and Ann Smith for their help in typing out the final draft. Finally, I should like to thank Shirley, Kate and Zoë for the patience and tolerance shown me in that last, desperate stage as I tried to meet (though in fact missed) the publisher's deadline.

I Introduction

1 The uses of melodrama

My idea of heaven is that there is no melodrama in it at all.
Ralph Emerson[1]

Il s'est rencontré, sous l'Empire et dans Paris, treize hommes également frappés du même sentiment, tous doués d'une assez grande énergie pour être fidèles à la même pensée, assez probes entre eux pour ne point se trahir, alors même que leurs intérêts se trouvaient opposés, assez profondément politiques pour dissimuler les liens sacrés qui les unissaient, assez forts pour se mettre au-dessus de toutes les lois, assez hardis pour tout entreprendre, et assez heureux pour avoir presque toujours réussi dans leurs desseins. . . . Enfin, pour que rien ne manquât à la sombre et mystérieuse poésie de cette histoire, ces treize hommes sont restés inconnus, quoique tous aient réalisé les plus bizarres idées que suggère à l'imagination la fantastique puissance faussement attribuée aux Manfred, aux Faust, aux Melmoth; et tous aujourd'-hui sont brisés, dispersés du moins. Ils sont paisiblement rentrés sous le joug des lois civiles, de même que Morgan, l'Achille des pirates, se fit, de ravageur, colon tranquille, et disposa sans remords, à la lueur du foyer domestique, de millions ramassés dans le sang, à la rouge clarté des incendies (v, 11).

This is an extract from the opening passage of the preface to *Histoire des Treize* and, strategically placed at the head of one of the earliest texts of the *Comédie humaine*, it reads like a sign, neon-lit, announcing the entry of the reader into the world of 'melodrama'. Although on the next page of the preface Balzac dissociates himself from cruder forms of narrative sensationalism, explicitly repudiating 'des drames dégouttant de sang, des comédies pleines de terreur, des romans où roulent des têtes secrètement coupées', the controlling literary intention seems clear: the hyperbolic, slightly lurid, exotic tone ('la sombre et mysterieuse poésie de cette histoire'), the excited emphasis on the theme of the secret society of heroic-demonic outlaws, the revealing references to the tradition of the *roman noir* (in the next paragraph Balzac describes his narrative as 'curieuse autant que peut l'être le plus noir des romans de

madame Radcliffe')—all these are so many indices (one uses the commercial metaphor advisedly here) of the kind of literary goods on sale.
And what follows in the three tales themselves that make up the
triptych of *Histoire des Treize* would seem, on the surface at least, to
furnish ample evidence that the somewhat dismaying promise of the
preface has been fully honoured—a leader of a secret society who
administers death by poisoning at the mere touch of a finger (*Ferragus*);
a viscount who abducts a duchess-turned-nun from a convent perched
on top of the ostensibly unscalable cliffs of a Mediterranean island (*La
Duchesse de Langeais*); the gory murder of a bisexual young woman by
her lesbian mistress (*La Fille aux yeux d'or*). Evidently, there is a strong
case here for viewing the text as a classic example of the invasion and
contamination of the Romantic sensibility by the idiom of contemporary and immediately pre-contemporary melodramatic writing.

Yet this is by no means the whole story. As Proust, probably the first
to make this decisive recognition, observed in his comments on *La Fille
aux yeux d'or*,[2] reading Balzac can be an experience full of very odd and
unexpected encounters; and, at the very moment Balzac seems to be
most hopelessly and predictably the victim of his celebrated 'bad taste',
his text yields levels of meaning and effect that the banal melodramatic
convention within which he is working could not, on the face of it,
possibly have accommodated. It is precisely this creative exploitation of
what is generally known as a highly limited, impoverished literary
mode, this remodelling and transformation of the conventions of 'melodrama' in the service of a major artistic purpose, that is the subject of this
book.[3] In it I hope to show, mainly through detailed attention to half
a dozen or so central texts of the *Comédie humaine*, that those features
of Balzac's work which criticism has habitually either passed over in
silence or discussed with open contempt, or at least an amused condescension, are in fact often rich in various kinds of literary achievement; that, indeed, what is often most radical and innovative in Balzac's
literary practice may paradoxically be grasped through a new way of
looking at what are normally construed as the most disabling qualities
of his work. What follows therefore is offered not merely as a reassessment of a particular aspect of the *Comédie humaine* but, by implication
and extension, also as a general reassessment, a new way of looking at
Balzac as a whole.

In order to give focus to this enterprise, I have gathered together these
various qualities under the common heading of 'melodrama'. This calls
for some preliminary clarification. What exactly is entailed in using the
term 'melodrama' as the focal point for a critical argument of this kind;
more specifically, in what senses can one use the term in relation to the
analysis of the novel? For in the strict sense, the word belongs, of
course, to the vocabulary of dramatic criticism and designates a particular kind of theatrical practice: 'In early nineteenth century use, a
stage play (usually romantic and sensational in plot and incident) in
which songs were interspersed and in which the actors were accom-

panied by orchestral music appropriate to the situations. In later use, the musical element gradually ceased to be an essential feature of the "melodrama", and the name now denotes a dramatic piece characterized by sensational incident and violent appeals to the emotions, but with a happy ending.' Thus the Oxford English Dictionary, within the necessarily somewhat stilted and compressed convention of a dictionary definition, nevertheless adequately summarizes the main outlines of the development of 'melodrama' as a dramatic form. It originates (probably with Rousseau's *Pygmalion* of 1770) as a kind of 'music drama' (Greek *melos*: 'music') and, in the course of the late eighteenth and early nineteenth centuries, while often retaining a musical component, it rapidly shifts in meaning to denote the kind of play established in the nineteenth century on the 'Boulevard du Temple'; the most famous and prolific representative of this was Guilbert de Pixerécourt, whose *Coelina ou l'enfant du mystère* (1800), in the words of James Smith, 'established overnight the pattern of popular melodrama for the next hundred years'.[4]

That melodrama, as a distinctive stage form, exercised a certain influence on the development of popular fiction is well known; given the spectacular commercial success of the form, it is in no way surprising that the nineteenth-century popular novelist turned to it as a source of inspiration for both subject matter and technique. We know, for instance, that Balzac paid close attention to it in the early 1820s and that several sketches for stage melodramas were among his early plans—he presented, unsuccessfully, one melodrama, *Le Nègre*, to the Théâtre de la Gaieté in 1822; more importantly, he consciously applied some of the current theatrical techniques to his early novels, *Clotilde de Lusignan* and *Le Vicaire des Ardennes*.[5]

To the extent, then, that in an exact sense the term 'melodrama' is a category of dramatic criticism, the title of this book would seem to imply that it is, or in principle ought to be, a study in the influence of theatrical melodrama on the novel. Such a study, conducted in detail, remains to be done, and would doubtless prove in some degree informative and instructive. For a variety of reasons, however, it is not the theme of this book. In the first place, viewed purely in terms of literary history, the actual pattern of historical facts is more complex. Thus, if it is true that stage melodrama exercised some influence on the development of a certain kind of prose fiction, the reverse is equally true; the process of interaction was essentially a two-way one. The boulevard theatres of the 1830s and 1840s, for example, were to a large extent sustained by dramatic adaptations of the texts of the popular novelists: Scott, Ainsworth, Dickens in England, Sue, Dumas, Balzac in France are major examples. Furthermore, if one were interested in trying to establish certain facts of historical priority, it could be shown that a primary impetus in the formation of the stage melodrama was in fact the novel itself, in particular the Gothic novel of Mrs Radcliffe, Walpole, Lewis, Mathurin and their manifold imitators in both England

and France.[6] One of Pixerécourt's most successful plays, for instance (*Le Château des Apennins*), was an adaptation of Mrs Radcliffe's *Mysteries of Udolpho*, while the decisively influential *Coelina ou l'enfant du mystère* was borrowed almost entirely from the *roman noir* of the same title by Ducray-Dumesnil. Above all, and of far greater importance for our purposes, it would be possible to demonstrate that the Gothic novel, rather than developments in the theatre, constituted the more active force in preparing the ground for the emergence of the kind of popular fiction with which Balzac was so intimately associated; any tracing of the line of descent of the popular novel, in particular the *roman-feuilleton*, of the 1830s and 1840s would have to point to the Gothic novel as a far more significant parent than the productions of the boulevards.

The pattern and sequence of transactions between the theatre and the novel form, therefore, a fairly complicated network, but unravelling it is probably an exercise of limited interest. If I have begun with this brief and somewhat awkward excursus into literary history, it is not because of a preoccupation with disengaging strands of influence for their own sake. 'Influence', borrowings, exchanges, lines of descent, whether between genres or in respect of the work of a single author, are not my concern, or only marginally. The references here to elements of interplay and overlap in the evolution of nineteenth-century popular forms, and in particular the stress on the centrality of the Gothic novel, are designed simply to show that in adopting the term 'melodrama' as a focus for the analysis of some of Balzac's narrative practices, I am using the term in a fairly large and flexible sense, in a manner that is not confined to its specifically theatrical heritage.[7] In short, 'melodrama' in the present context refers to a mode rather than to a formal genre, a mode which may be said to encompass certain dispositions of the novelistic imagination as well as the particular conventions and techniques of the stage.

One of the initial advantages of this approach to 'melodrama' as a loose, general category is that it enables one to bypass the rather arid territory of fine taxonomic distinctions and generic definitions. Just as this is not a study in influence, neither is it an essay in formal definitions. The question 'what is melodrama?', posed as a rigidly definitional problem, is not one to which we need address ourselves here. Seen as a general mode, 'melodrama' may manifest itself in a whole variety of different ways, not all of which we need investigate. Nevertheless, if the requirements of systematic definition can be dispensed with, some guiding perspective on what might be deemed the typical properties and tendencies of the melodramatic mode is essential as a base from which the main issues can be intelligibly discussed. One could, for instance, rehearse the familiar inventory of the basic formal devices and figures of melodrama. In formal terms, melodrama is organized by a decidedly limited number of devices, of which the most central are antithesis, hyperbole, stereotype, mystery, coincidence, poetic justice.

In varying degrees, all of these are to be found at work in the *Comédie humaine*, and it is indeed around the particular operations of these figures and devices that most of the critical discussion in subsequent chapters is organized. However, if we are properly to appreciate the significance of these operations, as against their more conventional uses in the popular fiction of the period, clearly more than a simple inventory of 'stock' devices is required by way of an introductory context.

In this respect, perhaps the most helpful approach to an account of the nature of melodrama, and in fact the one most frequently adopted by criticism, is by way of its psychological and emotional functions—the attempt to identify the 'melodramatic' by asking to what needs and desires it responds and in what ways it seeks to gratify them. All the major commentators are agreed in emphasizing that the crucial element of melodrama lies in its relation to fantasy (although the terms in which this emphasis has been cast have been generally somewhat restricted). Linking the prominence of melodrama in nineteenth-century popular culture to the development of certain social conditions, in particular the brutalities of industrial and urban growth, they have argued that melodrama, both on the stage and in fiction, answered primarily to the need to escape from the strains and stresses of daily social life; that it offered a grandiose, if somewhat tawdry, compensatory fantasy in which the longings and desires denied by the pressures and deprivations of social actuality could be vicariously released. Thus Michael Booth, in his study of English melodrama, has observed: 'Essentially, melodrama is a dream world inhabited by dream people and dream justice, offering audiences the fulfilment and satisfaction found only in dreams. An idealization and simplification of the world of reality, it is in fact the world the audiences want but cannot get.'[8] Eric Bentley, pursuing further the relation between melodrama and dream, and invoking explicitly the model of psychoanalysis, has written: 'Melodrama is the Naturalism of the dream life';[9] whether it be the journey into the 'paranoid' world of absolute terror (the fear of the monster), the gratifying world of indulgent self-pity (projection into the sufferings of persecuted innocence), or the euphoric world of moral triumph (exultation in the victory of order), melodrama unself-consciously articulates the desire for a return to the magical phase of childhood fantasy, 'the phase when thoughts seem omnipotent, when the distinction between *I want to* and *I can* is not clearly made, in short when the larger reality has not been given diplomatic recognition'.[10]

The dream offered by melodrama is thus neither prophetic nor analytic; it is reassuring and predictable, enacting a fantasy of wish-fulfilment within a plane that is an idealized version of the real world. At the heart of this idealization lies a set of simple, unambiguous moral presuppositions, articulated in the melodramatic text largely through the systematic use of two elementary rhetorical figures, antithesis and hyperbole. Antithesis serves to organize the universe in terms of the preconceived polarities of good and evil, vice and virtue, while hyperbole reinforces this naive antithetical ordering of experience by ensuring that each side of the moral polarity is represented in an extreme, intensely magnified form (whence the recurrent complement of stereotypic characters—the black villain, the noble hero, the pure heroine, the benevolent protector, etc.). In melodrama, antithesis and hyperbole combine to structure a pattern of response that Robert Heilman, in contrast to the complex response of the tragic catharsis, has called 'monopathy' ('the security of an ordering monopathy'),[11] a series of uncomplicated identifications and reactions which spring from and speak to our longing for an ordered moral universe. In its simplified manicheanism, its unremittingly reductive classification of experience in terms of clear-cut moral divisions, melodrama responds directly to the desire for a world characterized by the maximum moral clarity. And to the pleasures of clarity must also be added the satisfactions of re-assurance: the fear generated by the machinations of the villain is always to a certain degree factitious, for in the manichean struggle between the forces of good and evil, the convention generally guarantees the ultimate victory of the good (the famous 'happy ending'). Simple in structure, melodrama is also simple in dynamic, the movement of the plot being nearly always, despite the innumerable delays, obstacles, apparent uncertainties, towards the triumphal assertion of the rule of moral law; through the rewarding of the virtuous and the punishment of the transgressor, melodrama embodies, among other things, a power fantasy, a fantasy of mastery in which, as in the children's fairy story, the demons are banished and the angels govern. All the formal apparatus of melodrama—the unfolding of mysteries, providential coincidences, hyperbolic gestures, stereotyped characters, antithetical patternings—participates in the articulation of this stable and reassuring universe.

The dominant function of melodrama appears, therefore, to be that of making available an uncomplicated moral reading of the universe, and of locating the subject in a secure world of moral representations, free from doubt, uncertainty, ambiguity.[12] This release from moral tension into moral certitude is familiar territory, and it is almost entirely within these terms that criticism has normally discussed the role of fantasy in melodrama. However, the structure of melodramatic fantasy is more complex (although this complexity is not to be read as a sign of intellectual and literary strength) than Heilman's theory of a morally orientated 'monopathy' suggests. Booth and Bentley are right when they stress the relation between melodrama and dream but, just as the compensations and wish-fulfilments produced by the oneiric life cannot be confined to the fantasy of ethical mastery and triumph, so the 'primitive' appeal of melodrama by no means rests entirely on its invocation of an idealized 'dream justice'. This complexity resides essentially in the peculiarly ambiguous manner in which the melo-dramatic imagination handles the relationship between 'order' and 'dis-order'; in the way it allows the mind to shift ambivalently to and fro between the longing for order and the excitements of disorder,[13] to slip back and forth from the soothing caress of moral safety to the seductive attractions of danger and violence. The key to this peculiar dynamic is to be found in what is generally described, in the context of discussions of melodrama, as 'sensationalism', and can best be approached in terms of the presentation of evil in melodrama.

All the historians of stage melodrama have pointed out that, despite its moral pretensions, the real moving force of the form was the villain; as Peter Brooks has observed of nineteenth-century French stage melodrama, 'En baptisant le Boulevard du Temple le "Boulevard du Crime", le public contemporain reconnaissait implicitement que malgré le triomphe extérieur de la vertu, c'était l'instant du mal régnant qui fascinait.'[14] For the demonic spectacle of pure evil in melodrama arouses not merely fear and revulsion (the reactions demanded by the overt moral intentions of melodrama), but also, and more disconcertingly, fascination and vicarious complicity. We may will the destruction of the malefactor, and the convention accommodates that desire, but at the same time (the process is of course quite unselfconscious, a matter of the left hand not knowing what the right is doing) the evil and disorder he perpetrates strike a chord in our own fantasies of cruelty and destruction. A passage from a novel by one of the great ancestors of nineteenth-century popular writing (Mrs Radcliffe's *The Italian*) furnishes a perfect example of this type of ambiguity:

> A dark malignity overspread the features of the monk and at that moment Vivaldi thought he beheld a man whose passions might impel him to the perpetration of almost any crime, howsoever hideous. He recoiled from him as if he had suddenly seen a serpent in his path, yet stood gazing on his face with an attention so wholly occupied as to be unconscious that he did so. It seemed as if the evil power one attributed to the eye of envious malice held him in fascination to the monk.[15]

The gesture of moral recoil ('He recoiled from him as if he had seen a serpent') meets the conventional expectations, but the almost hypnotic fascination exercised by the 'evil power' of the monk registers another, quite different kind of response. And through Vivaldi's ambiguous feeling of revulsion and fascination, Mrs Radcliffe is instinctively giving expression to an experience that is at the heart of the 'sensationalism' of the early and mid-nineteenth century, that curious mixture of dread and delight, fear and attraction that typically accompanies the presentation of crime and violence in the melodrama of nineteenth-century *romantisme frénétique*. Examples from both the drama and the prose fiction of the period are abundant, but a particularly interesting case is that of Eugène Sue. Sue, the prince of the *roman-feuilleton*, always laid claim, at least in respect of his major work *Les Mystères de Paris*, to a certain literary seriousness. Not only did he assert that he was exposing the iniquities of the Parisian *bas-fonds* for serious social purposes, he also argued an impeccable sense of moral values in his treatment of violence. But such declarations of literary policy hardly explain the uncontrolled luridness of the following passage in which the sensational element, far from being harnessed by any impulse to moral realism or responsible social criticism, is quite clearly nothing other than an overt pandering to the unsophisticated reader's appetite for blood:

> Enchaîné par la jambe à une pierre énorme placée au milieu du caveau, Le Maître d'école, horrible, monstrueux, la crinière hérissée, la barbe longue, la bouche écumante, vêtu de haillons ensanglantés tournait comme une bête fauve autour de son cachot, traînant après lui, par les deux pieds, le cadavre de la Chouette, dont la tête était horriblement mutilée, brisée, écrasée.[16]

The passage is just one among many like it, and—this is the important point in terms of a discussion of the functions of melodramatic writing—it was undoubtedly episodes like these which were responsible for the novel's enormous popularity. In the nineteenth century in both England and France, public interest of a quite staggering morbidity in the details of crime and violence is attested by various factors outside literature itself. Hangings in England drew enormous crowds, many often arriving the night before to ensure a place at the 'spectacle'.[17] Newspapers thrived commercially on the extensive publicity they gave to crime and trials. Sainte-Beuve complained, in a significant conjunction of the social and the literary, that 'la publicité des cours d'assises va de pair avec les romans-feuilletons',[18] while Thackeray wrote ironically, 'A good murder is a great godsend. Light be the stones on Thurtell's bones; he was the best friend the penny-a-line men had for many a day.'[19] Vidocq's *Mémoires*, published in 1828 and immediately translated into English, broadsides, ballads, last-minute confessions, Newgate calendars, *causes célèbres* and *almanachs du crime* sold in their thousands and constituted a treasure-trove of excitement and identification. In terms of their effect on contemporary popular fiction, Sainte-Beuve made the important point when he wrote, in characteristic moralizing vein, 'La fatuité combinée à la cupidité, à l'industrialisme, au besoin d'exploiter les mauvais penchants du public a produit dans les oeuvres d'imagination et dans le roman un raffinement d'immoralité et de dépravation. . . . Il y a un fond de Sade masqué . . . dans deux ou trois de nos romanciers les plus accrédités.'[20]

The issue could, of course, remain a dead one, or at least more a matter for the social historian than the literary critic, if it did not implicate the work of more significant writers. An outstanding case in point is Dickens. Dickens's relationship with nineteenth-century melodrama was profound and sustained, and his example is one I shall be returning to at various junctures. For the moment let us consider one particular text, *Oliver Twist*. As John Bayley has shown,[21] Dickens's feelings towards evil and violence in *Oliver Twist* are just this mixture of dread and attraction, manifested above all in the morbid lingering over the details of the murder of Nancy ('the pool of gore that quivered and danced in the sunlight on the ceiling. . . . There was the body—mere flesh and blood, no more—but such flesh, and so much blood!').[22] That this episode testifies to an unconscious identification on Dickens's part with Sikes's brutality is a commonplace of modern criticism, supported by the evidence of the obsessive interest shown by Dickens, in later life, in his public readings of the murder scene. However, the instructive point for our purposes is the degree to which these speculations about Dickens's own feelings relate to the kind of responses evoked in his readers. It is no accident that the murder of Nancy proved to be one of the most 'thrilling' episodes of the novel. *Oliver Twist* may be described as 'melodramatic' in a variety of ways—its division of social reality into the 'wicked' and the 'virtuous', its fantasy of unsullied and triumphant innocence, its recourse to the operations of poetic justice. But unquestionably one of the points at which it exemplifies the melodramatic imagination at work is in its unconscious connivance at the darker impulses and fantasies of its readers.

This oscillation between the claims of order and the excitements of disorder, between the genuflection to virtue and complicity in the demonic, defines one of the central patterns of the melodramatic mode and demonstrates, despite its outward simplicity of design, its fundamental emotional and moral incoherence; in melodrama we simultaneously pay homage to the idea of moral order and yet secretly enjoy the violence which threatens it. Emotionally and morally incoherent, melodrama is also blind. The tension between its overt moral ideology and its subterranean feelings goes wholly unexamined. The conflict between the two levels of fantasmatic reality to which it addresses itself (the fantasy of mastery and the fantasy of destruction) can never be explored and resolved within the melodramatic mode itself, since its commitment to the value and ultimate victory of the moral good requires that its complicity with the dynamic of evil remain forever hidden and unacknowledged. In respect of its involvement with evil, melodrama is founded upon a dialectic of gratification and repression: it partially gratifies an impulse to destruction, but at the same time, through its insistence on triumphant virtue, represses any acknowledgement of that gratification. The villain may draw the crowds, provide all the 'thrills', but he must be finally punished. In *Oliver Twist*, after the excitements of the murder of Nancy, the text retreats back into the realm of moral sanctuary by mobilizing against Sikes the machinery of justice and revenge. Sikes, the ultimate transgressor, must be destroyed, not because of the inherent requirements of a rigorous narrative realism, but because the convention of melodrama demands it. For whatever satisfactions Sikes's frenzy may have secretly afforded us, they must remain secret, unspoken, and one way of ensuring this is by inviting the reader to exult in his annihilation, to disclaim any possible involvement with Sikes through unequivocally and enthusiastically siding with the forces of 'justice'.

But it is precisely here that the moral and emotional confusion of melodrama, its naively ambiguous manipulation of fantasy, is most acutely felt. For it is here, in the operations of nemesis, that the 'dark' taste for violence and the 'respectable' desire for order are simultaneously and indissociably met. In terms of what exactly is appealed to in the reader or spectator, the convention of retribution in melodrama (quite unlike its functioning in tragedy) is always morally ambiguous: we rejoice in the suppression or destitution of the malefactor not simply because the elimination of evil makes the world a morally safer and more agreeable place, but also because of the pleasure itself taken in the act of destruction; this pleasure can nevertheless be indulged without any undermining of the form's defence of the principle of order, since in this case it bears the stamp of social and moral legitimacy. Melodramatic nemesis, in short, presents the dubious pleasures of what can only be called self-righteous sadism. In a brief passage in his *Anatomy of Criticism*, Northrop Frye offers what is, I think, the most perspicacious comment on the nature of melodrama:

> In melodrama two themes are important: the triumph of moral virtue over villainy, and the consequent idealizing of the moral views assumed to be held by the audience. In the melodrama of the brutal thriller we come as close as it is normally possible for art to come to the pure self-righteousness of the lynching mob. We should have to say, then, that all forms of melodrama, the detective story in particular, were advance propaganda for the police state, in so far as that represents the regularizing of mob violence, if it were possible to take them seriously.[23]

If we set this passage alongside the closing chapters of *Oliver Twist*, some interesting implications emerge. The circumstances of Sikes's death will be recalled: Sikes is hounded through London by an angry mob and finally slips accidentally from a roof-top with a rope around his neck. The identification of the text at this point with the instincts of the mob is unmistakable, and the 'accidental' nature of Sikes's death cannot obscure the fact (although this is perhaps its unconsciously intended function) of the moral, if not material, involvement of the crowd—and, of course, the reader—in that death. It has been suggested that what Dickens, in an uncomprehending way, is dealing with here, or rather is implicated in, is the fury of the lynch mob and the ritual of a revenge hanging.[24] Dickens was later to arrive at a deep understanding of this disconcerting connection between violence and 'justice' (for example, in his presentation in *Barnaby Rudge* of the figure of Denis, whose dual role of sadist and servant of order is subsumed under the

single role of public hangman). But in *Oliver Twist* that kind of understanding was not yet available to him and, in that lack, it illustrates
perfectly the quintessential structure of melodramatic fantasy.

Seen in this light, 'melodrama' is clearly something of a liability. Despite
recent attempts at its rehabilitation,[25] whether in terms of a naive psy-
chologism or a highly suspect gesture towards the notion of a vital
'popular' culture, melodrama is the mode which, along with cognate
modes such as sentimentality and pornography, accommodates and
exploits the demands of the immature and uncritical sensibility; even
Eric Bentley, one of the more vigorous rehabilitators, has to concede
that 'melodrama is human but it is not mature. It is imaginative but it is
not intelligent.'[26] With few exceptions, it is in this disabling sense that
the presence of melodrama in Balzac's work has usually been discussed.
Its origins are well known, rooted in the literary apprenticeship served
by Balzac in the 1820s—the period of his enthusiastic and calculating involvement in the pot-boiling enterprises which produced the fictions
published under the various pseudonyms, A. de Viellerglé, Lord
R'Hoone and Horace de Saint Aubin, and which Balzac himself was
later to dismiss contemptuously as 'cochonnerie littéraire'.[27] The indebtedness of these texts, now generally known as the *oeuvres de jeunesse*, to
the stage melodrama and popular romances of the period has been elaborately documented, in particular by Prioult and Bardèche,[28] and is not a
subject that need be investigated here. The crucial question is the extent
to which the early encounter with the idiom of *le bas romantisme* affected
the writing of the *Comédie humaine*. Prioult has suggested that the
influence was not an entirely unhappy one, but his remarks rarely get
beyond the fairly trite reflection that in the juvenilia we can detect signs
of the later 'realism' of accurately observed milieu. The dominant
emphases in this area of criticism, however, have been almost
uniformly negative: Balzac's débuts were something of a disaster; they
formed a series of literary habits which, in his mature work, Balzac was
never able fully to discard, which indeed were actively nourished by his
involvement from 1836 onwards with the eminently commercial
enterprise of the *roman-feuilleton*, and whose consequences for the 'serious' novels were almost invariably harmful and often fatal. Sainte-
Beuve was probably the first to express this view ('Balzac, jusqu'en ses
meilleurs romans, a toujours gardé quelque chose de la bassesse et, pour
ainsi dire, de la crapule de ses débuts'),[29] and it is a view that has
consistently found an echo in the established critics since. Here are some
typical examples:

> Un romancier n'apprend pas impunément son métier à pareille
> école. On ne demanderait pas mieux que d'oublier les premiers
> écrits de Balzac, s'ils n'annonçaient à bien des égards ce qu'il a
> publié ensuite, s'ils ne s'y attachaient, s'ils n'y tenaient étroitement.
> Peu importerait l'action immédiate que de puérils ou grossiers

conteurs ont eue sur ses oeuvres de jeunesse, si elles n'expliquaient
l'action lointaine et trop forte encore qu'ils ont eue jusque sur les
oeuvres de sa maturité. Et qu'ils en aient eu une, en effet, c'est,
hélas! ce qui ne se voit que trop. . . . Il faut bien convenir: la
substance et les procédés du roman populaire et du mélodrame
ont passé chez Balzac et reparaissent, sauf d'heureuses exceptions, jusque dans les chef-d'oeuvres du roman balzacien.[30] (Le
Breton)

Balzac est déplorablement romanesque: la moitié de son oeuvre
appartient au bas romantisme, par les invraisemblables ou
insipides actions qu'il développe sérieusement ou tragiquement.
Mélodrame, roman-feuilleton, tous les pires mots sont trop doux
pour caractériser l'écoeurante extravagance des intrigues que
combine lourdement la fantaisie de Balzac. Il fait concurrence à E.
Sue et à Dumas père, dans *Ferragus* et les *Treize*, dans *la Dernière
Incarnation de Vautrin*, dans *Une Ténébreuse affaire*, dans *La Femme
de trente ans*, dans maints épisodes ou incidents des meilleurs
romans. (Lanson)[31]

Tout ce bas romantisme . . . Balzac l'a accepté, l'a goûté, lui,
homme de génie, à moins qu'il ne l'a exploité par connaissance et
mépris de son public; et il lui a donné une place considérable dans
son oeuvre. Il y a en lui un Eugène Sue, un Soulié . . . Il a perdu la
moitié de sa vie à cela et j'ajouterai, comme toujours, que cela me
serait indifférent, s'il n'était arrivé, comme presque toujours aussi,
que dans d'autres oeuvres les plus sérieuses, l'humeur folle du
romancier de cabinet de lecture éclate tout d'un coup, donne
soudain à l'ouvrage un caractère inattendu et le gâte. . . . L'imagination vulgaire et facile, l'imagination de l'étudiant ou de la
grisette a pris le dessus. (Faguet)[32]

He began his career as the anonymous author of what are now
called 'thrillers'—*Argow le Pirate* is the best known of them—and
the melodramatic element persists all through his work. . . . Our
experience in reading Balzac is not always very elevated and his
interests are by no means always those of an adult. . . . His world
with its duchesses mixed up with prostitutes, affords the same
vicarious satisfaction as a detective story. (Turnell)[33]

The erstwhile magisterial voices of Lanson and Faguet have since lost
a good deal of their authority, while the eccentricities of Turnell's
interpretation of the 'great tradition' of the French novel no longer
command the attention they once did. Cumulatively, nevertheless,
there is a case here that needs to be met. The usual response of the
committed 'Balzacian' is simply to bypass it and to go on to talk of other
things. Yet, in many of the major texts of the *Comédie humaine* the
'melodrama' is central, and any attempt at an assessment of them must
start from the fact of that centrality; it dictates a great deal of the terms

on which the question of their exact literary status must be decided. The case I want to argue, therefore, is not that the way to rescue these texts from their damaging critical heritage is by asserting an artistic achievement located, as it were, outside Balzac's use of melodrama. On the contrary, what needs to be stressed is an idea of wholeness, a deep unity of vision and technique, entailing above all the recognition that Balzac does indeed work in and through the conventions of the melodramatic mode, but that his achievement lies in the radical reworking of these conventions to support a serious and important artistic aim.

In this respect, Balzac is by no means alone in the history of nineteenth-century fiction. There are several major novelists whose work, in varying degrees, displays just this kind of transforming relationship between their own creative vision and the strategies of popular writing. Of Dostoyevsky, George Steiner reminds us that 'even where his purposes were most complex and radical, Dostoyevsky adhered to the stock situations of contemporary melodrama.'[34] One thinks, for instance, of the ways in which the stock melodramatic motif of persecuted innocence is refashioned by Dostoyevsky to produce his profound studies of the experience of humiliation or again, of the manner in which the device of 'coincidence' is used poetically to evoke his sense of the frightening instability and disorder of human personality. More surprisingly perhaps, the exquisitely refined sensibility of Henry James is modulated from a basic structure which has many of its roots in melodramatic representation. As has often been pointed out,[35] the typical melodramatic schema of 'innocence' and 'villainy' is central to the Jamesian *oeuvre*, but whereas in the very early works this is often handled in terms of a somewhat feverish theatricality of tone and method, in the mature work it is radically transformed to yield a deep and complex exploration of moral reality; the 'armature' of melodrama remains, but it is moulded, built upon, modified to create effects of great sophistication. Again, one might safely cite the case of Conrad: 'one word comes before long to haunt the mind of any persistent reader of Conrad's stories—the word melodrama. Why does he use it?'[36] The answer of course is that he uses it for special and serious reasons; thus, much of the raw narrative 'material' of *The Secret Agent*, for example, is the stuff of the 'thriller' but, as Leavis has rightly stressed,[37] the material becomes the occasion for creating a subtle and compelling pattern of psychological and moral ironies. Above all, and inevitably, the example of Dickens once again springs to mind. I have already referred to the complicity of *Oliver Twist* in the disingenuousness of melodramatic fantasy, yet—and this is one of the earliest manifestations of a process that will recur, in an increasingly controlled and complex form, throughout the whole of Dickens's career—at the very moment when the novel seems to be helplessly caught in the limitations of the melodramatic mode, it pulls off one of its most astonishing feats. Certainly, part of the meaning of Sikes's death lies in its pandering to what Frye, in his comment on melodrama, has called the 'self-righteousness of the

lynching mob'; but there is also another and far more intelligent meaning—the implicit and deeply ironic social comment in the fact that it is
only through the cruelty of the chase that the barriers of laissez-faire
isolation in Victorian London are broken down and some sense of
'community' achieved: 'Again and again it rose (the triumphant cry of
execration). Those who were at too great a distance to know its meaning took up the sound; it echoed and re-echoed; it seemed as though the
whole city had poured its population out to curse him.'[38]

The important point is that both these meanings spring from the
same moment in the text: at one level, 'melodrama' operates in the
conventional manner; at another level, however, it is imaginatively
transformed to embody a critical insight that reaches into the heart of
Victorian society. This capacity of the Dickensian text to organize
different levels of reference from the same source, to generate multiplicity from ostensible simplicity, paradoxically to transform a convention from within while outwardly accommodating its more ordinary requirements, is one of the defining features of Dickens's work as a
whole (and one we shall meet again in the context of his treatment of the
mystery story in his later novels). And it is just this multilayered
phenomenon that I want to examine in the work of Balzac. It is no
accident, moreover, that the careers of Dickens and Balzac were partly
contemporaneous. For the common ways in which melodrama enters
their respective novelistic worlds are directly related to the fact that, as
writers, both found themselves in a very similar set of social and
cultural circumstances. In particular, both were confronted with the
emergence of an expanding and changing reading public and with the
dramatic effects of this on the changing situation of the professional
writer. Both, although for a variety of different reasons, longed for and
actively sought 'popularity' (in Dickens's case there appears to have
been a very real psychological dependence on the 'applause' of an
audience), and both were acutely aware of the tensions that necessarily
arose between the desire for popular acclaim and the commitment to
the autonomy of the literary vocation. The complex manipulation of
the melodramatic mode, at once meeting the relatively untutored
demands of the new reading public and at the same time featuring its
deeper transformations, represents one of the ways in which they tried
to cope with these tensions. Hence, before going on to consider the
actual uses of melodrama in the *Comédie humaine*, it is necessary to look
in some detail at Balzac's attitudes to and relations with the new reading
public.

2 *Balzac and the reading public*

Of the various cultural changes wrought in France by the social, political and economic upheavals of the early nineteenth century, one of the most important and the most problematical is that which Sainte-Beuve, in his article *De la littérature industrielle*, describes as 'l'invasion de la démocratie littéraire'.[1] For a variety of reasons—the demographic explosion, the consolidation of middle-class interests and power, the expansion of the urban working class, the increase in literacy owing to the primary education acts of 1833, the development of commercial publishing and the press—the first half of the nineteenth century witnesses the spectacular growth of the reading public and consequently the radical transformation of the 'common reader', thereby bringing about a whole series of largely unprecedented cultural problems and predicaments vitally affecting the position and the activity of the writer. The contemporary recognition of that change, and its various attendant problems, can be illustrated from a wide variety of different sources. Sainte-Beuve's article (to which we shall return again) is central, as indeed are many other contributions to the *Revue des deux mondes*, a journal which in general is to play an important role in diagnosing, from a particular ideological standpoint, the consequences of a rapidly changing culture. But for a relatively neutral, dispassionate summary of the new situation, we might turn to the *Discours préliminaire* of the Academician, Sylvestre de Sacy, in that curious, fascinating document compiled for the Ministère de l'instruction publique, *Rapport sur le Progrès des Lettres*:

> On ne lisait guère autrefois que dans les salons; aujourd'hui ce sont peut-être les salons qui lisent le moins. Il s'agissait de satisfaire un petit nombre d'esprits délicats; il s'agit de répondre aux besoins d'une multitude affamée. . . . Le monde a changé. Ce ne sont plus des salons, une cour, un public de cordons bleus, de financiers et de grandes dames, des coteries littéraires ou philosophiques qu'il faut contenter; c'est la foule, un peuple de quarante millions d'hommes.[2]

The reference here to forty million is, of course, more a rhetorical flourish (for the Minister?) than a statement of actual fact, but in focusing the general shift in readership from a socially and culturally closed community of 'esprits délicats' to a 'multitude affamée', Sacy unquestionably captures an emphasis of major importance: the privileged apartness of the classic act of reading, founded on economic and social structures that permitted leisure and sophistication to a limited group of people, begins to give way to a large-scale 'democratic' extension of reading into other areas and layers of society, thus laying the foundations for the emergence of modern 'mass' culture and 'mass' communications.

Nowhere is this more apparent than in the development of the novel. Indeed it can be argued that the very rise of the novel to its position of dominance in the nineteenth century is closely linked to the kind of social developments we are here considering, and in particular to the growth of an increasingly literate urban population. The connection certainly exists in the minds of the nineteenth-century commentators, for many of whom the novel presents itself as the 'democratic' form par excellence. Thus Sacy in his ministerial report, describing the situation in terms of a series of highly significant and symptomatic metaphors, explicitly refers to 'le roman qui aujourd'hui forme à lui seul une littérature tout entière. L'offre peut à peine répondre à la demande, quoique l'immense atelier où se fabrique le roman ne se repose jamais et que les ingénieux ouvriers qui font mouvoir la machine ne connaissent ni les vacances du dimanche ni celles du lundi.'[3] The historian Duquesnel writes that the novel is 'la plus populaire de toutes les formes littéraires . . . il s'en publie un presque par jour' and that 'plus la société approche de la démocratie, plus le roman acquiert d'importance'.[4] Alfred Nettement, in a somewhat more concerned tone, affirms that 'les écrivains de talent se tournent instinctivement vers le genre qui conduit le plus vite et le plus sûrement au succès.'[5] The publisher Edmond Werdet, perhaps just a little carried away by the stupendous successes of commercial publishing in the early nineteenth century, records glowingly, 'Ce nouveau genre de littérature eut une telle expansion dès la fin de 1830, que la France entière semble ne plus former qu'un immense salon de lecture, où chacun attendit avec impatience son tour pour dévorer l'oeuvre fraîchement éclose. Partout s'élevait des cabinets littéraires. La librairie de nouveautés et de romans prit tout à coup un développement immense.'[6]

In accounting for the growth of the novel-reading public, Werdet's references are confined to the expansion of the book-selling trade and the appearance of the *cabinets de lecture*. Both these factors are of course important but, popular though they were, the *cabinets de lecture* were necessarily limited in number, while book buying, despite ventures in cheaper editions such as Charpentier's,[7] was still a relatively expensive business. Without doubt the most important commercial development in making the novel more available to the new reading public, and therefore in turn expanding that public, was the decision to publish fiction serially in the daily press. The origins of the *roman-feuilleton* are now well known and there is no need to rehearse these here in detail.[8] Suffice it to recall the general outlines of the venture launched in 1836 by Emile de Girardin and destined to have wide repercussions in nineteenth-century literary culture. Girardin set out to challenge the established newspapers costing 80 francs by marketing a daily news-paper at 40 francs; the loss of revenue at the level of prices was to be offset both by increased sales and the extensive use of advertising, but the prospective advertisers were prepared to make use of the news-papers only on condition that they reached a very wide public and, in particular, a public larger than that normally commanded by the politi-cal affiliations of the newspaper. The answer lay in the institution of the *roman-feuilleton*, of which the first French example was significantly Balzac's *La Vieille fille*. The impact of this innovation on the general diffusion of the reading habit was both immediate and dramatic, for it is quite clear that the phenomenal success of the cheaper press was the direct result of Girardin's policy on the serialization of fiction. René Bazin, for instance, records in *Questions littéraires et sociales* that 'dans la première semaine après le commencement d'un feuilleton, le tirage d'un journal montait ou s'abaissait de 50 mille, de 80 mille, selon que le feuilleton plaisait ou ne plaisait pas.'[9] It is therefore chiefly through the introduction of the *roman-feuilleton* that the reading of fiction became the pastime of a large and fairly diverse reading public; consequently, the problems created for the serious writer by the existence of that public we shall find recurrently, although not exclusively, defined in the context of the growth of this particular mode of writing. The *roman-feuilleton* becomes a symbol, representing and crystallizing in extreme form many of the dominant forces and tendencies at work in the emergence of Sainte-Beuve's *démocratie littéraire*, and the whole ques-tion of popularity and relations with the reading public, of standards and values in 'popular' culture, will be debated time and time again against the background of this particularly symptomatic phenomenon.

What then can one say in more precise terms about the nature of the new reading public? We know that in social character it is essentially middle class;[10] we know that an important component is made up from a substantial number of women with plenty of leisure;[11] an idea of overall size can be gauged from the compilation of statistics, on the basis of book sales and newspaper circulation, for instance.[12] Yet the prob-lems of description and analysis are in fact immense: how are we to investigate what Pedro Salinas has so aptly described as 'ce public qui, pour soumis qu'il soit aux statistiques et aux compatibilités, n'en reste pas moins essentiellement mystérieux et insaisissable'?[13] What is a public? When we speak of a public, we seem to imply the existence of some kind of 'collective consciousness'; yet the 'public' is made up of a multiplicity of different individuals, engaged in an activity (reading) which is essentially private and bringing to that activity highly different expectations and responses. The sociological and psychological method that would enable one to investigate empirically such diversity and resolve the results into some kind of synthesis (a 'public') simply does not appear to be available.[14] Pierre Barbéris has suggested, with specific reference to Balzac, the usefulness of a study of 'l'accueil de la critique', and has advanced the theory that 'il existe donc bien une dialectique Balzac-public et qui se saisit avec assez de clarté au niveau des rapports Balzac-critique.'[15] This approach has a certain validity, and, in a subsequent chapter, we shall return again to the question of possible relations between the assumptions of the nineteenth century critic and general social attitudes. In comprehensive terms, however, Barbéris's suggestion has to be seen as methodologically problematical, since the professional critics constitute a very specific group of individuals, with their own particular interests and demands, and cannot therefore be necessarily seen as fully representative. There is a further problem, peculiar to the period in question. The 'mysterious' nature of the public is not just a matter of a failure to discover the evidence or to elaborate adequate methods of research; it is rooted in the particular realities of the nineteenth century, where the anonymity of the reading public is of the essence. In earlier periods there is frequently a close relationship between artist and public; indeed many writers are directly acquainted with many members of an anyway severely restricted circle of readers. In the nineteenth century, however, that intimacy begins to disappear; the relationship between writer and reader tends to become a basically economic one, mediated by the workings of the market, that is, by something essentially impersonal. When therefore we speak of the nineteenth-century 'reading public', we are speaking rather of an image of that public, an image that comes down to us via the recorded statements and views of a relatively small group of highly articulate individuals, who furthermore generally see themselves not as included in, but as standing apart from that public.

The essential content of that image is now, of course, an integral, wholly familiar part of our general awareness of the nineteenth century. It is transmitted to us from a number of different sources, but can be adequately illustrated by means of the following extract from an article by Charles de Mazade, a regular contributor to the *Revue des deux mondes* and a fairly typical example of the sense of concern over the new developments that is so consistently focused by that journal:

> Il y a eu un moment, et ce moment n'est pas encore si éloigné de nous, où il s'est produit un phénomène extraordinaire: c'est ce que j'appellerai l'irruption de la démocratie dans le domaine de l'intelligence et des arts. Le nombre des lecteurs s'est accru dans une proportion incalculable. Il s'est levé tout à coup un public affamé d'une certaine nourriture d'imagination, affichant presque par vanité aristocratique le goût des arts, poursuivant les satisfactions d'esprit à bon marché et se jetant sur tout ce qu'on lui offrait, sans

distinction et sans choix, avec l'inexpérience d'un enfant excité et surpris. . . . C'est ainsi que s'est développé cette situation étrange où on pourrait dire que tout s'écrit, que tout se lit, où le succès n'est nullement en raison de la supériorité de l'art, et où la littérature, sous prétexte de se populariser, s'abaisse lui-même sans élever assurément le niveau intellectuel de ceux à qui elle n'offre qu'un aliment banal. Le résultat, c'est l'invasion de médiocrité bruyante et puérile, ayant sa place au soleil, satisfaite d'elle-même et se prenant quelquefois au sérieux parce qu'elle trouve des lecteurs.[16]

The 'irruption de la démocratie de l'intelligence' is thus directly equated with 'l'invasion de la médiocrité bruyante et puérile'. The extension of readers is seen to entail a corresponding decline in standards; the older, hierarchical unity of educated taste and discriminating response dissolves, ushering in the reign of a new intellectual and artistic barbarism. And, once again, it is with the growth of the novel that this process of disintegration and collapse is primarily associated; in Mazade's words, 'c'est une lutte bizarre entre la qualité et la quantité, entre le nombre envahissant et l'élite débordée ou envahie, entre l'art véritable et le métier, et nulle part plus que dans le roman cette lutte n'est visible.'[17] Mazade's reference to the novel as the area which most clearly reflects the threat to standards generated by the fragmentation of the public into 'le nombre envahissant' and 'l'élite envahie' may be further amplified by returning again to the specific phenomenon of the *roman-feuilleton*. The spectacular success of the latter appears to spring directly from an appeal to the lowest common denominator in the public, and is consequently seen as fundamentally incompatible with the aims of serious writing. In the words of the fictional newspaper editor in Louis Reybaud's satirical novel, *Jérôme Paturôt à la recherche d'une position sociale*:

Môsieur . . . brisons, s'il vous plaît. Ce que vous appelez la question d'art ne peut venir qu'en seconde ligne lorsqu'on s'adresse à un public nombreux. Voyons, ne sortons pas des réalités. De quoi se compose la masse des lecteurs de journaux? de propriétaires, de fermiers, de marchands, d'industriels, assaisonnés de quelques hommes de robe et d'épées; encore ce sont là les plus éclairés. Eh bien, dites maintenant quelle est la moyenne de l'intelligence de cette clientèle? Croyez-vous que vos théories sur l'art pourront la toucher, qu'elle s'y montrera sensible, qu'elle vous comprendra seulement? Quand on parle à tout le monde, môsieur, il faut parler comme tout le monde.[18]

The view of the nature and significance of the new reading public contained in these passages may be taken as fairly representative of nineteenth-century thinking on the subject. That the testimony of critics such as Sainte-Beuve, Mazade and Reybaud directly illuminates a central cultural reality and that their fears and concern are sincere and largely justified cannot be called in question. It would be quite wrong to dismiss them as the oversensitive reactions of high conservative minds adopting a sort of siege mentality towards the challenge to their position of supremacy. Yet in the quality-quantity debate, as it is typically conducted in the nineteenth century and, in particular, in the context of the violent denunciation of the idea of 'mass' culture, there are a number of dangers that need to be identified. For 'mass', along with related words, is a very problematical term. As Raymond Williams has put it, 'masses are other people',[19] our image of a collective other, to which we ourselves do not belong or rather do not see ourselves as belonging. The point is important not just because it poses problems of accuracy in historical description but also because it raises questions of values in the analysis and criticism of a culture. 'Masses' is frequently a semantic correlative of 'mob', and just as the latter carries overtones of a threat to social order, so the former is often made to speak of a threat to culture and sensibility. An analysis that operates the concept of 'mass' culture or 'mass' reading public generally tends to be coloured by highly conservative and elitist assumptions. This does not mean that in many of its central points of observation and diagnosis such an analysis is false; on the contrary, some of the best informed and most intelligent thinking of the period comes from just such conservative quarters. But as a total account of the cultural situation, it can be misleading both in matters of fact and in matters of emphasis. At the level of purely factual oversimplification it tends, in the image it constructs of the 'public', to ignore diversity—for instance, the significant number of intelligent and discriminating readers in the middle classes or again, the numerous working class autodidacts mentioned by Heine in his reports on France.[20] More important than this, however, is the tendency to think in terms of fixed definitions, to naturalize an historically specific state of affairs into some ineluctable 'law' of human culture, in terms of which the 'mass' reading public is, by definition, low, ignorant, philistine. It is the kind of thinking exemplified, for instance, by the novelist Paul Féval's formulation on the growth of the novel: 'L'auditoire acquis au roman s'est considérablement augmenté pendant les dernières vingt-cinq années. . . . En toutes choses, la loi est que l'élargissement d'une surface amène l'abaissement proportionnel de son niveau.'[21] It cannot be overstressed that the problem of quality is a crucial one, but assertions such as these grossly oversimplify; for the assumption that the spread of reading automatically entails a lowering of standards in fact rests on the narrowly mechanistic argument that there exists in the 'mass' reader a set of pre-existent, ineradicably 'vulgar' tastes which the apparatus of commercial publishing merely satisfies. Such an explanation, in its relative neglect of human possibilities, gives little weight to the cardinal historical point of the way the inexperienced nineteenth-century reader is systematically exploited by the new commercial speculators. The real problem, as Williams puts it, 'is always the relation between inexperience and the way it is met'.²²

Indeed, the more intelligent minds of the period are quick to realize that the problems thrown up by the emergence of the new reading public are inextricably linked to the growing 'capitalization of literature', to the radical nineteenth-century extension of 'that fatal revolution whereby writing is converted into a mechanic trade' (to take up Goldsmith's famous observation). Publishers, editors, booksellers and many writers, in grasping the new commercial possibilities of writing, come increasingly to see literature and above all the novel simply as a 'commodity', qualitatively no different from any other and whose value is merely its exchange value as determined by the laws of the market. Such an attitude is implicit, for instance, in Girardin's remark to Gautier on the latter's complaint that the columns of *La Presse* were rarely open to writers of genuine talent, a remark which may be said to sum up the whole nineteenth-century commercial-artistic antinomy: 'Vous êtes tous de grands écrivains, c'est entendu, mais vous n'êtes pas fichu de m'amener dix abonnés. Tout est là.'²³ It is implicit, to take another example, in the cynical admonitions of the newspaper proprietor in *Jérôme Paturôt*, 'Vous n'ignorez pas, môsieur, que le feuilleton a pris dans notre ordre social une importance au moins égale à celle de la tasse de café et du cigare de la Havane. C'est devenu un besoin chronique, une consommation obligée.'²⁴ The interesting definition here is that of 'need'; in its crude association with the goals of the 'consumer' society, it is the classic (and, for our own age, prophetic) definition of the commercial manipulator, who seeks to legitimize what he purveys on the grounds that he is simply responding to what 'the people want'.

Hence we have the scathing denunciation in Sainte-Beuve's article, 'Vérites sur la situation en littérature': 'L'argent, l'argent, on ne saurait dire combien il est vraiment le nerf et le dieu de la littérature aujourd'hui.'²⁵ Similarly, the journalist and critic, Philarète Chasles, records in the *Chronique de Paris*, 'La littérature est devenue en France, depuis quelques années, une spéculation toute pure; et il ne s'agit plus de bon goût mais d'intérêts matériels.'²⁶ Louis Reybaud writes in *Moeurs et portraits du temps*, 'Il ne s'agit plus alors des lettres dans l'honorable acception du mot, il s'agit d'une véritable industrie, et d'une industrie de mauvaise aloi.'²⁷ Charles de Mazade asks and answers the question, 'Qu'est devenu l'art livré à cette autre influence, sans force pour lutter contre cet ensemble de causes avilissantes? C'est devenu une industrie, dont on a subsisté, qu'on a exploité, perfectionné, qui a pu donner à un homme une certaine surface commerciale, ainsi que le disait l'auteur de *La Comédie humaine*.'²⁸ (The reference here to Balzac is an instructive one, for, as we shall see, Balzac's place in this diagnosis of the nineteenth-century cultural malaise is both central and seminal.)

The growth of the reading public and the commercial exploitation of writing are therefore closely related historical phenomena, and it is this particular combination of factors that engenders the deeply ambivalent changes in the position of the writer, and in particular in his relations with and attitudes to his readers. On the one hand, these factors(allied to the disappearance of patronage) tend to make of the writer a fully fledged 'professional', not only in a position to make a living from writing but often confronted with wholly new possibilities of wealth, fame and status. On the other hand, it is precisely these possibilities which are frequently seen by the writer as embodying a threat to his independence and integrity as an artist. For 'success' is here defined in terms of the market, an institution hardly equipped to make qualitative distinctions between cultural 'production' and other forms of pro-duction; its job is simply to regulate prices in terms of supply and demand, and it will discriminate between commodities on no other basis than this. It is out of this ambivalence in the situation of the writer that there emerge essentially three characteristic responses by the writer to that situation. Firstly, there is the complete capitulation to the pressures of the market, as with the 'popular' novelists such as Sue, Dumas, Soulié. Secondly, there develops the notion of the artist as 'leader' or 'educator', responsible to his readers in that it is his 'mission' to lead them out of their ignorance. Hugo, Vigny and to a lesser extent Leconte de Lisle would be key figures in this context, although it cannot be too heavily emphasized that especially for Vigny and Leconte de Lisle the idea of the writer-educator (the 'éducateurs d'âmes' in Leconte de Lisle's phrase,[29] 'les maîtres de la pensée et les guides éloquents des grandes nations', according to Vigny[30]) is firmly grounded in a basic distinction between the 'herd' and the 'leader'. The third and, without question, the most dominant response is that of a strong, often violent hostility to the reading public. The 'public', frequently assimilated to the satirical image of the detested 'bourgeois', is globally and somewhat crudely identified as the main enemy, whose very presence constitutes a threat to the dignity and seriousness of literature. In the words of A. W. Raitt, 'The bonds which once linked a writer and the public have been severed. . . . The public was indifferent to or suspicious of the country's finest artists; for their part, the artists were often scornful or hostile to their potential readers . . . a breach between author and public opens up and goes on widening throughout the century.'[31]

The central social experience of the serious writer during the nineteenth century is, then, his alienation from a public that presents itself to him as ignorant and vulgar. Far from reaching out to the society around him, the artist now tends to recoil in disgust, to emphasize his isolation, to address himself to an elite or an imagined posterity, or to withdraw totally into a highly esoteric conception of his art. Thus Stendhal significantly dedicates *La Chartreuse de Parme* to the 'Happy Few' or, as in one of the drafts of his letter to Balzac, affirms that it will be 'plus digne de plaire en 1880 quand la société ne sera plus pavée d'enrichis grossiers'.[32] Sainte-Beuve reacts to those who claim to write 'pour le peuple' by affirming that 'il faut viser à satisfaire ses égaux (pares) ou ses supérieurs, et non pas écrire pour ceux qui ont moins de goût et d'esprit que nous; en un mot, il faut viser en haut et non en bas.'[33] Vigny, moving with consummate ease from the abstraction 'humanity' ('J'aime l'humanité) to the more concrete reality of the reading public, finds himself compelled to distinguish between 'l'élite' and 'la masse idiote'; the contemporary reading public 'cherche dans les arts l'amusant et jamais le beau. De là le succès de la médiocrité.'; in 'cette société basée sur l'or', the poet is either condemned to poverty and solitude (Chatterton) or is forced to prostitute his gifts; publication, the attempt to establish contact with the reader, becomes a contaminated activity, from which the writer must try to dissociate himself as far as possible ('publier, ne voir personne, et oublier son livre'); while the possibility of true understanding and appreciation is located, as it is by Stendhal, in posterity and never in the present ('Il ne faut désirer la popularité que dans la postérité et non dans le temps présent').[34] The various attacks on the philistinism of the nineteenth century launched by Gautier in the preface to *Mademoiselle de Maupin* are also relevant here and, in similar vein, Baudelaire, after his early advocacy of the need to communicate with the 'bourgeois' public, finally recoils to denounce the forces at work in the new society, and largely responsible for the emergence of the new reading public, as fundamentally inimical to art ('L'industrie et le progrès, ces despotiques ennemis de toute poésie').[35] Even more vitriolic is the reaction of Flaubert: 'Dans le règne de l'égalité, et il approche, on écorchera vif tout ce qui ne sera pas couvert de verrues. Qu'est-ce que ça fout à la masse, l'Art, la poésie, le style? Elle n'a pas besoin de tout ça. . . . Il y a une conjuration permanente contre l'original, voilà ce qu'il faut se fourrer dans la cervelle. Plus vous aurez de couleur, de relief, plus vous heurterez.'[36] Flaubert withdraws into the 'ivory tower' of an aloof, aristocratic aestheticism ('De la foule à nous aucun lieu. . . . Il faut vivre . . . pour sa vocation, monter dans sa tour d'ivoire'),[37] to be followed there by a host of others. Among them are the Goncourts, who are to focus centrally on the problem of the writer-reader relationship, notably in a passage from the *Journal* which may perhaps be taken as the most direct and explicit description of the schism between the artist and public in the nineteenth century: 'Il me semble voir une séparation, un abîme de distance entre l'artiste et le public de nos jours. Dans les autres siècles, un homme comme Molière n'était que la pensée de son public. Il était pour ainsi dire de plain-pied avec lui. Aujourd'hui, les grands hommes sont plus haut et le public plus bas.'[38]

These few passages—and there are plenty more like them—may be taken as representing the dominant, recurrent attitude of the serious writer to the new reading public. It is an attitude that is frequently oversimplified in its assessments, somewhat narrow in its awareness of the underlying issues, at times just a little hysterical in its expression of contempt and disgust. But it plainly reflects a genuine and deep unease about the place and function of the writer in a cultural situation subject to unprecedented and ever increasing strains and stresses, and it must be taken centrally into account if we are properly to understand the profound modifications that take place in the relations between literature and society in the course of the nineteenth century.

The response of Balzac to the new situation of the writer, as this is shaped by the changing nature of the reading public, is a complex and ambivalent one. In a number of important respects, he would appear to be closely identified with many aspects of the emerging 'literary democracy'. The assertion, for instance, in a letter to Maurice Schlesinger, 'Je resterai toujours attaché au parti séditieux et incorrigible . . . qui croit que les livres sont faits pour tout le monde',[39] indicates an attitude to the general reading public far removed from that which we have identified as characteristic of the nineteenth-century writer; the distance between them may be gauged by juxtaposing Balzac's declaration that 'les livres sont faits pour tout le monde' with Sainte-Beuve's bitter attack on *la démocratie littéraire*. Gaining 'les sympathies du public'[40] unquestionably constitutes a major objective for Balzac. Symptomatic in this respect is the letter to Anselme Pettetin, the editor of the *Revue encyclopédique*, advising him of the forthcoming appearance of the *Scènes de la vie privée*: 'Heureusement, monsieur, mon ouvrage ne paraîtra guère que du 15 au 20 avril, et j'espère que vous pourrez alors en rendre compte dans la revue. Aujourd'hui, vous seriez bien aimable de l'annoncer, comme devant paraître et de piquer par avance la curiosité d'un public qui devient de plus en plus indifférent pour la littérature. Mais c'est de notre faute. Si nous avions du talent, nous le réveillerions sans doute.'[41] More than fifteen years later, when working on *Les Parents pauvres*, we find an almost identical sentiment, 'Le public s'endort, il faut tâcher de réveiller ce despote ennuyé par des choses qui l'intéressent et l'amusent.'[42] Evidently, for Balzac the public is not something to be simply ignored. Where many of his contemporaries and immediate successors feel repelled, Balzac is strongly attracted; where these find themselves engaged in a process of retreat from the public, Balzac on the contrary commits himself energetically to the conquest of that public: 'Manier le public', he writes to Mme Hanska on the eve of the first publication of the *Etudes de Moeurs*, 'n'est pas une petite affaire, le bien disposer pour un ouvrage de douze volumes est une entreprise. C'est une campagne.'[43]

Balzac's enthusiasm is unmistakable. The prosecution of the 'campaign', however, rapidly brings him face to face with the intractable problems thrown up by the great cultural upheavals of the period. The ideal of the universal accessibility of literature ('les livres sont faits pour tout le monde'), the dream of shaking the public out of its 'indifference' to serious writing come up against the harsh practical realities of the nineteenth-century literary world. As we have seen, the growth of the reading public is intimately connected with the development and exploitation of *la littérature industrielle*; the two are historically interdependent, with the result that the pursuit of popularity seems inevitably to leave the writer no choice but to involve himself in the commercial strategies and concessions that are the preconditions of large-scale success. For many of Balzac's contemporaries, this is indeed precisely the choice that Balzac opts for. Sainte-Beuve speaks for many when he consistently reproaches Balzac for what he sees as the latter's shameless pandering to the tastes of the public. A minor but instructive example is Sainte-Beuve's furious response to the mysterious dedicatory note that appeared in the *Journal des débats* prior to the publication of *Modeste Mignon*: 'Ce roman de Balzac était annoncé, il y a quelques jours, dans les *Débats* par une lettre de l'auteur, la plus amphigourique, la plus affectée et la plus ridicule qui puisse se lire, tout cela enfin de mettre en goût le public. Ceux qui insèrent de telles fadaises s'en moquent sans doute, mais ils croient qu'il faut servir au public ce qu'il demande. On est comme au café ou au restaurant et tout caprice de consommateur est tenu pour loi.'[44] Trivial though it is, this particular instance is significant in that it illustrates a wider attitude which, in stressing Balzac's ostensible concessions to the public, tends to place him as a writer in the company of the popular novelists of the *roman-feuilleton* rather than in that of the more serious and sophisticated artists. As Sainte-Beuve puts it in *Notes et Pensées*, 'Leur activité a été proportionnée à ce que demande le siècle . . . surtout ceux qui ont combiné la littérature et l'industrie: Balzac, Dumas, Sue, Soulié.'[45]

As a total judgement of Balzac, this is of course ill-considered, and probably coloured by personal resentment. But at a number of crucial points it is not entirely irrelevant. That there is in Balzac an ambitious arriviste not only conscious of the possibilities of wealth and acclaim offered by the literary 'profession', but who actively welcomes those opportunities, is a commonplace of Balzac studies. From the very outset of his literary career, Balzac speaks almost obsessively of two paramount concerns, 'la fortune' and 'la gloire'. Two of his earliest letters to his sister Laure sound the characteristic Balzacian note: 'Songe à mon bonheur si j'illustrais le nom de Balzac' and, at a somewhat less elevated but closely related plane, 'j'ai l'espoir de vendre un roman tous les mois, 600 francs; c'est assez pour me tirer d'affaire en attendant la fortune que je partagerais avec vous tous, car elle me viendra, je n'en doute pas.'[46] He is, of course, speaking here of the *oeuvres de jeunesse*; but the habit of referring to his work in financial terms, as the possible source of enormous wealth, is to remain with him all his life. 'Ma plume aura rapporté des monceaux d'or', he writes to Mme Hanska in 1838, detailing in very precise terms the specific income to be realized by each of his literary projects, '*Qui terre a guerre a*, plus de mille ducats, *Le Cabinet des antiques* cinq cents ducats; *Soeur Marie-des-Anges* mille ducats, etc, etc'.[47] The insistent preoccupation with sales and prices, intensified by his later involvement with the *roman-feuilleton,* reflects the deeply ingrained tendency of Balzac's mind to envisage his novels as a series of commodities, a form of 'property' subject, in the determination of its value, to the operations of the market. Indeed it is largely through the agency of Balzac and, in particular in his role as President of the Société des gens de lettres, that the very concept of *la propriété littéraire* may be said to have fully established itself in the currency of nineteenth-century critical vocabulary.

Such an approach to writing clearly lends weight to Sainte-Beuve's assessment and would seem to imply that the kind of relationship Balzac attempts to institute with the reading public is a purely economic one; just as he envisages writing as a mode of 'production', analogous to other modes, so he frequently sees the public simply as the 'consumer', there to provide a profitable return on the output of the producer: 'Heureusement que depuis 15 jours j'ai eu l'esprit de me faire assurer 100,00 écus à prendre sur le public et je vais les recevoir en échange de quelques romans.'[48] In this context, the attempt to establish contact with his readers is undertaken not in terms of lofty declarations on the need to make literature available for *tout le monde*, but simply as a calculated exercise in public relations. The phrase 'manier le public' in the letter to Mme Hanska captures an important emphasis in this respect; the public is there to be manipulated, exploited, to be subjected to the kind of self-publicizing operation mounted, for instance, on behalf of *La Peau de Chagrin*.[49]

Yet, if the arriviste in Balzac chases false gods, the artist in him (the artist that Sainte-Beuve will scarcely acknowledge) holds back. In the really vital decisions, D'Arthez triumphs over Lucien de Rubempré, as the temptation to surrender to the exigencies of immediate popularity is met with the refusal to compromise his integrity as an artist: 'Il y a en moi je ne sais quoi, qui m'empêche de faire consciencieusement mal. Il s'agit de donner de l'avenir au livre, d'en faire un torche-cul ou un ouvrage de bibliothèque.'[50] The whole drama of Balzac's complicated relations with the reading public, and the commercial ethos and apparatus that accompany the growth of that public, is contained in this remark. For all his parvenu opportunism, there is, simply, a price that Balzac is not willing to pay for the success he so desperately wants. That refusal can be illustrated in a number of ways, but its adequate symbol may be seen, as Salinas has suggested,[51] in the commitment to his art represented by the Herculean labours of the *épreuves*. The temptation of facility, of producing too much too rapidly for the voracious 'consumer', is one with which Balzac was wholly familiar. But in the crucial area of stylistic elaboration represented by the work on the *épreuves*, Balzac will not yield. Of capital importance in this respect is Balzac's approach to the business of the serial publication of his novels in the daily press. The normal method of work adopted by the professional *feuilletonistes* was to write and publish *au jour le jour*. The implications of such a method for a novelist conscious of higher formal and stylistic responsibilities are obvious; in Balzac's own words, 'tous ceux qui publient leurs ouvrages en feuilletons n'ont plus la liberté de la forme.'[52] Balzac's general procedure, therefore, was not to permit publication to begin until the work was completed in first draft and more or less fully revised and corrected as well. Eventually, however, editorial pressure forced him to make some concessions: publication of *Béatrix*, for example, began in *Le Siècle* while he was still correcting the proofs. The inevitable result was that the issue of instalments caught up on him and his basic method of revision was threatened. 'Donnez moins de *Béatrix*', he writes to the editor, 'et ménagez-moi deux ou trois jours de repos. Je suis exténué.'[53] The significant point here is not so much that Balzac gets himself into difficulty, but that, when in difficulty and therefore confronted with the two alternatives of either interrupting publication and irritating a public avid for the next day's instalment or publishing a text with which he is not personally satisfied, it is the former that he opts for.

The almost symbolic choice that the example of *Béatrix* poses serves to underline the very real difficulties and tensions inherent in Balzac's near daily encounters with pressures of this type. And it is in the direct, painful living of those tensions that the complexity and ambivalence of Balzac's position are properly to be grasped. In the prefaces and correspondence, beneath the brasher emphases of the arriviste, a deeper and more disturbing resonance is frequently struck; alongside the enthusiastic calculations of *fortune* and *gloire*, the energetic plans for the conquest of the public, there is registered the bitter yet ultimately tonic experience of the anguish and humiliation at having to write in a world dominated by the 'toute puissante pièce de cent sous'. Already in 1821, in a letter to Laure he formulates the dilemma, 'J'ai l'espoir de devenir riche à coup de romans. Quelle chute! . . . Pourquoi faut-il que je n'aie pas 1,500 livres de rente pour pouvoir travailler d'une manière glorieuse, enfin il faut s'indépendantiser, et je n'ai que cet ignoble moyen-là: salir du papier et faire gémir la presse.'[54] Almost twenty years later, in the preface to *Pierrette*, he makes the same complaint: 'Au lieu de vivre pour la science, pour l'art, pour les lettres, on est obligé de faire des lettres, de l'art et de la science pour vivre, ce qui est contraire à la production de belles oeuvres';[55] more passionate still is the denunciation in the preface to *Le Lys dans la vallée*, 'l'on nous vend cher la triste célébrité littéraire . . . nous avons de secrètes agonies . . . les travaux de l'intelligence sont accompagnés de persécutions horribles . . . les spéculateurs, les entrepreneurs sont de cruels bourreaux.'[56]

Any final assessment of passages such as these must take into account a certain degree of pose on Balzac's part (all the more marked in the letters to Mme Hanska, where the constantly reiterated invitation to see him as an outcast and persecuted Chatterton is one that we may perhaps wish to decline). But, while allowing for an element of self-dramatization, at bottom Balzac's grievances are unquestionably genuine ones. The literary speculator, who mediates the relationship between writer and reader, is a figure that haunts the life and imagination of Balzac. The opposition between the 'écrivain' and the 'marchand',[57] the latter seen as the great despoiler of literary values, remains one of the constants of Balzac's thinking, and constitutes the basis for a sustained and often violent critique of precisely that 'industrialization' of literature for which Sainte-Beuve held Balzac partly responsible. In the elaboration of this critique, and all that it implies for Balzac's attitude to the reading public, two texts in particular are of great importance. The first is the satirical story, *L'Illustre Gaudissart*, in which, around the figure of the *commis-voyageur*, Balzac presents at once a picture and a judgement of the impact of commercial values on contemporary intellectual and literary life:

> Depuis 1830 . . . les idées devinrent des valeurs. . . . Peut-être un jour, verrons-nous une Bourse pour les idées; mais déjà, bonnes ou mauvaises, les idées se côtent, se récoltent, s'importent, se portent, se vendent, se réalisent et rapportent. . . . En devenant une exploitation, l'intelligence et ses produits devaient naturellement obéir au mode employé par les exploitations manufacturières. . . . De là ce rapt des idées, que, semblables aux marchands d'esclaves en Asie, les entrepreneurs d'esprit publique arrachent au cerveau paternel à peine écloses, et déshabillent et traînent aux yeux de leur sultan hébété, leur Shahabaham, ce terrible public, qui, s'il ne s'amuse pas, leur tranche la tête en leur retranchant leur picotin d'or (IV, 16–17).

To be sure, the tone here is somewhat light-hearted, bantering, indulgent even, a tone consonant with the amiable, relaxed style in which Balzac recounts the adventures of his roguish salesman, but at the same time its critical focus is unmistakable.

More central and more serious in this respect is the seminal analysis of cultural crisis and disintegration offered in *Illusions perdues*. The reference in the preface to the 'maux [qui] accablent la littérature dans sa transformation commerciale'[58] points to the organizing theme of the novel—the pervasive corruption of literature as it is increasingly subjected to the values of the cash nexus. In its exploration of this theme, the text articulates a formidable vision of the threat to culture and creativity represented by the degrading initiatives of the speculators and the popularizers. The destiny of Lucien de Rubempré, hawking his manuscripts around the 'logiques marchands de papier noirci qui préfèrent une bêtise debitée en quinze jours à un chef-d'oeuvre qui veut du temps pour se vendre' (IV, 681), is the symbol of that degradation; the grasping Porchon and Vidal, the scheming Doguereau, the grotesque but sinister Daurat ('je fais de spéculations en littérature' (701)), the corrupted and exhausted Lousteau are the agents that make that degradation possible. As Lucien himself reflects after his first encounter with the Parisian booksellers, 'Ce qu'il avait compris de cet argot commercial lui fit deviner que pour ces libraires les livres étaient comme des bonnets de coton pour les bonnetiers, une marchandise à vendre cher, à acheter bon marché'(640).

The implications of Lucien's lesson are further underscored by the cynical Lousteau: 'En dehors du monde littéraire . . . il n'existe pas une seule personne qui connaisse l'horrible odyssée par laquelle on arrive à ce qu'il faut nommer, selon les talents, la vogue, la mode, la réputation, la renommée, la célébrité, la faveur publique, ces différents échelons qui mènent à la gloire et qui ne la remplaceront jamais. . . . Cette réputation tant désirée est presque toujours une prostitution couronnée' (IV, 679–80). The image of prostitution is at the very heart of the thematic and symbolic structure of *Illusions perdues*, and it recurs again and again in other contexts to designate Balzac's criticism of the encroachment of commercial standards on literature. In the preface to *Les Chouans* he speaks of 'cette prostitution de la pensée qu'on nomme la publication';[59] in a letter to Mme Hanska he laments, 'publier ses pensées, n'est-ce pas les prostituer?';[60] to his friend Victor Ratier he writes, 'Sacre Dieu. Mon bon ami, je crois que la littérature est, par le·temps qui court, un métier de fille des rues qui se prostitue pour cent sous.'[61]

To see literary success as entailing a form of artistic and moral prostitution evidently carries a number of significant implications for Balzac's attitudes to, and actual relations with, the contemporary reading public. One should not, for instance, be misled by the claims made in the *avant-propos* to *Les Comédiens sans le savoir:* 'Aussi, comme le public attentif à toutes les nouveautés s'inquiète de l'apparition d'un livre de M de Balzac. . . . Un livre de cet écrivain, c'est un succès; c'est-à-dire une fortune pour l'éditeur, une joie pour le lecteur; qu'on se reporte pour un instant à quelques années après 1831, et l'on se rappellera sans peine quelle émotion, quelle avidité, quelle curiosité folle, ardente, inouie accueillait chaque production nouvelle de M de Balzac. . . . C'est ainsi qu'ont paru, soulevant de tous côtés un concert unanime de bravos, la plupart des livres que vous connaissez.'[62] The facts of the matter are rather different from the state of affairs suggested by the exuberant tone of this passage; indeed, for most of his life, Balzac's relations with the public were uneasy, difficult, and at times actively hostile.

The context in which these tensions are most sharply felt is, once again, that of the popular *roman-feuilleton*. Although nearly all his novels from 1836 onwards were published serially, Balzac's career as a *feuilletoniste* was, as René Guise has shown,[63] by and large a highly troubled and relatively unsuccessful one, precisely because of a fundamental antagonism between the demands of public and Balzac's own conception of his art. In so far as it can be documented and verified, the response of the public to the vast majority of his novels published in the press was extremely unfavourable, and this for essentially two reasons. The first concerns the 'morality' of his work: Balzacian 'realism', especially in connection with sexual themes, was frequently more than the average middle-class reader could accept with equanimity. On the publication of *La Vieille fille*, for instance, there was an immediate flow of letters to *La Presse* complaining, as Girardin put it in a letter to Balzac,

that there were 'des détails trop libres pour un journal qui doit être lu par
tout le monde et traîner partout'.[64] This led in turn to editorial objec-
tions to the subject matter of *La Torpille*: 'Il nous vient de si nombreuses
réclamations contre le choix du sujet et la liberté de quelques descriptions que le gérant de la *Presse* demande à l'auteur de *La Vieille fille* de
choisir un autre sujet que celui de *La Torpille*, un sujet qui par les descriptions qu'il comportera soit de nature à être lu par tout le monde.'[65]

Criticisms of this sort were not confined to readers of *La Presse*; the
publication of *Béatrix* in *Le Siècle* brought about a similar alienation of
the public, the editor this time receiving complaints which, in their
concern for the 'cheek of the young person', remind us that literary
prudishness was by no means monopolized across the Channel in
Victorian England: 'C'est ce qui m'oblige', writes one reader, 'chaque
fois que vous composez votre feuilleton d'un roman de Balzac de le
séparer du journal afin que mes enfants ne puissent pas le lire';[66] the
result was a certain 'bowdlerization' of the text, Balzac bitterly informing Mme Hanska that his work has appeared 'mauvaise et châtrée'.[67]
Similar problems arose with the publication of *Pierrette*; in the unconsciously comic words of Desnoyers, 'Ci-joint le feuilleton de demain
qui me paraît devoir être atténué en ce qui concerne le danger pour les
vieilles filles de se marier, la santé [?] du colonel, les détails d'os et de
muscles qui ont perdu leur flexibilité pour les accouchements, et la
blessure que peut faire aux jeunes filles l'action de se frotter. Et aussi la
difficulté d'accoucher chez les vieilles filles qui sont restées sages et
toujours assises.—Cela est évidemment trop clair et trop charnel pour
Le Siècle.'[68]

The second major area in which the diffident or aggressive reaction of
the public manifests itself is located in what may be broadly described as
the problem of the 'interest' or 'readability' of his novels. If Balzac's
readers were often outraged, they were even more frequently simply
bored. The basic recipe of the popular novel was quite straightforward;
a narrative rich in dramatic incident, liberally studded with *péripéties*
and *coups de théâtre*, and which above all held the reader in suspense from
one instalment to the next; in the words of Louis Reybaud's fictional
editor, 'Il faut que chaque numéro tombe bien, qu'il tienne au suivant
par une espèce de cordon ombilical, qu'il inspire, qu'il donne le désir,
l'impatience de lire la suite. Vous parliez tout à l'heure de l'art, le voilà,
c'est l'art de se faire attendre.'[69] It cannot be denied that Balzac made
certain prima facie concessions to popular expectations, notably in
Splendeurs et misères des courtisanes and, to a lesser extent, in *La Cousine
Bette* (although the ultimate status and meaning of those ostensible
'concessions' require considerable discussion). But in general terms the
opposition between many of his normal modes of writing—heavily
descriptive, documentary, analytical—and the idiom of the *roman-
feuilleton* was plain to all. For those attuned to the excitements of novels
such as *Les Mystères de Paris* or *Les Trois Mousquetaires*, large sections of
the Balzac novel were quite simply tedious, devoid of 'interest'.

A characteristic reflection of this kind of response comes in a letter from Dujarier (one of the editors of *La Presse*) on the subject of *Les Paysans*: '*Les Paysans* vont très bien. Ils iraient mieux encore si vous vouliez faire le sacrifice de quelques descriptions. On les trouve généralement trop longues pour le feuilleton; ne pourriez-vous les rogner un peu, s'il en reste encore, sauf à les rétablir dans l'édition de libraire? Croyez-moi, ce serait dans l'intérêt de votre succès auquel je m'intéresse, vous le savez, autant que vous-même.'[70] The catastrophic result of this indifference on the part of the public to that key aspect of Balzac's art is well known: towards the end of 1844, the publication of *Les Paysans* was interruped to make way for Dumas' *La Reine Margot*. Balzac's sense of outrage and humiliation is so intense that it strikes at and damages the creative nerve itself and, despite many efforts, the novel was never completed. As Balzac himself explained in a letter to Girardin, 'Dujarier a interrompu la publication de l'introduction des *Paysans* dans l'intérêt purement pécuniaire de la *Reine Margot*. . . . Ce temps d'arrêt a été fatal à mes travaux.'[71] *Les Paysans* therefore offers an exceptionally dramatic example of this fundamental discrepancy between the nature of Balzac's art and the demands of his readers, but the conflict reappears in connection with many other novels. Thus, a disappointed and somewhat bewildered Balzac recounts to Mme Hanska the failure of *La Femme supérieure*: 'Il arrive vingt lettres par jour de réprobation au journal, de gens qui cessent leurs abonnements, etc., disant que rien n'est plus ennuyeux, que ce sont des bavardages insipides.'[72] The detailed analyses of *Une Fille d'Eve*, the nuanced art of *Béatrix*, the subtle delicacy of *Modeste Mignon*, all meet with a similar unappreciative reception. The fate of *Modeste Mignon*, at first proudly offered to the *Journal des débats* as the sequel to *Les Mystères de Paris* ('Pourquoi le feuilleton ne vivrait-il pas . . . par les contrastes?'),[73] finally elicits the comment that it is 'trop délicat pour aller au bas d'un journal.'[74] In the preface to *Béatrix* he writes wearily but defiantly, 'L'auteur sait que . . . ces sortes d'oeuvres obtiennent un succès moins éclantant que celles où les situations se succèdent, où le mouvement est vif et pressé; mais à la longue, les livres comme *Béatrix* . . . arrivent à réunir plus de sympathies et triomphent des trahisons du feuilleton.'[75] Again, in the preface to *Une Fille d'Eve*, 'Quand l'auteur publia cette oeuvre dans un journal, beaucoup de lecteurs s'attendaient à des catastrophes émouvantes, à des pages dramatiques, comme on dit, et le dénouement vrai, quoique brusque, fit paraître cette scène innocente et partant un peu fade.'[76]

In the atmosphere of discontent and incomprehension that surrounds the appearance of so much of Balzac's own work, it is not surprising that he often reacts against the reading public with an almost Flaubertian bitterness and indignation. In the *Lettres sur la littérature* he comments witheringly, 'Pour écrire une vulgaire et ignoble anecdote à la hauteur des abonnés d'un journal, il n'est besoin ni de savoir écrire ne d'instruction.'[77] To Mme Hanska he stresses the frustration and ultimate futility of writing for 'ce sultan imbécile qu'on appelle le public';[78]

'Le public', in the definition offered by the article 'Des Artistes' is the 'gent moutonnière [qui] prend l'habitude de suivre les arrêts de cette conscience stupide décorée du nom de vox populi'.[79] In the same article he inveighs against 'le dédain avec lequel on traite les artistes', a sentiment echoed both in the essay *De la mode en littérature* ('Le public dédaigne un homme de talent et s'amourache d'un sot')[80] and in the preface to *Une Fille d'Eve*, where the author speaks of 'l'indifférence de son époque en matière de haute et grave littérature'.[81] The preface to *Le Père Goriot* poses the question, 'Les habitués des cabinets littéraires s'intéressent-ils à la littérature? Ne l'acceptent-ils pas comme l'étudiant accepte le cigare?';[82] and the preface to *Le Lys dans la vallée* answers the question in terms of the familiar association of the growth in readership with a decline in standards: 'Si la masse lisante s'est agrandie, la somme de l'intelligence publique n'a pas augmenté en proportion.'[83]

The 'masse lisante' (the use of the concept itself is revealing) is, therefore, dismissed as incapable of appreciating serious writing. Where some possibility of sympathetic response and genuine understanding is envisaged, it is now seen as forthcoming only from the 'elite', from the privileged group of discriminating readers set apart from the ignorant and philistine 'mass'. In the preface to *La Peau de chagrin* Balzac insists that the author 's'est promis d'en finir avec un nombreux public . . . pour satisfaire le petit public';[84] in the preface to the *Scènes de la vie privée* he refers to the 'lecteurs choisis auxquels il s'est constamment adressé';[85] and of the *Mémoires de deux jeunes mariées* he writes that 'elle se place naturellement sous la protection de lecteurs choisis, rares aujourd'hui et dont les tendances d'esprit sont en quelque sorte contraires à celles de leur temps.'[86] Observations such as these are, of course, strongly reminiscent of the views expressed by many of Balzac's contemporaries. Similarly in the article on *La Chartreuse de Parme*, in which he is conscious of one great artist speaking to another, and where he is possibly even inspired by Stendhal's dedication of the novel to the 'happy few', he differentiates between 'ceux qui s'agenouillent devant le vox populi' and the 'constellation d'âmes . . . peuple d'élite pour lequel travaillent les vrais artistes', and speaks of the 'homme de talent immense qui n'aura de génie qu'aux yeux de quelques êtres privilégiés et à qui la transcendance de ses idées ôte cette immédiate mais passagère popularité que recherchent les courtisans du peuple et que méprisent les grandes âmes'.[87]

The censure of the reading public contained in these remarks combines with the fierce indictment made elsewhere of the literary speculators to suggest, therefore, that Balzac's deeper reactions to many of the changing patterns of nineteenth-century culture are in fact closely analogous to those of his major contemporaries and successors; that the area of response in which he is, finally, to be situated is that of the acute alienation from the public experienced by Stendhal, Vigny, Sainte-Beuve, Gautier, Baudelaire, Flaubert and the Goncourts. In short, despite his efforts to 'manier le public', in Balzac's actual encounters with the public there appears to be a crucial breakdown in communication of the kind we have seen to be endemic to the period in general. Deep down, and in spite of his purported belief that 'les livres sont faits pour tout le monde', he sees (paradoxically, just like Sainte-Beuve) the extension of the reading public in terms of a drastic erosion of the important values in favour of the cheap and the ephemeral: 'Si l'auteur écrivait aujourd'hui pour demain, il ferait le plus mauvais des calculs et pour lui le drap serait pire que la lisière; car s'il voulait le succès immédiat, productif, il n'aurait qu'à obéir aux idées du moment et à les flatter comme ont fait quelques autres écrivains.'[88]

Yet to conclude by incorporating Balzac into the familiar Romantic tradition of the 'alienated' artist would of itself be somewhat misleading. It is probably true that it is ultimately to this tradition that he belongs, but, as we have seen, arriving at such a conclusion has involved travelling a fairly tortuous path of contradiction and paradox. And even if we accept this conclusion as the finally valid one, a certain residue of paradox still remains. For, in the later stages of Balzac's career as a novelist, that is, at precisely the moment when the accumulation of disappointments and failures in Balzac's relations with the public encourages his various gestures of disdain and rejection, a curious breakthrough occurs. Two novels in particular, *Splendeurs et misères des courtisanes* and *La Cousine Bette*, achieve a huge success with precisely that *gros public* that Balzac professes to despise. Balzac's reactions to this suddenly acquired popularity are extremely interesting:

> 'J'ai vu hier Véron qui veut autant de feuilles que j'en pourrai faire, c'est une bonne nouvelle, cela veut dire que Sue dégringole.
>
> Encore une nouvelle qui te plaira, il y a une immense réaction en ma faveur, j'ai vaincu. Tous, par une acclamation générale, me mettent à la tête.
>
> L'immense succès de *la Cousine* a causé des réchauffements chez les journaux, ils voudraient tous de moi. . . . Je veux avoir coup sur coup, succès sur succès.
>
> Ma situation en ce moment est souveraine. G. Sand n'en peut plus. . . . A. Dumas est brouillé avec le *Constitutionnel* et la *Presse*. . . . Soulié est bien tombé. Je reste seul, plus brillant, plus jeune, plus fécond que jamais.[89]

Balzac's reactions to this enthusiastic reception of his work are therefore those of undisguised pleasure and delight, the reactions of a writer to whom recognition by the 'mass' public is, after all, of vital emotional and psychological importance, and consequently hardly consonant with the views on 'popularity' he expresses elsewhere: 'On est perdu en France du moment où l'on est couronné de son vivant. . . . Vous savez combien peu je tiens à ce qu'on nomme la gloire (c'est ici un privilège d'être calomnié, vilipendé, honni).'[90] In particular, what is interesting here is that Balzac's exultant sense of triumph ('j'ai vaincu') is defined precisely in relation to the popular novelists, and especially Eugène Sue ('Sue dégringole'). This is significant because it is above all in terms of Balzac's approach to Sue that the ambiguities and tensions in Balzac's attitude to the question of popularity are best understood and indeed partially resolved. The name of Sue recurs again and again in the pages of Balzac's correspondence; indeed it would not be an exaggeration to describe the preoccupation with Sue as an obsession (René Guise significantly refers to Balzac's attitude as 'le complexe-Eugène Sue').[91] As one of the *maréchaux du feuilleton,* Sue is the living image of the prosperity and popularity achieved by a particular style of writing. Hence, in Balzac's mind, Sue often appears as a kind of symbolic figure, an embodiment of everything that materially Balzac would like to possess and therefore, in terms of literary and creative values, of the temptations that in all conscience he must resist. Geneviève Delattre makes the point well: 'Sue et Balzac se ressemblent, mais Sue est comme le double de Balzac vu du mauvais côté. Il représente toutes les tentations auxquelles la conscience de son génie et une volonté de fer ont empêché l'auteur de la *Comédie humaine* à succomber.'[92]

Sue is, of course, the archetypal purveyor of *la littérature industrielle* and, as such, the standard-bearer of the new *démocratie littéraire.* Although in the early years of their acquaintanceship relations between the two were cordial, Balzac never suffered any illusions about his qualities as a writer: 'Chez Sue il y a un *plat* qui permet au public de l'aborder.'[93] In his attitude to Sue's phenomenal success and everything which that success represents there is consequently a profound resentment at the injustice of a second-rate talent reaping the rewards of enormous popularity with the reading public, while genius remains in relative obscurity, unacknowledged and unrewarded: 'Mes ouvrages, au lieu d'être humblement demandés, sont offerts par moi. Il en résulte deux dommages: dommage d'argent, qui frappe la marchandise offerte, dommage de considération et perte de temps. On va chez Eugène Sue: on trouve un grand homme. Dans sa maison on fait antichambre, on est frappé de son luxe, on subit ses conditions.'[94] The dangers are obvious, and Balzac is fully aware of them. At moments of extreme depression his nightmare is to descend to the level of Sue: 'Je fais du Sue tout pur', he writes to Mme Hanska, 'Oh, combien j'ai besoin de repos.'[95] For the basic urge—and it is here that the complex strands of Balzac's attitudes to popularity come together—is not really to rival Sue on his own ground, but to outdo him in wealth and reputation without at any stage compromising his own talent. In this respect, the most important statement of literary aims and values in relation to Sue's work comes in a letter to Mme Hanska, and it is necessary to quote it at length:

> Je ne peux pas, je ne dois pas, je ne veux pas subir la dépréciation qui pèse sur moi par les marchés de Sue, et par le tapage que font ses deux ouvrages, je dois faire voir, par des succès *littéraires*, par des chefs-d'oeuvre, en un mot, que ses oeuvres en détrempe sont

les devants de cheminée, et exposer des Raphaël à côté de ses Dubufe. Vous me connaissez assez pour savoir que je n'ai ni jalousie ni aigreur contre lui, ni contre le public. Dieu merci, mes rivaux sont Molière et Walter Scott, Lesage et Voltaire, et non ce Paul de Kock en satin et à paillettes; mais, *mio tesoro*, il s'agit de payer 120,000 fr. de dettes, d'avoir sa case et une vie décente, ce qui, pour un homme comme moi, à 45 ans, est une nécessité, et si je n'envie rien de ce triomphateur à mirliton, vous me permettrez de déplorer qu'on lui paye ses volumes 10,000 fr. tandis que je n'obtiens que 3000 des miens. Or, en frappant deux grands coups, en étant *littéraire*, de *grand style* et plus *intéressant*, en étant *vrai*, si j'éteins à mon profit cette *furia francese*, qui se porte aux *Mystères* comme à la polka, comme à la *Grâce de Dieu*, je puis trouver 200,000 fr. pour 10 volumes des *Scènes de la vie militaire*, et j'ai du pain.[96]

This letter to Mme Hanska is a crucial document in any evaluation of Balzac's attitude to popularity and success; it contains the key which unifies the complexities and resolves the apparent contradictions of his position. With what a more experienced and disillusioned twentieth century can only regard as astonishing naivety, Balzac is demanding, in a commercially oriented world, the public and popular acclaim of genius; he is demanding that the nineteenth-century reader declare a preference for the *chef-d'oeuvre* over the 'faux dieux de cette littérature bâtarde',[97] of which Sue's work is the prime representative. This indeed is why the case of Balzac is such an instructive one. He is one of the first writers to be confronted with the modern realities of cultural fragmentation and the consequent loss of a relatively stable and satisfactory relationship with the public at large. This he has in common with many of his contemporaries but, whereas these are quick to withdraw, Balzac finds himself working through a highly complex and often contradictory process. Although the ultimate lesson of experience is a bitter one, there is nonetheless a side to Balzac's personality which seems at times genuinely to believe in the possibility of resisting and overcoming the schism separating the artist from the public, a belief attested, for instance, by the naive hope that a minor masterpiece such as *Modeste Mignon* might conceivably prove as successful with the public as Sue's *Mystères de Paris* ('le feuilleton, pourquoi ne vivrait-il pas par les contrastes?'). The failure of *Modeste Mignon* symbolizes the larger failure of Balzac's demand for a more discriminating response from the nineteenth-century reader. On the other hand, there were large-scale successes, notably with *Splendeurs et misères des courtisanes* and *La Cousine Bette*, but the problem (posed especially by *Splendeurs*) is whether or not Balzac achieved this belated popularity on his own terms or by providing, in part at least, simply a variation on the style and mode of Eugène Sue. Balzac may well have felt that 'le moment exige que je fasse deux ou trois oeuvres capitales qui renverseront les faux dieux de cette littérature batarde', but it is equally possible—the possibility needs, of course, to be tested through concrete analysis of the texts themselves—that he finally submitted to precisely that iron 'law' of modern popular writing he himself so contemptuously formulated in the preface to *Splendeurs*: 'Il faut bien accorder quelque chose au Dieu moderne, la majorité'[98] Indeed, it is because of their peculiar centrality in Balzac's problematical and ambiguous relationship with the con-temporary reading public, that these two novels, *Splendeurs et misères des courtisanes* and *La Cousine Bette*, occupy a particularly large place in the discussion which follows. Because of their relative success with the public, they provide a major focal point from which to consider the central question of this study: whether the various external pressures on the *Comédie humaine* are substantially reflected in the quality of the writing itself; or, alternatively, whether Balzac succeeded in negotiat-ing a position from which he was able, at one level, to accommodate some of the conventions and techniques associated with those pressures (what broadly I have called the conventions of 'melodrama'), while, at another level, pursuing within the novels themselves a strategy of transformation which recasts these conventions in radically new and challenging ways.

II Transformations

3 Chance and reality

Le hasard est le plus grand romancier du monde.
                                                    Balzac (I, 7)

Since Aristotle's discussion of the foundations of peripeteia in tragedy, the presence of 'chance' in literature has had an extremely bad press, characteristically seen as figuring among the more disreputable or irresponsible elements of the writer's repertoire. More specifically, the device of chance or coincidence is generally defined as belonging properly to the domain of low melodrama, exploited either, in T. S. Eliot's words (from his discussion of chance in the work of Wilkie Collins), 'simply for the sake of seeing the thrilling situation which arises in consequence',[1] or to furnish the easy moral reassurance that arises from the frequent association in melodrama of the coincidental with the mysterious workings of a just and benevolent providence. With certain rare exceptions, of which the grandest is *Oedipus Rex*, its appearance in a serious work is therefore likely to provoke in the reader feelings of dismay or embarrassment. Perhaps the most famous example of these forms of response is in the critical controversy that has always surrounded Shakespeare's *Romeo and Juliet*. Tragedy or melodrama?[2] The question is posed, of course, because—at the level of the dramatic action—the death of the lovers is immediately dependent upon the contingent fact of the friar's undelivered message; this dependence, in the familiar critical argument, represents either a serious violation of the inner aesthetic logic of tragedy or, at the very least, a somewhat trivial catalyst for the resolution of a dilemma whose deeper shaping forces lie elsewhere. But whether read as major lapse or minor embarrassment, the general response to the coincidence is characteristically negative; the security of the form and the tragic vision the form is designed to articulate would be greater if it were not there.

Tragedy, however, is a special case and to extrapolate from its central conventions a general law binding on all literary forms, including the novel, has no axiomatic validity. For manifold reasons, the history of tragedy is deeply implicated in notions of inevitability and fatality, but there is no necessary reason to assume that the premises on which tragedy is typically founded have to be identical to those regulating the form of the novel. It is true that analogies between drama and the novel have constituted a recurrent strategy in thinking about fiction, and they have often been highly fruitful at the level of both theory and practice. Equally, however, the analogies can prove to be reductive and restrictive, and this may well have been the case where the role of chance in the novel is concerned. On such analogies, a very simple set of evaluative equivalences can present itself: the novel of coincidence corresponds to the crudity of melodrama; the novel of consequential logic corresponds to the high seriousness of tragedy. Such a formula is not one that should be totally ignored, since some of the greatest effects in fiction have sprung from concentrations and inexorabilities of a kind that we tend to associate with the structure of tragedy. Yet the formula is of a narrowly schematic and simplifying order and, rigidly applied, often entails a serious neglect of the specific potentialities and achievements of the novel form. Unlike the highly codified nature of tragedy, the history of the novel, that most 'lawless' of forms as Gide once described it,[3] has not been marked by anything like the same degree of prescriptive rules and constraints; any attempt at formulating a legislative poetics of fiction is continually resisted by the stubborn flexibility and eclecticism of the form, so that what externally or mechanically is exactly the same structural device may, in one text, be seen as an index of the inferiority of the writing, but, in another text, may well operate as a significant element in the representation of a serious vision of the world.

The example of chance is a major case in point, its function and value varying quite considerably according to the different contexts and intentions which support and define it. In Wilkie Collins's *The Frozen Deep*, for instance, the two main protagonists (the accepted and the rejected lover), whose identities are unknown to each other and who in normal circumstances could not possibly have met, are joined by 'the long arm of coincidence' in a common adventure; we have no difficulty in recognizing that the sole purpose of the fortuitous encounter is to afford the mechanical excitements of the sensational plot. Similarly when, in *Les Mystères de Paris*, Eugène Sue climaxes the death of the arch-villain Jacques Ferrand through the latter stumbling quite by chance on the grave of the son he himself has murdered ('Poursuivi par la punition vengeresse de la luxure, le hasard le ramenait sur la fosse de son enfant... malheureux fruit de sa violence et de sa luxure . . . son front s'inonda d'une sueur glacée, ses genoux tremblants se dérobèrent sous lui, et il tomba sans mouvement à côté de cette tombe ouverte'), the intention and the effect of the device are quite clear: the glib narrative symmetry engineered by the coincidence is designed solely to intensify the atmosphere of crude horror and, by a specious effect of contiguity, to suggest the workings of a providential retribution ('il y avait quelque chose de fatal dans ce rapprochement').[4]

In the examples from both Collins and Sue (although it must be said that, in his best work, the former is greatly superior to the latter), the manipulation of chance is exclusively part of the melodramatic stock-in-trade of the popular entertainer. However, the picture is quite different if we turn to the work of, say, Dostoyevsky or Hardy, Proust or Pasternak, where chance often plays a decisive role in the structure of their novels but in a manner which demands and generally obtains from the reader a response of a much more sophisticated kind. In Dostoyevsky's *Crime and Punishment* the multiple coincidences of the plot are linked in a profound symbolic relationship with the psychological indeterminacies and unpredictabilities of character which are at the very heart of Dostoyevsky's exploration of human personality. In Hardy's *The Return of the Native*, chance finds its place in the elaboration of a deeply felt metaphysic, equivalent in seriousness and intensity to, for example, the anguished play on *hasard* and *destin* in Nerval's poetic cosmology. In Proust's novel we find the paradox that the discovery of the 'essential self', the self transcending the contingencies of experience ('hors des contingences du temps'), depends entirely on the purely random and contingent encounter with the objects which trigger the process of self-discovery ('Cet objet, il depend du hasard que nous le rencontrions avant de mourir, ou que nous ne le rencontrions pas').[5] Pasternak's *Dr Zhivago* offers a narrative dominated in many key areas by an elaborate network of coincidence; it is by what in the text itself is called 'an astounding coincidence'[6] that Strelnikov and Zhivago meet in the depths of the Russian countryside, and the encounter is at once utterly sensational and absolutely decisive: it precipitates the suicide of Strelnikov and the decision by Zhivago to embark on a new life. A similarly astonishing set of circumstances frames and shapes the ending of the novel: Lara, after several years' absence and having completely lost contact with Zhivago, not only returns to Moscow on the very day of the latter's death, but fortuitously discovers the fact of his death by going, on simple impulse, to the long since abandoned flat of her former husband in which Zhivago himself happens to have been living. Here the long arm of coincidence appears to stretch exceedingly long indeed. Yet this is far from representing a capitulation to banal and facile sensationalism. The incidents in question can certainly be named in terms of the familiar melodramatic convention, but can be properly appreciated only when it is understood that the convention from which they spring has been reworked and transformed to create a poetic device which contributes directly to the informing vision of the novel. At one level, it corresponds to Pasternak's deep sense of 'the interwovenness of all human lives'[7], as he describes it earlier in the novel, a sense of connection and convergence which transcends our customary rationalistic and causal ordering of things and yet which is completely different from the trite moral reference to 'providence' that accompanies Sue's use of coincidence. At another level—and this is a perspective we might bear in mind in relation to Balzac—the use of coincidence in *Dr Zhivago* derives from a mode of social and historical understanding. It serves to register, in a heightened form, one of the im-

portant perceptions offered by the novel, that of society in the midst of
the experience of revolution, a society in which nearly all the regulated
and predictable patterns of living have been so massively dislocated and
fractured by the upheavals of the revolution that almost anything is
possible, that even the most unsuspected turns of events, the most
spectacular criss-crossings and convergences of otherwise disparate
individual destinies become an integral part of the common experience;
in short, a society in which chance and accident—conventionally
known as the very antithesis of the 'realistic'—assume paradoxically a
kind of social normality.

The particular example of Pasternak is moreover of special interest in
that elsewhere he sketched an explicit rationale of his technique which,
for several reasons, it is worth quoting in part here. In his article, *A Visit
with Pasternak*, Ralph Maitlaw reports Pasternak as having said:

> In the nineteenth-century masters of the novel, Balzac, Tolstoy,
> Stendhal, if you take away the characters, the imagery, descrip-
> tion and so on, you still have left causality, the concept that an
> action has a consequence. . . . For me reality lies not there, but in
> the multiplicity of the universe, in the large number of pos-
> sibilities, a kind of spirit of freedom, a coincidence of impulses and
> inspirations. . . . Even modern science and mathematics, about
> which I know little, or better, nothing, is moving in that direc-
> tion, away from simple causality . . . . Nature is much richer in
> coincidence than is our imagination. . . . I have frequently been
> asked about the coincidences in the book. . . . Of course I made the
> coincidences on purpose, that is life, just as I purposely did not
> fully characterize the people in the book. For I wanted to get away
> from the idea of causality. The innovation of the book lies pre-
> cisely in this conception of reality.[8]

This passage is of great interest in at least two fundamental respects. In
the first place, it provides the spectacle of a great creative novelist
defending, with authority and conviction, the innovative possibilities
of a literary device generally viewed with the utmost contempt. Secondly, however, and of immediate relevance to the argument being
conducted here, Pasternak emphasizes the originality of his conception
by consciously setting it against what he construes as the typical practices of the classic nineteenth-century narrative tradition—a tradition
marked by the names of Balzac, Tolstoy, Stendhal, and defined by a
common stress on the importance of causality. At first sight the contrast
seems self-evident, even rather commonplace. Yet, on closer inspec-
tion, matters turn out to be rather more complicated. We are all familiar
with the essentially linear, sequential structure of the Stendhalian novel,
yet it could hardly be claimed that it is a clear-sighted vision of 'causality' which governs, for instance, Stendhal's presentation of the Battle
of Waterloo in *La Chartreuse de Parme*; on the contrary, what is drama-

tized here is a vision of history in the making in terms of an experience of pure contingency, where the disjunctions between 'cause' and 'effect', intention and result, the manifold reversals, surprises and coincidences, conspire in an elaborate network of ironies to confront the hero's expectations of order with a shapeless and derisory chaos. We are equally familiar with Tolstoy's 'determinism', his radical obsession with the causation of historical events, but that insistent concern has to be situated in the context of a complex, often extremely difficult meditation that incorporates the casual as well as the causal, the random as well as the inevitable, into its field of reference. (At the level of the narrative action, *War and Peace* abounds in coincidence, and it is perhaps also worth recalling that, in relation to the presentation of the war episodes, Tolstoy acknowledged a specific debt to Stendhal.)

What then of Balzac, the other of the three novelists Pasternak names as the major representatives of causal narrative? Initially, he seems to represent the least equivocal of cases. Indeed, in certain important areas of Balzac's literary and intellectual preoccupations, the term 'chance' figures as something of a dirty word or, more accurately, as part of the vocabulary of fools ('le nom de hasard, le grand mot des sots' (VIII, 700)). To ordinary mortals, life may present itelf as 'une espèce de loterie' but, continues Balzac, 'ce n'est que bien tard que le philosophe aperçoit la fatalité des existences individuelles, entraînée par le courant du système';[9] this is a view directly echoed by Louis Lambert: 'Si le hasard n'est pas, il faut admettre le Fatalisme, ou la co-ordination forcée des choses soumises à un plan général' (x, 415). The insistence upon the fundamental unity of the world, upon an order and an intelligibility hidden beneath the chaotic and random flux of surface appearances (and accessible only to the 'genius') is, in fact, a recurrent feature of Balzac's thought. The emphasis can fall on the idea of a determinist causality governing the unfolding of events in time ('De part et d'autre, tout se déduit, tout s'enchaîne. La cause fait deviner un effet, comme chaque effet permet de remonter à une cause.' (IX, 475)), or, in a more spatial perspective, it can fall on the idea of the world as a network of correspondences and analogies ('tout dans la nature est analogie'[10]) which finds its source—and here Balzac shares the concerns of the mystical thought of the period—in the unifying presence of God ('Dieu n'a-t-il pas agi par l'unité de composition?'(x, 556)).

The philosophical commitment to the idea of the universe as regulated by the principles of unity and fatality evidently carries implications for Balzac's conception and practice of the novel. Seen in the most general terms, these implications are essentially twofold. In the first place, there is a direct connection between the philosophical assumptions and the adoption, within the novels, of the posture of the omniscient narrator, who transcends the contingencies of time and space to see and apprehend things as a system of interrelated parts. In this respect, we might recall here the revealing speech of Antiquaire in

La Peau de chagrin, clearly related to Balzac's conception of the art of the novelist: 'Comment préférer tous les désastres de vos volontés trompées à la faculté sublime de faire comparaître en soi l'univers, au plaisir immense de se mouvoir sans être garrotté par les liens du temps ni par les entraves de l'espace, au plaisir de tout embrasser, de tout voir, de se pencher sur le bord du monde pour interroger les autres sphères, pour écouter Dieu'(IX, 41). Secondly, and closely related to the first implication, the novelist's passionate appetite for unity leads to the familiar Balzacian idea of the structure of the novel as constituting a kind of 'system': 'Quel que soit le nombre des accessoires et la multiplicité des figures, un romancier moderne doit les grouper d'après leur importance, les subordonner au soleil de son système.'[11] What is envisaged, in this metaphor, is a novel that embodies a consciously planned and fully integrated network of necessities, a rigorous chain of cause and effect, and of which the cornerstone, in concrete structural terms, is the famous 'art des préparations'. Whether the justifying reference be to the philosophical notion of a transcendent fatality or to the model of classical tragedy and its pattern of inexorability[12] or to the 'scientific' laws of historical and environmental causation, the characteristic narrative mode of the *Comédie humaine* is that of a relentless determinism shaping the destiny of the individual, from its major outlines down to its minutest detail. As is well known, the typical Balzacian novel is built around a central dramatic scene or episode which decides the fate of the individual but which is itself, so to speak, announced from afar, causally grounded in an elaborately constructed framework of preceding circumstance; 'les vicissitudes de la vie sociale et privée', writes Balzac in *Les Paysans*, 'sont engendrées par un monde de petites causes qui tiennent à tout' (VIII, 154). The model of narrative structure proposed, therefore, is one in which every component is subordinated to the exigencies of a systematic causality, and from which consequently every element of the contingent and the accidental has been mercilessly stripped—in short, a structure which, in the words of Antoine Allemand, enacts 'une perpétuelle répudiation du hasard'.[13]

Such a view of the Balzacian novel, retraced here in a highly condensed and schematic form, is one that has been fully consecrated by the Balzac critics. Nevertheless, it overlooks a great deal of evidence, suggesting that both Balzac's conception and his literary practice are, in fact, more complex than scholars such as Allemand have argued. For if we accept that Balzac's practice can be described in terms of a conscious and systematic 'repudiation' of the contingent, how are we to account for a number of insistently recurring phrases in the text of Balzac's work—'par l'un de ces hasards qui n'arrivent pas deux fois dans la vie' (V, 20), 'par un singulier hasard' (II, 138), 'le hasard de la vie sociale' (I, 420), 'voici le futile et niais hasard qui décida de la vie de cette jeune fille' (I, 398), 'par un de ces hasards qui n'arrivent qu'aux jolies femmes' (I, 1035), 'par un hasard assez naturel' (VIII, 130), 'par un de ces hasards qui ne sont invraisemblables que dans les livres' (IX, 645), etc? What is the status of remarks of this nature? Are they merely the residual verbal reflexes of an author who occasionally dabbled in the melodramatic idiom of *le bas romantisme*? Are they simply evidence of a vestigial contamination by the style of the *roman noir*, reinforced by Balzac's later involvement with the commercial *roman-feuilleton*, in which spectacular coincidence and abrupt reversal of fortune were commonplace ingredients of the normal fictional brew? Undoubtedly this is part of the answer. For example, in the story, *La Duchess de Langeais*, the second of the triptych *Histoire des Treize*, the dénouement of the central drama hinges on the facile exploitation of the classic melodramatic device of *le trop-tard*: at the crucial moment of their tortured relationship, Antoinette de Langeais sends a letter to Armand in which she states that if he does not leave his home at eight o'clock in the evening to come to see her, she will withdraw from the world into a convent; Armand fully intends to comply, but his departure is delayed because 'sa pendule retardait, et il ne sortait pour aller à l'hôtel de Langeais qu'au moment où la duchesse, emportée par une rage froide, fuyait à pieds dans les rues de Paris' (V, 246). The sequence of events that ensues thus springs from the banal incident of a clock happening to be a quarter of an hour slow, and from precisely that moment where 'chance' takes a hand in the unfolding of the narrative, what had hitherto been an absorbing and complex study in the interaction of desire, pride and humiliation collapses into the triviality of the *roman d'aventures*.

What happens in *La Duchesse de Langeais* suggests, therefore, that the appearance of chance in Balzac's work is something of a disaster, a disabling capitulation to a debased narrative idiom. But this is by no means the end of the matter, and the case to be argued here is that the presence of chance as a structural determinant in many of the novels of the *Comédie humaine* is a much more complicated business altogether; that chance in the novels of Balzac enters in a direct and significant way into the comprehension of reality the novels seek to project. Balzac may well have described the concept of 'hasard' as 'le grand mot des sots', but elsewhere he is equally capable of stressing the exact oposite: 'Il y a en ce monde des hasards auxquels les gens de petit esprit n'accordent point de créance, parce que ces dites rencontres semblent supernaturelles; mais les hommes de haute imagination les tiennent pour vraies, parce qu'on ne saurait les inventer';[14] and, despite the somewhat specious logic of that last clause, it is a stress that needs to be borne in mind if a vital and generally neglected aspect of Balzac's conception and technique are to be properly understood. For, set against the demiurgic impulse to create a novelistic 'system' shaped by an implacable determinism, there is also in Balzac a haunting awareness of the fragility and unpredictability of lived experience, a sense of its frequent dependence on the operation of purely random and fortuitous circumstances. In more precise terms, it is an awareness that is directly linked to a particular form of social and historical seeing, to a mode of understanding the specific nature of the society which constitutes the main subject matter of the *Comédie humaine*.

We may begin to approach this socio-historical meaning of chance in the *Comédie* if we consider for a moment the general experience of modern history, as it is registered in the work of most of the representative social thinkers of the nineteenth century. The crux of that experience is, of course, the enormously disruptive effect produced by the ideology and practices of the new individualism. From Chateaubriand and Burke down through Saint-Simon, Carlyle and Ruskin to Marx and Arnold, and cutting across a wide range of differing ideological and political perspectives, we meet a common emphasis: individualism, springing from and feeding off a society at the moment of crisis, breakdown and transition, equals disorder, the play of anarchic forces over which neither men nor institutions can exercise meaningful social control. The characteristic form or model through which this perception of contemporary historical change is articulated is that of the opposition between past and present. Saint-Simon's distinction between 'creative' and 'critical' periods, Carlyle's distinction between order and chaos, his opposition of the 'hard organic' society of the middle ages and the 'pulpy inorganic' society of the industrial ages, Tocqueville's differentiation of 'aristocratic' and 'democratic' societies and Arnold's of 'epochs of concentration' and 'epochs of expansion'—all tend towards the view which, schematically, identifies the past, or certain moments of the past, with order, hierarchy, with a state of affairs in which the basic patterns of social living are precisely determined, known and therefore predictable, in radical contrast to the present grasped as flux, disorder, fragmentation, where since nothing is stable, little is predictable. As Marx put it:

> Constant revolutionizing of production, uninterrupted disturbance of all social conditions, everlasting uncertainty and agitation distinguish the bourgeois epoch from all earlier ones. All fixed, fast-frozen relations, with their train of ancient and venerable prejudices and opinions, are swept away, all new-formed ones become antiquated before they can ossify. All that is solid melts into air.[15]

Or, to cite Carlyle, from one of the more apocalyptic passages of *Past and Present*:

> Our Epic having now become *Tools and the Man*, it is more than usually impossible to prophesy the Future. The boundless Future does lie there, predestined, nay already extant though unseen . . . but the supremest intelligence of man cannot prefigure much of it . . . . Straining our eyes hitherto, the utmost effort of intelligence sheds but the most glimmering dawn, a little way into its dark enormous deeps: only huge outlines loom uncertain on the sight; and the ray of prophecy, at a short distance, expires.[16]

This conflation of nineteenth-century social and historical analysis represents a drastically reductive simplification and totally ignores the manifold divergencies, complexities and ambiguities that distinguish each of the thinkers in question. (Saint-Simon, for instance, believed that the individualistic jungle of capitalism could be tamed, while Tocqueville, on the model of America, perceived real possibilities of stabilization in 'democratic' societies.) But these are not our concern here; in terms of the immediate argument, what is important is the recognition, above and beyond all difference and complexity, of a common emphasis in the apprehension of nineteenth century history and society, for it opens up a general space of experience and discourse in which certain aspects of Balzac's vision, and the narrative techniques which serve that vision, can be comprehended.

Thus, at one level, history and historical change are seen by Balzac as being governed by wholly intelligible general 'laws':

> A l'envisager philosophiquement, l'espèce humaine peut être considérée comme un être collectif qui se développe suivant des lois que l'on peut observer de telle sorte que, d'après le passé, on puisse établir la tendance et conclure l'avenir. L'histoire a pour objet d'étudier ces lois. . . . Elle devient une science positive qui a pour objet l'étude de l'humanité. Elle est plutôt la science générale qui comprend toutes les sciences et leur perfectionnement, tous les sentiments et toutes les révolutions politiques.[17]

At another level, however, that of the individual's immersion in the flux and immediacy of events (a level that the novelist in Balzac, in the interests of fidelity to actual experience, must respect), historical change is frequently felt as a sequence of bewildering, unpredictable, contingent occurrences. More specifically, the great historical upheavals of the Revolution, Empire and Restoration are seen as bringing about a huge dislocation of the essentially stable, hierarchical and therefore predictable way of life assumed as characteristic of the pre-revolutionary social order. The perspective is there, for instance, in the curious little fable Balzac wrote in 1842, 'Voyage d'un Lion d'Afrique à Paris':

> Ce détaché . . . vous a parfaitement expliqué comment ce pays était dans une époque de transition, c'est-à-dire qu'on ne peut prophétiser que le présent, tant les choses y vont vite. L'instabilité des choses publiques entraîne l'instabilité des positions particulières. Evidemment, ce peuple se prépare à devenir une horde. Il éprouve un si grand besoin de locomotion que, depuis dix ans surtout, en voyant tout aller à rien, il s'est mis en marche aussi: tout est danse et galop.[18]

Stability now gives way to the mobility, uncertainty and confusion of the new individualism, to what Balzac in *Béatrix* calls 'l'incertitude et l'inconstance de notre époque' (II, 335). The essential spectacle is of a series of historical transformations generating a fundamentally unsettled society, in which almost anything is possible, in which roles and functions are no longer determined by a rigid hierarchy but can fluctuate up and down the social scale according to unforeseen and apparently fortuitous shifts and turns of circumstance. As the conservative Balzac puts it in *L'Interdiction*, commenting bitterly on the breakdown of a fixed social structure occasioned by historical events: 'le hasard s'est arrogé le droit de faire des nobles' (III, 64); an emphasis echoed in *La Duchesse de Langeais* where, discussing the peculiar mobility of the epoch in terms of a shifting class structure, Balzac distinguishes firmly between the ancient hereditary aristocracy and the recent parvenu aristocracy, described significantly as 'les aristocrates de hasard' (v, 150). A particularly striking example of this kind of relationship between the turbulence of history and the vagaries of individual destiny is to be found in the opening section of *Modeste Mignon*, where the multiple vicissitudes of Charles Mignon's early career (aristocratic birth, dispossession and poverty during the Revolution, ascendancy during the Empire, financial collapse under the Bourbons) are presented as springing directly from the kaleidoscopic, rapidly changing and, from the individual's point of view, uncontrollable and unexpected course of historical events (I, 372–7).

This general sense of modern times as inherently insecure and unpredictable may be further specified in terms of two particular and central themes in the *Comédie humaine*—those of money and the city. Much has been written on the centrality of money in the *Comédie*, as the vantage point from which Balzac describes and evaluates the fundamental characteristics of his society. Relatively unnoticed, however, is the close connection in Balzac's imagination between the accumulation of wealth and the agencies of chance. The major context here is, once again, the contrast between past and present. Balzac tends to see wealth and property in pre-revolutionary times as being allied to birth and expressed largely in land and, as such, the foundations of a relatively secure, cohesive and productive system. The point is explicitly made in *La Duchesse de Langeais*, where the value Balzac accords to the idea of a patrician social order is specifically predicated on the economic commitment of the old aristocracy to 'le domaine': 'Ces avantages sont acquis à l'aristocratie française, comme à toutes les efflorescences patriciennes qui se produisent à la surface des nations aussi longtemps qu'elles assiéront leur existence sur le domaine, le domaine sol comme le domaine argent, seule base solide d'une société regulière' (v, 147). One of the main indices of the changing times, of the breakdown of a 'société regulière', is the abandonment of that commitment as the aristocracy increasingly exchanges its land for cash in order to enter the alluring but treacherous zone of speculation: 'le faubourg [Saint Germain] vendait ses terres pour jouer à la Bourse' (151). In the new society, wealth is increasingly transformed into finance capital, into an autonomous agent, abstracted from the immediate context of material production (recall the exchange between César Birotteau and Claparon: 'La Spéculation, dit le parfumeur, quel est ce commerce? C'est le commerce abstrait, reprit Claparon' (523)), and placed into a feverish circulation which is subject only to the anarchic and hazardous forces of the 'market'. Thus, where wealth was once a source of cohesion, money or capital now becomes an instrument of dissolution, responsible for the emergence of a fluid, shifting, disordered social reality. As Lionel Trilling has remarked, commenting on the role of money in general in the novel, and perhaps consciously echoing Carlyle's account of the 'cashnexus' as that which 'absolves and liquidates all engagements of man',[19]: 'Money [is] the great solvent of the solid fabric of the old society.... Money is the medium ... that makes for a fluent society.'[20]

In such a context, the making of money becomes, literally and metaphorically, a gamble,[21] a wager on chance, realizing either the dream of instant wealth or the nightmare of instant ruin. Indeed, the analogy between gambling and modern economic practice is a recurrent motif in nineteenth-century European literature and social criticism. In Dostoyevsky's *The Gambler*, the narrator remarks: 'However ridiculous it may seem to you that I was expecting to win at roulette, I look upon the generally accepted opinion concerning the folly and grossness of hoping to win at gambling as a thing even more absurd. For why is gambling a whit worse than any other method of acquiring money? How, for instance, is it worse than trade?'[22] Trollope's sense of the profound disturbances threatening the social landscape of Victorian England is centred on the movement from the 'solidities' of land into the risk-laden speculative enterprises of the City of London; his novel *The Prime Minister*, for example, is built to a large extent around the contrast, designed as typical of a general tendency, between the modern City operator, Lopez, a kind of high-class gambler, and the dependable Fletcher, representative of the traditional landed gentry:

—I am engaged in foreign loans.
—Very precarious I should think. A sort of gambling, isn't it?
—It is the business by which many of the greatest mercantile houses in the city have been made.[23]

One of the characteristics stressed by Carlyle in his description of the 'lawless anarchy' of laissez-faire capitalism is the growth of what he calls 'gambling speculation'.[24] In *The Roots of Honour*, Ruskin observed that 'the tendency of all modern mercantile operations is to throw both wages and trade into the form of a lottery, and to make the workman's pay depend on intermittent exertion and the principal's profit on dexterously used chance';[25] the French social historian, Eugène Buret, similarly stressed the vulnerability of the economic system, and in particular the livelihood of the working class, to the play of apparently random forces: 'Pour le prolétaire de l'industrie . . . la vie est à la merci des chances du jeu, des caprices du hasard.'[26]

At the heart of this radically unstable economic system, there stands the Stock Exchange, like some vast, institutionalized gaming table, legitimizing the principle of 'risk' in the circulation and exchange of capital. An editorial in the newspaper, *Le Constitutionnel*, of 1838 declares that 'la Bourse a remplacé Frascati et la loterie.'[27] In *Moeurs et portraits du temps*, Louis Reybaud speaks critically of 'le spectacle de ce succès insolent, de cette surprise faite aux divinités du *hasard*' offered daily by the activities of the Bourse: 'Il existe maintenant une manière de faire fortune qui n'exige ni travail de corps ni d'esprit, et suffit pour convertir, du matin au soir, un pauvre diable en millionnaire. C'est à la Bourse que se professe cet art nouveau de faire fortune en un clin d'oeil. . . . C'est donc un jeu, un jeu public, le seul qui survive aux jeux abolis.'[28] In the *Comédie humaine*, it is, above all, the Stock Exchange which furnishes the main context for the analogy between the economics of speculation and the game of chance. Described by Balzac, in *Melmoth réconcilié*, as 'une grande table de bouillotte' (IX, 306), the Stock Exchange consistently appears in Balzac's work as at once the symbol and the central institution of an economic order founded upon the vagaries of chance, dominated by individuals such as Nucingen or Claparon, 'négociant assez connu pour hasarder de grands coups qui pouvaient aussi bien le ruiner que l'enrichir (IX, 306). Du Tillet sets in motion the plot of *Cesar Birotteau* by advising Roguin 'de prendre dès à présent une forte somme, de la lui confier pour être jouée avec audace dans quelque partie quelconque, à la Bourse, ou dans quelque spécu-lation choisie entre les mille qui s'entreprenaient alors' (V, 373). In *La Maison Nucingen*, a story whose structure turns entirely on the man-ipulation of capital, the foundations of the baron's spectacular fortune are established partly through careful and cunning financial planning, but just as much as the result of a 'une circonstance inouïe' (V, 691) whereby a precarious speculation miraculously pays off.[29] Conversely, rapidly accumulated wealth can, in the shifting sands of speculation, give way to equally rapid disaster; in *Un Début dans la vie*, Balzac traces the relationship between political change and sudden capital move-ments in describing the effect of Napoleon's advent to power on the fate of the capitalist, Husson, 'un fournisseur qui gagna des millions et que Napoléon ruina en 1802. Cet homme . . . devint fou de son passage subit de l'opulence à la misère, il se jeta dans la Seine' (I, 627). Again, to return to the example of *Modeste Mignon*, Charles Mignon amasses a fortune, only to find himself in ruins overnight because of the unpredictable vicissitudes of the stock market: 'En janvier 1826, au milieu d'une fête, quand le Havre tout entier désignait Charles Mignon pour son député, trois lettres venues de New-York, de Paris et de Londres, avaient été comme autant de coups de marteau sur le palais de verre de la Prosp-érité. En dix minutes, la ruine avait fondu de ses ailes de vautour sur cet inouï bonheur, comme le froid sur la Grande Armée en 1812' (I, 377).

Money is, thus, one of the main thematic contexts in which the contingent and the unpredictable appear not as crude narrative devices, but as the sign of an instability which Balzac sees as being at the very core of his society. But perhaps the context in which chance is above all of central importance is that of Balzac's treatment of the theme of the city, and it is this that I should like to consider in some detail, with special reference to one particular novel, *Splendeurs et misères des courtisanes*. *Splendeurs* is generally reckoned to be the most 'melodramatic' of Balzac's mature novels. Jean-Louis Bory, for instance, has remarked on the degree to which the shape and movement of the narrative are dictated by *le hasard* and *le trop-tard*;[30] it is as a result of 'un hasard de grand'route' that, at the end of *Illusions perdues*, Vautrin meets Lucien and thus launches his renewed attempt at the conquest of Paris. By a fine irony, Nucingen, whose position as the prince of speculation has been achieved precisely through the manipulation of *les hasards* of the Stock Exchange, initiates a complex concatenation of events through a purely fortuitous encounter with Esther in the Bois de Vincennes; if Lucien is saved from suicide by a chance meeting with Vautrin, then his ruin is also brought about by the chance failure of the news of Esther's inheritance to arrive in time. Again, Vautrin arrives just 'too late' at the bedside of the poisoned Esther, Europe and Paccard have disappeared with the money extracted from Nucingen, and Lucien will be arrested on a charge of theft; Madame de Sérizy succeeds in obtaining the dismissal of the charges against Lucien, but a few moments before she brings the news to him, Lucien hangs himself. These are but the most immediate and important elements of a narrative packed with the unpredictable and the coincidental, in which everyday causality, the commonplace order of things, yield to the fantasmagoric, often nightmarish world of quasi-magical transformations.

The typical response of criticism has been to assess this aspect of the novel in terms of an ostensible lapse in artistic integrity, as representing a capitulation, under commercial pressure, to the mode of the *roman-feuilleton*, and, more particularly, to the kind of popular novel written by Eugène Sue. Certainly, and as we have seen in the previous chapter, much of the external evidence indicates the painful choice between resistance and accommodation with which the novel of Sue confronted Balzac, and it is clear from a number of sources that a significant strand of Balzac's career in the 1840s points in the direction of a move towards accommodation. In 1843-4, for example, there appears a collection of stories by different writers, including Balzac's *Dinah Piedefer* (*La Muse du département*), under the significant title of *Les Mystères de Province* [31] (Sue's most famous novel was, of course, *Les Mystères de Paris*). In 1844, Balzac describes to Mme Hanska his plan for *Les Bourgeois de Paris*, the title suggested by Hetzel and of which Balzac writes that it will comprise 'trois volumes semblables à ceux des *Mystères* [de Paris].'[32] In the same year he enters into an agreement with the projected but abortive newspaper, *Le Soleil*, to supply a *roman-feuilleton* whose title is to be none other than the obviously derivative *Les Enfers de Paris*[33]—perhaps the clearest indication of the extent to which the vogue for Sue was beginning to influence Balzac, especially in his growing concern with the more lurid and sensational aspects of Parisian life. By the middle of 1844, his objectives have become quite explicit, since he mentions the various projects 'qui me permettront de battre les généraux, E. Sue, A. Dumas, Soulié et autres gens de plume'.[34]

It is against this background that the writing of *Splendeurs*, more particularly the last two parts, has to be seen, and it is one that seems to speak unequivocally of a fatal yielding to commercial pressure in the interests of that large-scale, immediate success Balzac so desperately longed for; as Balzac himself put it, in the revealing moment of fatigue and despair during the composition of the second part of the novel: 'Je fais du Sue tout pur. Oh, combien j'ai besoin de repos!'[35] Yet against these admissions, one must set the various occasions when, in the correspondence with Mme Hanska, Balzac insists that in fact *Splendeurs* makes no concessions to the style and methods of Sue; that, on the contrary, in its imaginative treatment of the Parisian lower depths, *Splendeurs* exemplifies a serious realism fundamentally different from the melodramatic crudities of Sue's novel. In June 1843, he declares to Mme Hanska, '*Esther* est une horrible peinture. Il fallait la faire et elle me sera reprochée, comme on m'a reproché *La Fille aux yeux d'or*. Mais il faut faire Paris vrai';[36] and some time later, 'Vous lirez l'étrange comédie d'Esther; je vous l'enverrai bien corrigée et vous y verrez un monde bien autre que le faux Paris des *Mystères*.'[37] This insistence on sociological accuracy is to be found elsewhere; for example, in the text of the novel itself, Balzac talks of presenting 'le monde des filles, des voleurs et des assassins' in the context of that 'reproduction littérale de notre état social' (v, 1046) which, like the 'reproduction rigoreuse' of the *Avant-propos*, constitutes one of the foundations of Balzac's approach to the task of the novel. In the preface to the de Potter edition of *Splendeurs* (in which incidentally he specifically denounces the *roman-feuilleton*), Balzac again affirms the social veracity of his text, 'un livre où sont peintes les existences, dans toute leur vérité, des espions, des filles entretenues et des gens en guerre avec la société qui grouillent dans Paris'—a text 'composé de détails profondément vrais' and which he implicitly distinguishes from mere current fashion by designating its natural place in the *Comédie humaine* ('la grande et immense figure de Paris au XIXe siècle sera terminée (xi, 416–17)).

Declarations of intent are, of course, no guarantee of achievement, and equally, a conception of the novel as a 'reproduction littérale' of society is not one that will take us very far. Yet it is in relation to these assertions of some kind of meaningful fidelity to social reality that the 'melodramatic' apparatus of chance and coincidence in *Splendeurs et misères des courtisanes* assumes much of its significance, to be grasped as working not so much in contradiction to Balzac's 'realist' intentions, but rather as a direct extension of them. More specifically, and as

Donald Fanger has suggested in a more general context, it may be postulated that melodrama in *Splendeurs* finds part of its artistic rationale 'in the myth of the modern city';[38] that is, it forms part of a complex imaginative response to the often bizarre and extraordinary situations generated by the disordered, frenetic rhythms of life in the metropolis, a response which can therefore be adequately articulated only through the elaboration of a form of writing to which Dostoyevsky was later to give the name 'fantastic realism'.[39] The association of the 'romanesque' (in the sense of the extravagant and the improbable) with the actual nature of the modern city, a deeply rooted awareness of the fortuitous and the unforeseen as natural properties of the modern urban landscape, is indeed one of the constants of Balzac's imagination. In *Les Comédiens sans le savoir* we are told that 'tout est possible à Paris' (vii, 15), an emphasis repeated in *Illusions perdues*, 'la nature sociale est si fertile en inventions que rien n'y est impossible' (iv, 782); in *Ferragus*, Balzac speaks of Paris, in a conscious echo of *The Thousand and One Nights*, as the 'monstrueuse merveille . . . la ville aux cent mille romans' (v, 19) ('roman' to be understood here in terms of the connotations of 'romanesque'); in the preface to *Le Cabinet des antiques*, the example of *Histoire des Treize* is again adduced to support a view of the 'romanesque' as a form of the 'vrai': 'Mais quant à l'ensemble des faits rapportés par l'auteur, ils sont tous vrais pris isolément, même les plus romanesques, comme ceux si bizarres de la *Fille aux yeux d'or*' (xi, 368); in Félix Davin's *Etudes de moeurs au XIXe siecle*, probably written under Balzac's dictation, the analogy with *The Thousand and One Nights* reappears and Paris is seen as the centre of a society 'incessamment dissoute, incessamment recomposée . . . sans liens, sans principes, sans homogenéité' (xi, 230), perpetually unsettled, endlessly variegated, continually fertile in the sensational and the unexpected, in short the source of 'tout ce qu'il est permis à notre époque de comprendre et d'accepter de fantastique' (xi, 247). In the novels, this emphasis is again found in the recurring imagery of sea, ocean, storm, used to evoke the restless, ever-changing, ceaselessly astonishing rhythms of metropolitan life—'l'immense mer des intérêts parisiens' (v, 593), 'le grand mouvement de Paris' (iv, 478), 'Paris . . . un vaste champ incessament remué par une tempête d'intérêts' (v, 255), 'les fluctuations de la mer parisienne' (v, 812), 'l'agitation quasi-marine de cette grande cité' (v, 845). Above all, there is the celebrated passage in *Le Père Goriot* in which the metaphor of the mysterious and inexhaustible ocean is introduced to focus the novelist's sense of the special kinds of inspiration furnished by the spectacle of Paris:

> Mais Paris est un véritable océan. Jetez-y la sonde, vous n'en connaîtrez jamais la profondeur. Parcourez-le, décrivez-le, quelque soin que vous mettiez à le parcourir, à le décrire; quelque nombreux et intéressés que soient les explorateurs de cette mer, il s'y rencontrera toujours un lieu vierge, un antre inconnu, des

> fleurs, des perles, des monstres, quelque chose d'inouï, oublié par
> les plongeurs littéraires (ii, 806).

This tissue of metaphor and analogy points to a reading of the role of chance in the plot of *Splendeurs et misères des courtisanes* which is radically different from that generally proposed by Balzac's critics. The omnipresence of the contingent in the novel suggests that this is more than mere facile contrivance, but that it contributes directly to the understanding of social reality the novel mediates. Thus, the violent and disordered world of thieves and criminals may present itself as utterly incredible, but its authenticity is attested 'par de célèbres drames judiciaires' (iv, 725) enacted at the Courts of Assize. The fragile existence of the prostitute, situated on the extreme margin of society, frantically oscillating between wealth and poverty, joy and despair, life and death, is subject more than any other to the haphazard and uncontrollable vicissitudes of fortune: 'extrêmes dans tout, dans leurs joies, dans leurs désespoirs, dans leur irreligion; presque toutes deviendraient folles si la mortalité qui leur est particulière ne les décimait, et si d'heureux hasards n'élevaient quelques-unes d'entre elles au-dessus de la fange où elles vivent.' (682-3); although by no means exhausting her as a character, this generalization fits, in almost all its aspects, the particular shape of Esther's life. Most important of all is the theme of 'arrivisme', the risks and hazards encountered by the aspiring parvenu in his engagement with the treacherous terrain of the capital. In his essay on Henry James's *The Princess Casamassima*, Lionel Trilling, commenting generally on the theme of 'arrivisme' in nineteenth-century European fiction, has written: 'It is the fate of the Young Man to move from an obscure position into one of considerable eminence in Paris or London or St Petersburg. . . . His situation is as chancy as that of any questing knight of medieval romance.[40] (In this respect it is an interesting linguistic fact that the term 'chancer' has come into English idiomatic use as a synonym for 'opportunist'.) Certainly, 'chanciness' is a central feature of the multiple explorations of the theme offered by the *Comédie humaine*, and it should come as no surprise to discover, in this context, the reappearance of the analogy with the gambler. Thus, Rastignac's combative assertion, 'je réussirai' is described by Balzac as 'le mot du joueur' (ii, 918), echoed by Vautrin's remark, 'pour s'enrichir, il s'agit ici de jouer de grands coups' (937) and by Rastignac's observation to Bianchon, 'Il est, vois-tu, des circonstances dans la vie ou il faut jouer gros jeu et ne pas user son bonheur à gagner des sous' (961). Indeed in Rastignac's case, the gambling motif assumes a literal form: at a decisive moment of his career he wins a small fortune at roulette, thus enabling Delphine de Nucingen to pay off her debts and in turn laying the foundations of his own social success: in a straight act of exchange, Delphine becomes his mistress and hence a vital stepping-stone on the upward journey to fame and fortune. In *Z Marcas*, the central character remarks, 'Pour les ambitieux, Paris est une immense roulette, et tous les jeunes gens croient y trouver une victorieuse martingale' (vii, 747), a view repeated by Henriette de Mortsauf in the advice she gives to the young Félix on the ways of the world: 'A qui voit ainsi la société, le problème que constitue une fortune à faire, mon ami, se réduit à jouer une partie dont les enjeux sont un million ou le bagne' (viii, 887); the critical moment in the life of the young Oscar Husson, in *Un Début dans la vie*, is presented as entirely dependent on the forces of chance: 'le hasard qui perd les gens et le hasard qui les sauve firent des effets égaux pour et contre Oscar dans cette terrible matinée.'

Similarly, in the tracing of Lucien de Rubempré's perilous career throughout *Illusions perdues* and *Splendeurs et misères des courtisanes*, *le hasard* is a recurring and strategic leitmotif. Lousteau observes, 'Tout est hasard, voyez-vous. . . . Le hasard fait pour vous en un jour un miracle que j'ai attendu pendant deux ans' (iv, 705, 716); Balzac himself adduces the metaphor of the 'coup de baguette' to account for the way 'Lucien était si promptement passé de l'extrême misère à l'extrême opulence' (802); the final encounter with Vautrin is presented under the chapter heading of 'un hasard de grand'route', while in this same chapter Vautrin himself speaks of the social game to be played as analogous to the game of 'bouillotte' and instructs his protégé: 'embusquez-vous dans le monde parisien, attendez une proie et un hasard' (1027). In connection with Lucien's initially spectacular but ultimately disastrous re-entry into Parisian society in *Splendeurs*, we find an identical series of attitudes and comparisons. Lucien, exploiting the uncertainties and the mobility engendered by the new individualism, stakes his fate on a sacrifice 'au dieu le plus courtisé de cette cité royale, le Hasard' (656). The chance discovery of Esther, for instance, provides the basis for Vautrin's machinations and prompts from him the remark, 'Le hasard nous a mieux servi que ma pensée, qui depuis deux mois, travaillait dans le vide . . . il y a dans ce coup de roulette du bon et du mauvais, comme dans tout' (724). Lucien's destiny is a fragile construction pecariously poised between 'les bancs de la pairie . . . ou les bancs [du bagne]' (705); between the two extremes, anything can happen, nothing is predictable—a stroke of fortune, and Lucien is a marquis and an ambassador's secretary, a slight mishap, however, 'pouvait faire crouler le fantastique édifice d'une fortune si audacieusement bâtie' (728). Eventually, the unforeseen erupts sensationally to destroy the carefully laid plans, and in a matter of hours, Lucien experiences the dizzying descent 'du faîte des grandeurs sociales au fond d'un cachot' (918). It is true that in retrospect Lucien's fate seems the inevitable outcome of some iron law of necessity, but in the actual process of living that fate with Lucien, the reader may well feel inclined to give greater weight to a sense of pure contingency than to that of a transcendent determinism.

Several of the major social themes of the novel, the themes of criminality, prostitution and 'arrivisme', are thus directly served by a plot which establishes a central point of reference for them through its

continual insistence on the importance of the accidental and the indeterminate in certain areas of human affairs. More specifically, it should
be clear that a particular approach to the relation between literary
'realism' and the nature of the modern city is capable of yielding a
number of fruitful results in the interpretation and evaluation of some
of the narrative strategies of *Splendeurs*. That approach does, however,
raise almost as many problems as it solves. A particular kind of criticism
will concern itself not with whether the events and situations of *Splendeurs* have their analogues in real life, but with whether they properly
belong in a work of art. Like Balzac, Dickens was fond of asserting that
his elaborate and fantastic plots faithfully reflected the nature of his
society and, in particular, the nature of London. A contemporary critic
however, commenting in the *Westminster Review* on precisely this claim
in respect of the plot of *Our Mutual Friend*, wrote: 'Truth is not always
probable. And it is probability which is required in a work of art.'[41] The
problem, that of the relation between the true and the probable, is as old
as Aristotle's *Poetics* ('It is not the function of the poet to relate what has
happened but what may happen—what is possible according to the law
of probability or necessity'),[42] but it assumes a special edge in the
context of a realistic fiction whose 'realism' is in part defined by the
attempt to engage with what is apprehended as the diffuse and random
multiplicity of life. The problem is stated with exemplary clarity in the
text of *Splendeurs* itself:

> Une des obligations auxquelles ne doit jamais manquer l'historien
> des moeurs, c'est de ne point gâter le vrai par des arrangements en
> apparence dramatiques, surtout quand le vrai a pris la peine de
> devenir romanesque. La nature sociale, à Paris surtout, comporte
> de tels hasards, des enchevêtrements de conjectures si cap-
> ricieuses, que l'imagination des inventeurs est à tout moment
> dépassée. La hardiesse du vrai s'élève à des combinaisons inter-
> dites à l'art, tant elles sont invraisemblables ou peu décentes, à
> moins que l'écrivain ne les adoucisse, ne les émonde, ne les châtre
> (IV, 1087).

This passage is of capital importance in any discussion of the role of
'melodrama' in *Splendeurs*. On the one hand, it explicitly acknowledges
the sensational as an authentic component of the modern urban scene,
but on the other calls in question the extent to which it is the legitimate
terrain of literature. While the city is grasped as intrinsically 'melodramatic', Balzac nevertheless places important limitations on the literary exploitation of what that reality has to offer and, in so doing, raises
the more general question of the possibilities and limits of realism in the
novel: the metropolis is so exuberantly fertile in its invention of the
'romanesque' ('l'imagination des inventeurs est à tout moment dépas-
sée') that it has to be held in check and toned down. The rationale of this
imperative to modify what is given comes from the implicit rec-

ognition here of a logic operating independently of the immediate experience of the real, an autonomous logic of art to which everything must be subordinated and which demands the supression or modification of those elements which violate that logic. The conflict of aims we find in this passage (an immediate responsiveness to the 'extravagant' nature of the modern city against an urge to contain and modify that extravagance through reference to a pre-established artistic logic) may be said to dramatise a central tension of the novel in general. In the words of Virginia Woolf, 'It is the gift of style, arrangement, construction to put us at a distance from the special life and obliterate its features, while it is the gift of the novel to bring us into close touch with life. The two powers fight if they are brought into combination.'[43] The conflict between the disordered flux of life and the systematizing nature of art has long been one of the focal points of modern thinking about the novel, and evidently it raises theoretical and critical problems, the full elucidation of which cannot be undertaken here. However, in relation to the role of chance in the *Comédie humaine*, the essential issue is clearly in the opposing claims of the *vrai* and the *vraisemblable*, a dilemma which in France was made familiar largely by the debates of seventeenth-century literary theory. The plot of *Splendeurs* may well lay claim to exemplifying *le vrai* of city life, but it is not necessarily *vraisemblable* and, as Balzac puts it in *Les Paysans*, 'l'historien des moeurs obéit à des lois plus dures que celles qui régissent l'historien des faits; il doit rendre tout probable, même le vrai' (VIII, 154); thus he signals his apparent adherence to that cardinal law of classical poetics which demands the working of the diffuseness and contingency of the real into ordered aesthetic patterns.

Yet in Balzac's actual practice as a novelist that adherence is far from being a rigidly fixed, unnegotiable literary policy, and when the pressures of a particular vision demand it, Balzac is perfectly willing to set the 'classical' commitment on one side; the emphasis of *Les Paysans* is flatly contradicted, for instance, by *La Recherche de l'absolu* where a particular development in the narrative is introduced with the phrase 'par un de ces hasards qui ne sont invraisemblables que dans les livres' (IX, 645). The important point, however, is that this transgression of the inherited legalities of poetics is not necessarily a sign of literary weakness or betrayal, but is often a sign of strength. Such an emphasis gains support from the experience of literary history. For, if in the name of a particular *vraisemblable*, the critic is tempted to dismiss *Splendeurs* as 'extravagant', we should bear in mind that in the seventeenth century Bussy-Rabutin used precisely the same epithet in relation to *La Princesse de Clèves* ('L'aveu de Mme de Clèves à son mari est extravagant'[44]), on the grounds that it transgressed the codes and norms of the *vraisemblable*. However, it is in just that transgression that the modern reader will locate much of the psychological realism and artistic originality of Mme de la Fayette's work. That disjunction is rich in implication; to pre-empt briefly discussion of an approach that will be more fully elaborated in the final chapter, it lends weight to the thesis advanced by Roman Jakobson,[45] in an essay of seminal importance for the theory of realism, that the function of a given *vraisemblable* is to reflect and reinforce a particular society's habitual definitions of reality; that is, it mediates a particular social construction of reality stabilized in what Husserl was to call the 'natural attitude' and Proust 'habitude'. The major works of literary realism, using the term in the widest historical sense, have always stood in an ambiguous relation to the socio-cultural 'idéogramme'[46] reflected in and supported by the conventions of the *vraisemblable*. On the one hand, they conform to it, repeating the socially accepted conceptions of the real (the measure of Balzac's conformity has been stressed by Roland Barthes in his analysis of the 'cultural code' in *Sarrasine*);[47] on the other hand, they 'deform' it (to use one of the favourite terms of the Russian Formalists), breaking through the horizons of its limited space into a wider perspective. It may well be that it is in the 'strangeness', the 'extravagance' of *Splendeurs* (as in the 'sensationalism' of *Sarrasine* or the 'exaggeration' of Goriot and Hulot) that the radical gesture of Balzac's writing is in part located, the mark of a breakthrough the stereotype towards the realization of Dostoyevsky: 'What the majority call almost fantastic and exceptional sometimes signifies for me the very essence of reality.'[48]

4 Connection and totality

> The endless labyrinth of connections which is the essence of art.
> Tolstoy[1]

In one of its primary functions, coincidence may be described as disjunctive: through its unexpectedness it introduces, to recall Barthes's phrase, 'un trouble de la causalite',[2] a rupture in our habitual constructions of reality, a momentary breakdown or transformation, which in the hands of a second-rate writer is usually but a pretext for easy excitement, but with a serious writer can be instrumental in the expression of his vision of the world. Equally, however, coincidence can be a device of conjuction: while at one level it disjoins what are assumed as established patterns of experience, at another level it conjoins, forges connections between things and persons otherwise assumed to be quite separate. 'Coincidence', writes Dorothy van Ghent in a discussion of Dickens's *Great Expectations*, 'is the violent connection of the unconnected.'[3] The context of this remark is interesting since Dickens himself laid explicit and particular stress on the relationship between coincidence and connection. In his *Life of Dickens*, Forster records: 'On the coincidences, resemblances and surprises of life Dickens liked especially to dwell. . . . The world, he would say, was so much smaller than we thought it; we were all so connected by fate without knowing it and people supposed to be so far apart were so constantly elbowing each other.'[4] In a letter explaining the organizing strategy of *Little Dorrit* Dickens himself wrote: 'It struck me that it would be a new thing to show people coming together, in a chance way, as fellow-travellers, and being in the same place, ignorant of one another, as happens in real life; and to connect them afterwards and to make the waiting for that connection a part of the interest.'[5] 'Connection', in a multiplicity of senses, does indeed play a vital role in the vision and structure of Dickens's novels, especially the later ones (and we shall return subsequently to the example of Dickens). But what is of special interest here, as the phrase 'to make the waiting for that connection a part of the interest' indicates, is that the theme of connection is articulated through one of the most elementary structures of melodrama—that of mystery.[6] From *The Mysteries of Udolpho* to *Les Mystères de Paris* (the change from the remote Gothic castle to the modern urban setting being a fact of major literary and sociological importance), mystery has been at the core of the melodramatic imagination: a mystery is posed and its unravelling consists, precisely, in the revelation of a connection hitherto unknown or repressed. Within the classic tradition of melodrama, the mystery is usually one of identity and the connection revealed usually one of kinship. In the nineteenth-century theatre, the model for this kind of plot was furnished by Pixerécourt's *Coelina ou l'enfant du mystère* (1800) which is built around the story of a young girl, thought to be an orphan, but who after numerous misfortunes discovers the mysterious stranger of the play to be none other than her long-lost father. After Pixerécourt, the formula developed into a spectacularly successful one: variations on the trammelled formula of the dismembered family, with its array of orphans, bastards, half brothers and sisters, lost fathers and mothers, and its climatic moments of recognition and reunion, become the stock-in-trade of the Victorian music halls and the Parisian boulevards. The theatrical pattern has its precise parallel in the development of fiction, and much of Pixerécourt's plot was in fact borrowed from the romance of the same title by Ducray-Dumesnil. The mysteries and revelations of kinship constitute one of the mainsprings of the Gothic novel; they find their place in some of Balzac's *oeuvres de jeunesse*, notably in *L'Héritière de Birague* and *Jean-Louis ou la fille trouvée*; and they are frequently exploited by most of the popular novelists of the first half of the nineteenth century. Sue's *Martin ou l'enfant trouvé* announces its adherence to the convention in its very title; Rodolphe of *Les Mystères de Paris* rescues la Goualeuse, ignorant at that moment of the fact that she is his daughter; the climax of Dumas's *Les Trois Mousquetaires* depends for much of its impact on the disclosure in the final chapters that the enterprisingly infamous Lady de Winter turns out to be, among other things, the lost wife of one of the musketeers; the adventures of Luizzi recounted in Soulié's *Mémoires du Diable* are strewn with unknown and miraculously encountered half sisters liberally and conveniently supplied by Luizzi's licentious father.

The mystery-of-kinship narrative represents an extremely primitive form of plotting and, in the hands of Soulié *et cie*, yields little or nothing beyond the simple recipe which combines the suspense of the mystery with the sentimental pathos of the recognition. It fulfils, that is, two of Wilkie Collins's three famous precepts for the popular novel—'make 'em wait', 'make 'em cry', and perhaps also, the more uncharitable might suggest, quite unconsciously the third—'make 'em laugh'. Yet, although a primitive structure generally aiming at crude effects of narrative tension, in certain hands it can undergo significant processes of transformation. In Dickens's *Oliver Twist*, for example, the convention is central: in that quite appalling last chapter, not only does the mysterious Monks, the chief though relatively unseen engineer of Oliver's sufferings, 'turn out' to be the latter's half brother, but

Brownlow the protector-figure quite fortuitously happens to have been the close friend of Oliver's defunct father. Most would agree that as such the plot of *Oliver Twist* is hardly its strongest point, but it is arguable that it provided a form peculiarly hospitable to the exploration of one of Dickens's greatest themes, that of the abandoned child, as well as representing a tentative and embryonic stage in his progression towards the superbly organized and mature transformation of the mystery tale in the late novels. In other words, Dickens's use of the convention in *Oliver Twist*, for all its stumblings and falterings, at once revealed and released a potential in the form which was subsequently to generate the great artistic triumphs of *Bleak House, Little Dorrit* and *Our Mutual Friend.*

A similar case can, I think, be made for Balzac's *La Fille aux yeux d'or*, a text whose debt to the extravagances of the *roman noir* is quite evident ('il reconnut cette sensation que lui procurait la lecture d'un des romans d'Anne Radcliffe' (v,293)), but which is nevertheless intrinsically more interesting and complex than any of its immediate literary ancestors and which, at the same time, announces possibilities of creative transformation that will be brought to fruition in *Le Père Goriot* and *Splendeurs et misères des courtisanes.* Viewed in terms of its plot, *La Fille aux yeux d'or* is conventional enough: it is a mystery story which turns on the sensational revelation of a kinship connection between the two lovers of Paquita Valdès (Henri de Marsay is the half brother of Margarita de San Réal, both the offspring of the profligate Lord Dudley). In the elaboration of the narrative, Balzac displays most of the customary trappings of this type of story—ignorance, suspense, allusion, detour, leading finally to the disclosure of connection by means of the standard 'recognition scene'.

> 'Qui est-tu?' lui dit-elle en courant à lui le poignard levé. Henri lui arrêta le bras, et ils purent ainsi se contempler tous deux face à face. Une surprise horrible leur fit couler à tous deux un sang glacé dans les veines, et ils tremblèrent sur leurs jambes comme des chevaux effrayés. En effet, deux Ménechmes ne se seraient pas mieux ressemblé. Ils dirent ensemble le même mot: Lord Dudley doit être votre père?
> Chacun d'eux baissa la tête affirmativement (v, 322).

The tone here is crudely theatrical and is scarcely to be distinguished from that which informs the countless similar narratives of the period. Yet through this outwardly banal structure Balzac succeeds in articulating a quite unusual range of theme, insight and implication. In the first place, the set of connections which forms the basis of the plot serves the exploration of the theme of forbidden sexuality; it is directly instrumental in structuring the entry of the text into the more obscure and alarming zones of sexual feeling and experience. In this respect, *La Fille aux yeux d'or* seems to me to be one of the few Balzacian works which supports Albert Béguin's general argument that the way in which 'melodrama' in the *Comédie humaine* is redeemed, assumes high literary seriousness, is through its transfiguration into 'myth' (in the sense in which this term is used in psychoanalytical and anthropological models of analysis);[7] it enacts a 'myth-drama' of sexuality, its figures participating in a kind of ancestral ritual of interdiction and transgression in which fundamental principles of sexual differentiation and constraint (masculine/feminine, heterosexual/homosexual, the incest taboo) dissolve into a pandemic flux of indeterminate desire. *La Fille aux yeux d'or* is a text which consciously places itself at a certain limit,[8] at the point where culturally fixed definitions and distinctions of sexual identity begin to collapse in a wild transfer and interchange of sexual attribute and function. This is not just a question of what is most frequently commented upon in *La Fille aux yeux d'or*—the sexual ambivalence of Paquita, simultaneoulsy involved in both a heterosexual and a lesbian relationship. More interesting is the disturbing field of sexual implication opened up by a plot which makes her two lovers half brother and half sister. It has been suggested that in the symbolic scheme of the story Henri and Margarita represent the archetypal male and female ('les Dieux Mâle et Femelle'[9]) engaged in a demonic struggle for the body of Paquita. The story is, of course, one of intense sexual competition, reflected in the agony of Paquita and culminating in the revenge murder of Margarita. But this is to misplace the real emphasis, and wholly leaves out of account the vital fact that Paquita's lovers are not only a man and a woman but also brother and sister. What is crucial is not difference but similarity, not division—and it is here that the deep meaning of the mystery plot is located—but connection. In the context of the sexual drama of which Paquita is the central, mediating figure, what is continually brought out is the physical resemblance of the two lovers, a motif not simply designed to reflect the fact that they are blood relations, but also powerfully charged with sexual connotations, shading into two of the profoundest themes of the text, those of androgyny and incest.

As we know from *Séraphita*, Balzac was deeply attracted by the androgynous theme and, although only hinted at rather than fully elaborated, its presence comes through strongly in *La Fille aux yeux d'or*. Thus, the scene where Paquita, before making love with Henri, dresses him in female clothes is not just an indication of her lesbian attachment; it also corresponds to a certain femininity in the person of de Marsay himself. This trait is explicitly marked in the early description where the obvious 'virile' qualities of de Marsay ('un courage de lion', etc.) are offset by the references to 'une peau de jeune fille, un air doux et modeste, une taille fine et aristocratique, de fort belles mains . . . cette suave figure qui n'eût pas déparé le corps de la plus belle d'entre elles [les femmes]' (v, 273); rewritten by Proust—and we know how much of Balzac was assimilated and reworked in the text of the latter—de Marsay would doubtless have turned up in the male brothel of

A la recherche. There is certainly more than a suggestion of ambivalence here and, in the general design of the book, it finds its counterpart in the 'virile' aspect of Margarita, the stress on her masterful and aggressive nature. Indeed a mind bent on symbolic interpretation—and such interpretation, outlandish though it may seem, would gain support within the text from Margarita's strange remark as she murders Paquita, 'Pour le sang que tu lui as donné, tu me dois tout le tien' (321)—might well see in the dagger a phallic substitute and in the frenzied stabbing the hysterical displacement of the desire for male penetration. But it is above all in the recognition scene, discreetly yet powerfully, that the notion of an ambiguity or interchange of sexual identity is felt. What is remarkable in this scene is that, with the recognition, the murdered Paquita, previously the object of such violent sexual passion and jealousy, is instantaneously and almost entirely forgotten, as each of the two lovers becomes completely absorbed by the presence of the other. 'Elle [Paquita] est fidèle au sang' (322), murmurs de Marsay, implying, among other possibilities, that it is as if Paquita had loved but one, though split, person. As they stare at each other across Paquita's corpse, Henri and Margarita act as mirror images of each other;[10] what is 'recognized' is not just the fact that they are siblings but also the dark sense of a shared sexual duality. Seen in conjunction with other elements of the text, the implications of the recognition scene point towards a radical transgression of the sexual divide, a confusion of masculine and feminine which seems to re-produce the intuition of an ambivalence at the heart of nature itself, the contradictoriness of primordial sexuality before the differentiations imposed and demanded by culture; each both 'masculine' and 'feminine', taken together Henri and Margarita symbolically duplicate the figure of the Androgyne.[11]

The undercurrents of the recognition scene suggest, moreover, another level at which the sexual themes of *La Fille aux yeux d'or* might be read, that of incest. At no point is incest explicitly mentioned in the text, but obliquely—the obliqueness of method is a source of literary strength here—we glimpse it surfacing briefly from the depths of the text in the closing pages. There is, for instance, the ambiguous embrace (fraternal or sexual?—the text deliberately refuses to be specific) given by de Marsay to Margarita as she declares her intention of withdrawing to a convent: 'Tu es encore trop jeune, trop belle, dit Henri en la prenant dans ses bras et lui donnant un baiser '(v, 323). More important are the implications of the symbolism of 'le sang'. The bloody murder of Paquita by Margarita is of course primarily a venge-ful and compensatory act of appropriation ('pour le sang que tu lui a donné, tu me dois tout le tien'): the blood spilt in the breaking of the hymen (before her encounter with de Marsay Paquita is a virgin) is, as it were, retrieved through her destruction, the blood given to one lover in intercourse compensated by the blood taken in death by the other lover. But in the recognition scene another, quite different sense intervenes.

Henri de Marsay, we recall, remarks 'Elle est fidèle au sang.' With the realization that the two lovers are brother and sister, the blood spilt in the loss of virginity and in her murder no longer articulates the theme of division, but the theme of union; it is as if the blood of the deflowered Paquita and of the murdered Paquita is absorbed into the blood relation itself, as if, in loving Paquita, they have loved each other. In other words, the symbolic and rhetorical structure of *La Fille aux yeux d'or* can be read as representing a mode of indirection or displacement through which the text approaches the troubling zone of incest. Of course, in touching upon the theme of incest, *La Fille aux yeux d'or* can state no claim to uniqueness. On the contrary, as Mario Praz has abundantly shown in *The Romantic Agony*,[12] incest along with lesbianism, androgyny and sadism were commonplace ingredients of the *romantisme frénétique* of the 1830s. And Balzac's text is by no means entirely free of the melodramatic horrors characteristic of this type of writing (stylistically, the murder scene falls squarely into the tomato-ketchup syndrome of the blood-and-thunder melodrama of the period). Nevertheless, compared with the histrionics and sensation-mongering of, say, Dumas' *La Tour de Nesles* or Hugo's *Lucrèce Borgia*, both of which deal in incest, Balzac's treatment shows a tact and discretion, an ability to work at the level of implication which far outstrips his contemporaries. Proust was deeply appreciative of *La Fille aux yeux d'or*, and although it cannot be seen as comparable to the subtlety and complexity which mark the exploration of sexual inversion and ambiguity in *A la recherche*, it was Proust, as usual, who made the essential point, when he wrote of Balzac's story: 'Là, sous l'action apparente et extérieure du drame, circulent des mystérieuses lois de la chair et du sentiment.'[13]

A mystery story in which the unravelling of the mystery is transformed and raised to a high level of significance through the injection of a complex awareness of sexuality, *La Fille aux yeux d'or* also offers a further dimension for consideration, of decisive importance for the subsequent pattern of our argument—namely, the grafting of the sexual themes onto a large-scale social vision. The famous account of modern Paris which constitutes the *ouverture* of *La Fille aux yeux d'or* has frequently been the subject of critical commentary, but generally in isolation from the main body of the narrative itself. Apart from the obvious point that de Marsay is the blasé product of a cynical Parisian environment or the somewhat flat observation that the function of the opening section is to guarantee the 'authenticity' of the exotic tale of passion and violence by setting it a contemporary framework, the really deep relationship between the two parts has generally been missed. This relationship, essentially one between plot and metaphor, is best approached by way of the polyvalent colour symbolism of the text, in particular the play on the motif of 'gold'.[14] Gold is both colour and metal and, in that dual status, it circulates, in terms of a complex series of metaphorical transfers, throughout the whole of the book, and in particular articulates the connection between the opening social description and the narrative proper which succeeds it. As colour, that is, in relation to Paquita, 'the girl with the golden eyes', gold functions as a sign of sensuality, the object of sexual desire: 'et d'abord ce qui m'a le plus frappé, ce dont je suis encore épris', remarks de Marsay to Paul de Manerville, 'ce sont deux yeux jaunes comme ceux des tigres; un jaune d'or qui brille, de l'or vivant, de l'or qui pense, de l'or qui aime et veut absolument venir dans votre gousset' (v, 279). This motif is taken up later in the actual love scene: 'Tout ce que la volupté la plus raffinée a de plus savant, tout ce que pouvait connaître Henri de cette poésie des sens que l'on nomme l'amour, fut dépassé par les trésors que déroula cette fille dont les yeux jaillissants ne mentirent à aucune des promesses qu'ils faisaient' (306). On the other hand, as precious metal, it functions as a sign of wealth, the object of cupidity. Associated therefore with both pleasure and wealth, gold forms a metaphor whose structural function, to adopt I.A. Richards's definition of metaphor, is to generate a 'transaction between contexts',[15] to create a link between the central sexual drama and the opening social analysis of Paris. The desire for Paquita parallels the desire for material possession, this latter impulse presented, in a conscious echo of the multilayered yet integrated structure of Dante's Inferno, as pervading the whole of society, as running through the 'totality' (a term we shall return to later) of the social life of modern Paris:

> Qui domine en ce pays sans moeurs, sans croyance, sans aucun sentiment; mais d'où partent et où aboutissent tous les sentiments, toutes les croyances et toutes les moeurs? L'or et le plaisir. Prenez ces deux mots comme une lumière et parcourez cette grande cage de plâtre, cette ruche à ruisseaux noirs, et suivez-y les serpenteaux de cette pensée qui l'agite, la soulève, la travaille (v, 256).

The metaphorical changes rung on the theme of gold thus produce yet another level of implied meaning for the plot of *La Fille aux yeux d'or*, more precisely a further gloss on the motif of 'la parenté' which we have seen to be the core of the intrigue. Just as the girl with the golden eyes acts as the source for the revelation of the kinship bond between Henri and Margarita, so money is seen as the source of a 'bond' that unites all levels of society in a common 'family', an analogy made explicit in the remark, 'il n'y a là [à Paris] de vrai parent que le billet de mille francs' (256). This sentence occurs on the second page of the text and on the closing page it receives a distinct and macabre echo with the appearance of Paquita's 'parent', the silent and sinister old woman who is the former's mother. For the girl with the golden eyes is not only an object of sexual desire; sold by her mother to Margarita, she is also the object of a commercial arrangement, an item in an exchange transaction. Her death represents therefore not only a sexual loss but also, for the parent, an economic loss which has to be paid for—and this provides the 'last incarnation' of this multivalent theme, the final link in the metaphoric chain of gold-sex-kinship-money-society—by precisely, 'l'or':

> En ce moment apparut l'horrible figure de la mère de Paquita.—Tu vas me dire que tu ne l'avais pas vendue pour que je la tuasse, s'écria la marquise. Je sais pourquoi tu sors de ta tanière. Tais-toi.
> Elle alla prendre un sac d'or dans le meuble d'ebène et le jeta dédaigneusement aux pieds de cette vieille femme. Le son de l'or eut le pouvoir de dessiner un sourire sur l'immobile physionomie de la Géorgienne (v, 322).

I have attempted to argue that in *La Fille aux yeux d'or* the raw materials of 'melodrama' undergo a profound transformation at various levels. At the same time, an attempt to build a major critical argument on that text alone would entail a serious loss of perspective; its flaws and weaknesses are manifold and obvious, and have been fully documented by other critics. Rather, what I want to suggest is that, like Dickens's *Oliver Twist*, though in quite different thematic and emotional registers, it is at once heavily contaminated by the baser elements of contemporary melodrama, but at the same time can be seen to exploit the conventions of melodrama to yield something far more interesting and serious than the characteristic products of the genre in the period. In particular, the extension, by way of the analogical play of the text, of the sexual and familial intrigue into the social, and specifically urban, domain of modern life, with its tentative gesture at the comprehension of a whole social structure, marks the first stage in a literary itinerary that will result in deeper and more complex realizations.

In terms of the history of nineteenth-century popular fiction, the key development in this respect is the change in the scope of the mystery novel. Without abandoning the kinship narrative, the structure of the mystery novel is no longer exclusively confined to connections of this type, but tends to move towards the elaboration of larger, more complicated systems of connection; these bring into unexpected relationship a set of characters from across a whole range of social classes, and the unifying context is provided less by the individual family, although this convention remains, than by the phenomenon of the modern city. In his study of Baudelaire, Walter Benjamin has pointed to the link between the growth of the mystery story and a developing urban history,[16] and it is clear that the experience of the size, anonymity and complexity of the modern city provided an extremely fruitful terrain for the increasingly labyrinthine ramifications of the mystery story. In the sphere of French popular fiction, the paradigm of this development is of course Eugène Sue's *Les Mystères de Paris*. Both of the major terms of Sue's title have to be given equal emphasis: a huge, rambling structure, the novel weaves and unravels a vast network of mysteries into which are drawn and interconnected criminal, aristocrat, proletarian, bourgeois, and whose rudimentary unity is founded on the shared context of contemporary Paris. To adduce Sue's text as the exemplary case of this type of development is, of course, to make no assumptions about its inherent literary value. In fact *Les Mystères de Paris* is primarily of interest to those concerned with the theory and history of cultural forms in the modern urban age. For the literary critic, however, its value is essentially of a symptomatic nature: it focuses the emergence of a popular form, which can be interestingly related to a number of nineteenth-century social developments, but which in strictly literary terms fails to transcend the stratagems of mechanical entertainment. Its symptomatic value is nevertheless of capital importance to us, for it provides a model for an increasingly dominant popular form which, in the hands of the serious writer, was manipulated to produce artistic meaning and effect of the highest order.

It is here that the comparison of Balzac with Dickens, rather than with Sue and the other popular novelists, is perhaps most illuminating. It is now a commonplace of our reading of Dickens that what distinguishes novels such as *Bleak House, Little Dorrit* and *Our Mutual Friend* from both Dickens's early work and other Victorian novelists is their imaginative grasp of Victorian social reality as a total system; and that the conventions of what Orwell once called 'the awful Victorian plot',[17] in particular the complexities of the mystery story, contribute directly to the formal organization of that vision. *Bleak House*, for instance, is built around the opposition between an ostensibly fragmented, atomized society (dramatized in Esther's experience of the 'daily spin and whirl', the disconnected rhythms of London life) and the various connections which eventually bind this disordered picture into an organic whole. What initially presents itself as disparate and uncoordinated, finally converges in the creation of a closely woven fabric that is rich in moral and social meaning; as the Chancery suit gradually draws nearly everyone into its atmosphere of inertia and atrophy, as the disease which springs from the squalor of Tom-all-Alone's spreads outwards and upwards until it begins to affect the whole social organism, the novel's themes of guilt, responsibility and complicity become so all-embracing that eventually it is a complete social order that is called in question. The specific funcion of the plot in the articulation of this way of seeing society is underscored by the questions introduced by the narrator in chapter 16:

> What connection can there be between the place in Lincolnshire, the house in town, the Mercury in powder and the whereabout of Jo the outlaw with the broom, who had that distant ray of light upon him when he swept the churchyard step? What connection can there have been between the many people in the innumerable histories of this world who, from opposite sides of great gulfs, have nevertheless been very curiously brought together?[18]

The plot of *Bleak House* gives the answers to these questions, but in such a manner that the merely mechanical unfolding of the mysteries and the connections they conceal is transformed into a comprehensive vision and judgment of Dickens's society. Put in more abstract terms, the focus of this transforming activity is in a particular relationship that Dickens (and Balzac) establishes between 'melodrama' and 'realism', in the creation of what may paradoxically and yet very exactly be called a 'melodramatic realism', whose purpose is to demonstrate the inter-relationships of things in a way that other modes of nineteenth-century social 'representation' could not accommodate. Among the various approaches to the intensely problematic category of literary 'realism', there is one in relation to which the ramifications of the type of plot represented by *Bleak House* and *Little Dorrit* or *Le Père Goriot* and *Splendeurs et misères des courtisanes* prove to be of great significance. That approach, which has occupied a central and fruitful place in literary theory, in particular in the work of Georg Lukács and Raymond Williams, derives essentially from an emphasis on the idea of totality. 'The condition of realism in the nineteenth century', writes Raymond Williams, 'was in fact the assumption of a total world.'[19] The terms 'total' and 'totality', like the cognate terms 'totalizing' and 'total-ization',[20] require careful definition, but their general bearing serves to illuminate the way in which the tradition of classic realism attempts to show man and society in their completeness, as a complex network of interrelations. With regard to Balzac, the notion of 'totality' is habitu-ally invoked in the description of two crucial levels of his writing. The first and most obvious concerns the 'totalizing' impulse that lies behind the classificatory scheme of the *Comédie humaine*—its division into *scènes*, and the related technique of recurring characters. The re-appearing characters extend the economy and widen the perspectives of the individual novel; in forging connections between the disparate novels of the *Comédie*, they form a 'mosaic' (Balzac's term)[21] of fluid yet integrated patterns, suggesting finally a whole society, a 'total' world that remains nevertheless unfinished and theoretically open-ended, open to addition and change and therefore continually at the service of the 'totalizing' vision. Secondly, there are the implications of the imporatant Balzacian idea of the 'type'; in the words of Lukács, 'The central category and criterion of realist literature is the type, a peculiar synthesis which organically binds together the general and the par-ticular both in characters and situations. . . . [The] live portrayal of the complete human personality is possible only if the writer creates types. The point in question is the organic, indissoluble connection between man as a private individual and man as a social being, as a member of a community.'[22] Although the principle of typicality contains its own set of critical problems (which we shall consider in a later chapter), it is nonetheless decisive in the organization of the generalizing vision of the *Comédie humaine*: through the creation of the typology, the novelist dramatizes the interaction of the public and the private domains of experience, generalizes the particular, shows how the individual life, however densely particularized and idiosyncratic, is woven into and reflects the dynamic of the larger social process. In *La Vieille fille*, for example, by making the two wooers of Rose Cormon, Valois and Bousquier, the 'typical' representatives of the Restoration aristocracy and the newly arrived bourgeoisie, Balzac transforms the narrow, local drama of a provincial courtship into an illustration of the clash and interplay of broader social and historical forces. The focus of this account of 'completeness' in the realist novel is thus not on a notion of 'total' representation in any naive quantitative sense (this will be the stress of later naturalist theory, the fallacy of which is captured in the breakdown of the self-conscious attempt at exhaustive transcription in Michel Butor's *Degrés*), but on an imaginatively realized system of connections which operates as a paradigm of the laws governing the functioning and development of society in general. And it is through an analogy with this idea of paradigmatic representation of whole social processes and structures that we can approach the deeper significance of the 'melodramatic' plot in both *Le Père Goriot* and *Splendeurs et misères des courtisanes*.

Le Père Goriot, as has often been observed, draws extensively on the repertoire of melodrama (for Martin Turnell the degree of its involvement is such as to place it irretrievably beyond the pale of serious fiction[23]) but of the various melodramatic modes it uses (hyperbole, theatrical climax, etc.) none is more powerfully present than that of mystery, a presence strongly marked from the outset of the novel. Careful analysis could doubtless show that the closely textured and semantically rich description with which *Le Père Goriot* begins is in fact regulated by a limited number of general figures and codes. Central among these is the figure of the enigma or, in Barthes's phrase, the operation of the 'hermeneutic code';[24] at almost every point, diction and rhetoric combine to saturate the reader's consciousness with a sense of mystery. The text speaks of its 'désir de pénétrer les mystères d'une situation épouvantable, aussi soigneusement cachée par ceux qui l'avaient créée que par celui qui la subissait' (II, 854), and of its intention to explore 'les secrètes infortunes du père Goriot' (848), an exploration that will call upon considerable resource—'Ce fut à qui devinerait les causes de cette décadence. Exploration difficile!'(866). Of Vautrin it is remarked that 'il y avait au fond de sa vie un mystère soigneusement enfoui' (859), while the appearance of Mlle Michonneau generates a whole series of questions and speculations ('quel acide avait dépouillé cette créature de ses formes féminines? (855)), a rhetorical procedure immediately echoed in the presentation of Poiret ('Quel travail avait pu le ratatiner ainsi? quelle passion avait bistré sa face bulbeuse?' etc. (855)). It is no wonder that the newly arrived Rastignac reflects to himself: 'Voilà bien des mystères dans une pension bourgeoise' (876). Some of these mysteries are incidental, others are central. The primary mystery, that of Goriot and his daughters, is once again one of kinship, but here it is ramified in such a way that its unravelling encompasses whole social structures; it leads us through the secret corridors of 'le labyrinthe parisien' towards an understanding of the 'superposition des couches humaines qui composent la société' (871), grasped as a network of inter-connections which unmasks and plays havoc with that society's self-image.

The image is essentially that of a broken vertical line, evoking a hierarchical structure in which each class or group is not only marked by differences of wealth and status, but also remains entirely separate and self-contained, acknowledging no resemblance to, and with cer-tain allowable exceptions, rarely entering into contact with, the others. This image receives what is perhaps its first explicit formulation by Balzac in the account of the Faubourg Saint Germain in *La Duchesse de Langeais*:

> Partout, lorsque vous rassemblerez des familles d'inégale fortune sur un espace donné, vous verrez se former des cercles supérieurs, des patriciens, des première, seconde et troisième sociétés. . . . Cet espace mis entre une classe et toute une capitale, n'est-il pas une consécration matérielle des distances morales qui doivent les séparer (v, 145)?

The emphasis here on geographical separation as indices of social and moral distinction is taken up and developed in *Le Père Goriot*, mainly through the opposition between the shabby world of the Pension Vauquer and the glittering salons of the *haut monde*, a bosic polarity which organizes a whole series of antithetical terms—high/low, wealth/poverty, success/failure, beauty/ugliness, power/impotence, delicacy/vulgarity, grandeur/pettiness, etc. Yet running through this neatly defined outer structure there is a trammelled vein of mystery, and the unfolding of the plot will trace a pattern in which separation gives way to connection, difference to similarity, in which the vertical axis will be increasingly displaced onto the horizontal through a developing insistence on the theme of a moral uniformity enveloping the whole system.

In terms of the functioning of the plot, the pivotal figure is, of course, Rastignac, who, by virtue of his special mobility, serves at once to create and to reveal connections; himself a point of connection between ostensibly separate worlds, the process of his 'education' will be the discovery of further and more disconcerting relationships. The essential pattern is formed with the social call Rastignac makes on Anastasie de Restaud, an occasion which gathers together a triple set of con-nections between the worlds of the Pension Vauquer and high so-ciety—Rastignac and Goriot, Rastignac and Anastasie, Anastasie and Goriot—and which may be represented diagrammatically as follows:

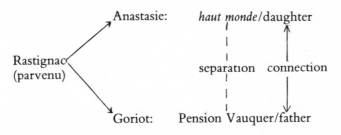

The first two of these three connections, those centred exclusively on Rastignac and his acquaintanceship with Goriot and with Anastasie, are in themselves fundamentally unproblematical. The ambiguity of Rastignac's social position troubles no one, and the conjunction between different layers of society engendered by that ambiguity disturbs nothing. Socially, Rastignac is two people—the young aristocrat with the 'magical' name that can open the doors of the most illustrious salons and the impoverished student living in one of the seedy boarding houses of Paris. But the co-existence of the two social personae in the one individual, although it creates personal problems for Rastignac (he has to learn the 'haute jurisprudence sociale' (II, 906) of Parisian life, to don the right clothes, utter the correct phrases, cultivate the right people), entails no deep implication of the one social world in the other. Rastignac's poverty represents a phenomenon with which the upper classes are fully accustomed and relatively at ease—the dispossession of the aristocracy by the Revolution of '79. He is simply the victim of a misfortune of history, which in no way tarnishes the 'purity' of his origins and which enables him to surface from the murky lower depths of the Pension Vauquer armed with an accredited 'alibi'. His mobility does not threaten the dividing wall of the social antithesis; the links between the two worlds created by that mobility are merely tenuous and circumstantial, and will disappear as soon as he makes his fortune.

The third connection, between Anastasie and Goriot, is of a quite different order, infinitely problematical. In Rastignac's own mind, his connection with Anastasie, on the one hand, and that with Goriot, on the other, remain quite separate, precisely because the third is unknown; opaque, shrouded in mystery, the object of systematic concealment, Rastignac has intimations of its existence, from a previous conversation in the Pension Vauquer, but remains ignorant of its nature ('cette femme . . . liée secrètement au vieux vermicellier lui semblait tout un mystère' (II, 897)). That ignorance is not an accidental matter, but goes to the very heart of the novel to yield a significance at once psychological, ideological and structural. Psychologically, it corresponds to a mode of perception in Rastignac, which is in turn complicit in and nourished by the ideology of high society (the myth of separation, of 'distinction'), and which, in formal terms, is projected along one of the major structural axes of the novel, that of antithesis. In his daily journeys to the upper regions of society and his nightly returns to the Pension Vauquer, Rastignac habitually and not unnaturally organizes his impressions in terms of the principle of contrast:

> D'un côté, les fraîches et charmantes images de la nature sociale la plus élégante, des figures jeunes, vives, encadrées par les merveilles de l'art et du luxe, des têtes, passionnées pleines de poésie; de l'autre, de sinistres tableaux bordés de fange, et des faces où les passions n'avaient laissé que leurs cordes et leurs mécanismes (II, 914).

The sense of radical contrast and separation which informs Rastignac's perception of society is focused with particular sharpness when he first enters the Restaud salon: 'Une soudaine lumière lui fit voir clair dans l'atmosphère de la haute société parisienne, encore ténébreuse pour lui. La Maison Vauquer, le père Goriot étaient alors bien loin de sa pensée' (896). The counterpoint of 'lumière' and 'ténébreuse' here is deliberately ironic; Rastignac's assumptions and his state of mind constitute the very reverse of 'illumination' and 'clear-sightedness'. Goriot may be 'bien loin de sa pensée', but he is by no means far from the Restaud house; indeed, a moment earlier Rastignac has caught an astonished glimpse of Goriot furtively leaving the house 'près de la porte cochère par le petit escalier' (893). And a few moments later, the process of true illumination will begin, as Rastignac naively plunges into what is at once a major social error and the first stage of an important discovery: 'je viens de voir sortir de chez vous un monsieur avec lequel je suis porte à porte dans la même pension, le père Goriot' (898). As Peter Brooks has pointed out,[25] Rastignac's 'gaucherie' represents what is perhaps the most decisive moment of the novel. The immediate effect of his innocent remark is like that of a bomb going off at a tea party, and its long-term effect will be that of the initiation of the hero into a total understanding of the society he has set out to master.

In accidently unearthing the secret which lies buried in the mystery, Rastignac perpetrates the unconscious transgression of a fundamental taboo; through his verbal awkwardness he trespasses inadvertently on forbidden territory, stumbles into an area of knowledge which is the object of complete censure and repression, and the price he pays is instant rejection and exclusion ('Toutes les fois que monsieur se présentera, dit le comte à Maurice, ni madame ni mois nous n'y serons' (899)). More specifically, Rastignac brings to the surface an anxiety, even a neurosis, of origin, an anxiety generated by the new social formations of the Restoration period and in particular by the movement, on the basis of marriage and money, of the lower middle class into sectors of the *haute bourgeoisie* and the aristocracy. That transaction is the inevitable product of a society in a critical period of transition but, because of its attendant social ambiguities and uncertainties, it is also a transaction that cannot be openly faced, which is accompanied by a guilty conscience, bad faith, a radical lack of confidence. Goriot's fortune buys his daughters' entry ticket into high society, a purchase which, by implication, represents the problematical and uneasy alliance between bourgeoisie and aristocracy in the early nineteenth century. But it is purchase which must go unacknowledged: Goriot, the visible reminder of a dubious origin, must be hidden from sight. By a cruel logic, the very 'arrival' purchased through Goriot demands his own suppression; his relegation to the twilight world of the Pension Vauquer becomes an essential condition of maintaining the daughters' outward display of social brilliance:

> —Elles ont renié leur père, répétait Eugène.
> —Eh! bien, oui, leur père, le père, un père, reprit la vicomtesse, un bon père qui leur a donné, dit-on, à chacune cinq ou six cent mille francs pour faire leur bonheur en les mariant bien, et qui ne s'était réservé que huit à dix mille livres de rente pour lui, croyant que ses filles resteraient ses filles, qu'il s'était créé chez elles deux existences, deux maisons où il serait adoré, choyé. En deux ans, ses gendres l'ont banni de leur société comme le dernier des misérables (909).

Thus, the glamour of the daughters and the squalor of the father are functions of each other, totally interdependent—a perspective dramatically realized in Rastignac's reflection at Mme de Beauséant's ball: 'Il revit alors, sous les diamants des deux soeurs, le grabat sous lequel gisait le père Goriot' (1061). And the cruelty of this logic is further accentuated, and Goriot's suffering futher intensified, by the fact of an ongoing dependence: rejected and despised, Goriot nevertheless still acts as a source of income to which covertly and furtively, as witnessed by the secret night visits and whispered pleadings, Anastasie and Delphine turn when in need. Behind the scenes, contact between father and daughters remains, but because the actual relationships it sustains are founded exclusively on exploitation and humiliation, that contact is void of human content.

This then is the secret, repressed reality which Rastignac unwittingly discovers. In unveiling the mystery, he raises the barrier of the social antithesis, brings about, as Peter Brooks has aptly put it, 'the juxtaposition of a public social style and its unavowable genetic and financial substructure'.[26] The image of the broken vertical line, with its apparent divisions and separations, its assumption of disparate and autonomous worlds, now appears as pure illusion, dispelled in the revelation of the troublesome 'unity' that lies beneath the outward facade of a confident social differentiation. As the novel unfolds, the essential spectacle it offers is that of 'high' and 'low' united by a dehumanized system of connections, the nodal point of which is money. In *Le Père Goriot* money is not only an atomistic agent (source of division and conflict in an individualistic society), but also—and here we find an echo and an expansion of the opening pages of *La Fille aux yeux d'or*—a force which circulates throughout the social organism, providing the points of contact between its otherwise divided parts, a kind of 'bond' but one which paradoxically represents a travesty and a negation of primary human bonds. In terms of the conventions of the mystery story, this idea is, of course, most fully developed in the relationship between Goriot and his daughters. But, from this central base, it is thematized at all levels of the text through a network of parallelism and analogy in which the operations of buying and selling, exploitation and theft are seen to implicate everyone from top to bottom of the social structure, indeed to make a mockery of the very notions of 'top' and 'bottom' as meaningful distinctions. Symbolically, Anastasie sells herself to Maxime de Trailles, just as, in order to meet the terms of that contract, she literally sells her diamonds to the usurer Gobseck, an episode whose general significance is clarified by Vautrin: 'Hier en haut de la roue chez une duchesse . . . ce matin en bas de l'échelle chez un escompteur: voilà les Parisiennes. Si leurs maris ne peuvent pas entretenir leur luxe effréné, elles se vendent' (884). Similarly, though at a vast social remove, Mlle Michonneau, appropriately described as a 'vieille vendeuse de chair' (1015), collaborates with Poiret to sell Vautrin to the police for a few hundred francs. Madame Vauquer haggles over clean sheets for the dying Goriot and only releases them when Rastignac guarantees payment in advance. Even Goriot himself, the lamb devoured by wolves, is not exempt from the critical vision. Goriot may be the innocent victim of others, but the fortune so shamelessly appropriated by those 'above' him is itself far from innocent in origin: Goriot's money has come directly from the sordid manipulation of the black market in flour during the famine of the Revolutionary period ('il . . . a commencé sa fortune par vendre dans ces temps-là des farines dix fois plus qu'elles ne lui coûtaient' (910). By a vicious paradox of history, and one which gives a further, deeply ironic twist to the theme of 'connection', the wealth which finances the social successes of the immediate post-revolutionary period rests on the exploitation of the starving masses whose interests the Revolution was supposed to serve; from the *disette* of '79 to the brilliant appearance at Mme de Beauséant's ball, the chain is an unbroken one. Again, Vautrin, whose great dream is to trade in men as the owner of a slave plantation, attempts to buy the soul, and probably also the body, of Rastignac with the offer of the handsome dowry to be obtained through the murder of Victorine Taillefer's brother. Rastignac of course refuses the bargain (though the temptation to complicity is indicated in the famous 'mandarin' question he puts to Bianchon), but in other contexts he proves less squeamish. His arriviste enterprise is financed initially by the cunning extraction of his sisters' hard-won savings, an act which he himself, in a moment of remorseful lucidity, has to describe as one of 'theft' ('J'ai donc volé mes soeurs' (942)). His relationship with Delphine de Nucingen is a straight *quid pro quo* deal. At one point Delphine, commenting bitterly on her marriage, remarks: 'C'est une association improbe et voleuse à laquelle je dois consentir sous peine d'être ruineé. Il m'achète ma conscience et la paye en me laissant être à mon aise la femme d'Eugène' (1038). The remark is absolutely on target, expresses a fundamental truth, but the bitterness is hardly free from hypocrisy, for not only has Delphine been a willing accomplice in the business of the 'bought' marriage, but, as mistress and lover, she and Rastignac will repeat exactly the same moral pattern as that which has governed her marriage. Delphine exchanges her body in return for Rastignac's social ticket, the invitation to Mme de Béauseant's ball, while Rastignac gives her the ticket because he needs a rich mistress, the monetary image entering even into the description of the physical relationship itself ('Infâme ou sublime, il adorait cette femme pour les voluptés qu'il lui avait apportées en dot, et pour toutes celles qu'il en avait reçues' (1057–8)). Hence, from the large-scale gesture to the petty gesture, and cutting across all social boundaries (aristocrat, banker, student, landlady, ex-prostitute, policeman, criminal), the model for conduct remains morally identical, that of exchange, a continual trafficking in relationships and values in the pursuit of private gain; not surprisingly, Rastignac learns to see 'dans la fortune l'*ultima ratio mundi*' (914).

The model or metaphor of exchange constitutes, therefore, a major focus for the 'totalizing' vision of the novel; it is, so to speak, one of the lamps with which the narrator guides both reader and hero through the mysteries of the Parisian 'labyrinth' towards an understanding of its interconnected moral design. It links moreover with another metaphor, which fulfils a similar function—the metaphor of 'dirt'. Some indication of the potential of this metaphor in the organization of a comprehensive social vision can be gauged by briefly returning once again to the early text *La Duchesse de Langeais*. In the passage which speaks of the physical distance of the Faubourg Saint Germain as the expression of its assumed social and spiritual superiority, the narrator comments:

> Pour les gens accoutumés aux splendeurs de la vie, est-il en effet rien de plus ignoble que le tumulte, la boue, les cris, la mauvaise odeur, l'étroitesse des rues populeuses? . . . De là, des moeurs diamétralement opposées (v, 144).

Later in the story, however, Montriveau, when confronted with the moral truth about the behaviour of one of the supreme representatives of that class, observes: 'A mesure que l'on monte en haut de la société, il s'y trouve autant de boue qu'il y en a par le bas; seulement elle s'y durcit et se dore' (v, 213). The meaning derives, of course, from the ironic echoing, across the text, of the literal sense of 'boue' (index of social difference) by its figurative sense (index of moral sameness), and this simple echo may be said to furnish the matrix for a schema that will be extensively deployed in *Le Père Goriot*. In this respect the opening description of the Pension Vauquer is of great strategic value. In one sense, the boarding house at once mirrors and parodies the structure of Parisian society generally: it is a mirror in that the precise calculations of wealth and status, according to which Madame Vauquer regulates the hierarchical distribution of her lodgers throughout the various storeys of the house, reflect the norms which organize the social world at large; a parody in that Goriot's 'upwards' movement from the relative comfort of the first floor to the squalor of the garret forms a kind of reversed image of the vertical structure of society and its concomitant idea of 'progress' as ascent up the social ladder. More important, however, is the way in which the description, in its detailed itinerary through the various levels and rooms of the house, tends towards the complete obliteration of these fine distinctions through its persistent spotlighting of the omnipresence of filth and decay ('ordure', 'le moisi', 'le rance', 'crasse', 'pourriture', 'fange', 'l'air chaudement fétide', etc.). That the physical setting of the boarding house acts as a global image for its inhabitants is a commonplace of Balzac criticism. What needs to be stressed however is the manner in which this image, by way of an expansion of the figure of metonymy,[27] reaches out from its local context to evoke the whole of the social reality of Paris, including those regions ostensibly so different from the world of the Pension Vauquer; in a continual sliding between literal and figurative levels of meaning, the motif of dirt, so emphatically brought out in the description of the pension, encroaches totally on those other areas of society which define themselves or would like to be defined as 'clean'. At the literal level, its presence or absence signifies, as it does in *La Duchesse de Langeais*, the notion of distance and difference— for instance, in the contrast between the muddied boots of Rastignac, who makes his way to Mme de Restaud's salon on foot, and the polished boots of Maxime de Trailles who arrives in a carriage ('Maxime avait des bottes fines et propres, tandis que les siennes, malgré le soin qu'il avait pris en marchant, s'étaient empreintes d'une légère teinte de boue' (II, 894). At the figurative level, however, the motif, as it were, turns against itself, ironically subverting the very connotations which its literal context supports. Thus, of Delphine de Nucingen, whose life style naturally protects her from the muddy streets of Paris, Mme de Beauséant remarks that 'elle laperait toute la boue qu'il y a entre la rue Saint-Lazare et la rue Grenelle pour entrer dans mon salon' (913), pointing to a disjunction between surface and depth, manners and morality generalized elsewhere in the novel as a universal condition, in the early exchange between Vautrin and Rastignac:

> Mais, dit Eugène, avec un air de dégoût, votre Paris est donc un bourbier.
> Et un drôle de bourbier, reprit Vautrin. Ceux qui s'y crottent en voiture sont d'honnêtes gens, ceux qui s'y crottent à pied sont des fripons (886).

Vautrin's use of metaphor here in effect summarizes the whole novel: in a neat reversal of meaning which replaces the idea of separation with that of connection and uniformity, Vautrin's reply to Rastignac takes up the distinction symbolized by moving about Paris on foot or in a carriage, along with its pretence at moral division ('honnêtes gens'/ 'fripons'), only to annihilate that distinction through the metaphorical application to both groups of the very motif ('se crotter') which at the literal level sustains the distinction; as with dirt and disease in Dicken's *Bleak House* and *Our Mutual Friend*, 'mud' in *Le Père Goriot* is everywhere. According to the rules of Vautrin's pedagogy, therefore, the question of differentiation is not one of morality, but solely one of cosmetics: 'Voilà la vie telle qu'elle est. Ça n'est pas plus beau que la cuisine, ça pue tout autant, et il faut se salir les mains si l'on veut fricoter, sachez bien vous débarbouiller: là est toute la morale de l'époque' (937); this a problem to which Vautrin suggests his own particular solution, again in exactly the same metaphorical terms: 'je suis un bon homme qui veut se crotter pour que vous soyez à l'abri de la boue pour le reste de vos jours' (981).

   This view of society is not confined to Vautrin. In conversation with Mme de Beauséant and Rastignac, Antoinette de Langeais observes 'le monde est un bourbier', but then goes on to add 'tâchons de rester sur les hauteurs' (911). The diagnosis is correct, but the advice hardly carries conviction. True, Mme de Beauséant will retain her integrity by retiring to a convent, but withdrawal to a convent can scarcely be said to offer a meaningful solution to the whole of the moral problematic opened up by the novel. The essential point is that there are no 'heights', only appearances—hence one of the significances of the famous closing episode of *Le Père Goriot*, when from the 'heights' of Père Lachaise Rastignac surveys the city and throws out his challenge 'à nous deux maintenant'. Unlike analagous situations in Stendhal, altitude here in no way signals moral and spiritual superiority. Far from representing a moment of redemption and rejection, Rastignac's posture is but the prelude to a descent and an acceptance. A few pages earlier we are told that 'il voyait le monde comme un océan de boue dans lequel un homme se plongeait jusqu'au cou s'il y trempait le pied' (1056), and his return from Père Lachaise into the city will constitute just such a plunging into the mire ('Et pour premier acte de défi qu'il portait à la société, il alla dîner chez Madame de Nucingen' (1085)). The physical location of Rastignac's last appearance represents rather a moment of total understanding; from the heights of the cemetery, he can see Paris literally and figuratively as a whole: 'Rastignac, resté seul, fit quelques pas vers le haut du cimitière et vit Paris tortueusement couché le long des deux rives de la Seine' (1085); he can, to go back to the 'aerial' vision introduced by the narrator on the first page of the novel, run his gaze over 'cette illustre vallée de plâtras incessament près de tomber et de ruisseaux noirs de boue' (847) to seize it, not only physically but also intellectually, in the 'totality' of its interconnections.

Rastignac's position on the last page of the novel thus resembles that of the narrator on the first page. His journey might therefore be described as a movement towards the kind of 'total' understanding available to the narrator. In this respect, Rastignac is one of Balzac's privileged creatures. Lucien de Rubempré is not so privileged, and the disasters which befall him spring, precisely, from his inability to see society as a whole, to achieve that understanding of its multiple and complex interrelations which is the precondition of mastering it. This returns us once more to the crucial text of *Splendeurs et misères des courtisanes*, of all the major novels of the *Comédie humaine* the one which, from the point of view of certain structural devices, stands in the most interesting relationship to nineteenth-century melodrama. This relationship is essentially of a twofold order, in that *Splendeurs* simultaneously employs two basic structural forms of melodramatic fiction in the organization of its meaning—the 'disjoining' mode of the plot of coincidence and the 'conjoining' mode of the plot of connection. The previous chapter examined the relationship between melodramatic plot structures and *Splendeurs* in terms of the role played by chance and coincidence, where these are directly linked to the charting of Lucien's individual destiny, and in particular to the consequences of his inability to perceive society clearly. At this level, the plot of *Splendeurs* exploits a stock melodramatic device to enhance our sense of the fragility of the hero's projects, of the gap between aspiration and achievement into which, unprotected by sufficient foresight and control, the fortuitous can intervene to shatter the hero's most carefully calculated designs. Ill-equipped to negotiate the unpredictable terrain of modern Paris, Lucien is the natural victim of its fluid and ostensibly uncontrollable vicissitudes and, through its emphasis on disjunction and collapse, the melodrama of unfortunate coincidence serves to accentuate that particular way of experiencing the social world.

Off-setting this pattern, however, and throwing it into ironic relief, there is another pattern which equally derives from the conventions of popular fiction. Lucien may experience society as a bewildering, inchoate sequence of unexpected reversals, he may fail to see the connections which bind its disparate elements together, but the connections emphatically exist. Indeed in *Splendeurs* the technique developed in *Le Père Goriot* becomes at once more pervasive and more explicit. Of the various intrusions made by the narrator to comment on the text itself, unquestionably the most important are those which draw attention to the plot as a connecting and unifying agent. There is not the space to list all of them, but the following passage, introducing part IV of the novel, may be taken as a characteristic reflection on general narrative strategy:

> Ce dernier acte du drame peut d'ailleurs compléter la peinture de
> moeurs que comporte cette étude et donne la solution des divers
> intérêts en suspens que la vie de Lucien avait si singulièrement

enchevêtrés, en mêlant quelques-unes des ignobles figures du Bagne à celles des plus hauts personnages (v, 1015).

The primary task of the plot in *Splendeurs* is the bringing of different groups of characters into relationship with one another, and the primary effect of these various conjunctions is the impression the novel creates of dealing with a whole social system. By creating links between characters from different social classes, by knitting together worlds as socially remote from each other as that of the banker, the prostitute, the criminal, the aristocrat, the plot, for all its cumbersome machinery, provides the formal means through which the novel projects a coherent image of a social reality grasped in its totality, seen and judged across the divisions which otherwise fragment it. The plot therefore mediates a comprehensive vision which is also, and by the same token, a moral vision, a 'total' critique of contemporary society in that, through the interweaving of the different strands of the intrigue, it emphasises the theme of an all-pervasive moral disease, a community of interests defined by a universal complicity in corruption and decay. High and low, base interest and calculation interact with each other; a class-divided society finds its common factor in a moral anarchy that runs from top to bottom throughout the whole social structure.

The play of social differences and moral similarities that will constitute the controlling scheme of the novel is in fact evoked from the very outset of the novel, in two of its opening sequences. It will be recalled that the novel begins with the episode of the annual masked ball at the Opéra. Described as the occasion on which 'les différents cercles dont se compose la société parisienne se retrouvent, se reconnaissent et s'observent' (v, 656), it adumbrates symbolically the interaction of different social groups that will take place in the main body of the narrative. It forms a sort of neutral ground upon which social differences are temporarily suspended; the wearing of the mask, in concealing social identity, establishes an anonymity, a kind of grotesque equality that prefigures the real moral equivalences explored later in the novel, and which is explicitly focused here by the narrator's comment on that 'loi fatale' according to which 'il existe peu de différence, soit physique, soit morale, entre le plus distingué, le mieux élevé des fils d'un duc et pair, et ce charmant garçon que naguère la misère étreignait de ses mains de fer au milieu de Paris' (v, 656). Equally significant is the chapter which immediately follows the presentation of the masked ball and which begins with a description of the *quartier* in which Esther lives:

> La rue de Langlade, de même que les rues adjacentes, sépare le Palais-Royal et la rue de Rivoli. Cette partie d'un des plus brillants quartiers de Paris conservera longtemps la souillure qu'y ont laissée les monticules produits par les immondices du vieux Paris, et sur lesquels il y eut autrefois des moulins. Ces rues étroites, sombres et boueuses, où s'exercent des industries peu soigneuses

de leurs dehors, prennent à la nuit une physionomie mystérieuse et pleines de contrastes. En venant des endroits lumineux de la rue Saint-Honoré de la rue Neuve-des-Petits-Champs et de la rue de Richelieu, où se presse une foule incessante, où reluisent les chefs-d'oeuvre de l'Industrie, de la Mode et des Arts, tout homme à qui le Paris du soir est inconnu serait saisi d'une terreur triste en tombant dans le lacis de petites rues qui cercle cette lueur reflétée jusque sur le ciel (v, 670).

As in *Le Père Goriot*, the geographical landscape may be taken as a symbol of the human and moral landscape. But whereas the former text uses the geographical symbolism ironically, to focus the ideas of distance and separation which it then proceeds to undermine, here physical setting relates to moral meaning in a more direct way: the streets interconnect in the way the characters will interconnect;[28] the smart and respectable areas of the rue Saint-Honoré and the rue de Rivoli are intersected by and joined to the squalid areas represented by the rue de Langlade, the former indelibly marked by the 'souillure' of the latter, just as the diseased world of Tom-all-Alone's is linked to the aristocratic world of Sir Leceister and Lady Dedlock. In their stress on the theme of interdependence, the two initial scenes of *Splendeurs* define in miniature the larger dialectic of the novel which, as in *Bleak House*, may be described as the oposition and interplay of a pattern of disconnection and a pattern of connection. The term 'disconnection' refers to a society divided along lines of class and wealth (socially there is nothing in common between Mme de Sérizy and Esther, Vautrin and M. de Granville); that of 'connection; however, refers to a moral uniformity that is to be found beneath the separations imposed by social difference (Vautrin abducts Lydie, de Marsay rapes her, and in a shared act of brutality the social barriers which separate the criminal from the aristocrat are raised). As Balzac puts it (echoing Vautrin's observation in *Le Père Goriot* that 'l'homme est le même en haut, en bas, au milieu' (ii, 937) and his celebrated distinction in *Illusions perdues* between 'l'Histoire officielle' and 'l'Histoire secrète' (iv, 1020)): 'A Paris les extrêmes se rencontrent par les passions. Le vice y soude perpétuellement le riche au pauvre, le grand au petit' (v, 826). The whole narrative structure of *Splendeurs* may be seen as an extended imaginative meditation on the implications of that remark.

To pursue this relation between plot and vision at the level of detailed analysis is to encounter a great variety of critical and interpretative possibilities. We shall limit ourselves to the essentials, concentrating on the three basic sequences of the narrative (the intrigue built around Nucingen's passion for Esther and Lucien's incursions into the *haut monde*; the web of interlocking interests that surrounds Lucien's arrest and imprisonment; the drama of Vautrin's 'last incarnation') in terms of their expression of two of the major themes of the novel—sexuality and prostitution, politics and justice. For it is from the interrelations of these two themes that the informing vision of a general moral bankruptcy takes its essential shape and substance.

Of the many corrupt and corrupting bonds which unite characters from different social levels, perhaps the strongest and most insidious is that of a debased sexuality, hawked around the market place of society, prostituted and exploited throughout the entire social hierarchy. Like *La Cousine Bette*, *Splendeurs* is a novel absolutely saturated in instances and images of an elemental, at times frenzied sexuality, whose power and pervasiveness are such that it forms a kind of community of its own that cuts across social and class divisions. Maurice Bardèche has commented on the centrality of the prostitution theme in *Splendeurs* and its function as the 'lierre monstrueux qui tapisse toute la façade de la société capitaliste et qui unit mystérieusement la pègre et les grands'.[29] In this context, the figure of Esther is crucial; although her self-sacrificing love finally redeems her from the general moral squalor, through her irresistible sensuality, her capacity to arouse and exploit 'l'Animal', she operates as a symbol of society's degeneracy and, in the narrative realization of that symbol, as a cornerstone of the novel's action. Early in the novel, her past as a prostitute is significantly described by Lousteau in the following terms: 'A dix-huit ans, cette fille a déjà connu la plus haute opulence, la plus basse misère, les hommes à tous les étages. Elle tient comme une baguette magique avec laquelle elle déchaîne les appétits brutaux si violemment comprimés chez les hommes qui ont encore du coeur en s'occupant de politique ou de science, de littérature ou d'art. Il n'y a pas de femme dans Paris qui puisse dire comme elle à l'Animal: 'Sors'. . . ! Et l'Animal quitte sa loge, et il se roule dans les excès' (v, 666). The important emphasis here is in the reference to Esther's experience of 'les hommes à tous les étages' and in the suggestion of a diffuse corruption infecting the whole body politic. In the mainstream of the narrative, this suggestion will be exemplified chiefly through Esther's relationship with the banker Nucingen, where calculated seduction and libidinous desire combine to evoke a point of connection at which two disparate worlds meet and interact. There are, moreover, a number of moral parallels between these worlds. The 'official history' would undoubtedly present the financier as a respected and valuable citizen, while the 'secret history', containing an account of 'les moyens secrètement honteux auxquels le baron devait sa fortune colossale' (861), would place him at the same level as that of the criminal and the prostitute. Just as Esther, and through her, Vautrin, exploits Nucingen's sexuality for gain, Nucingen (appropriately described as a 'Jacques Collin légalement et dans le monde des écus' (1136)) exploits others in the amassing of his millions; as Esther puts it in a sardonic moment, 'Fille et voleur, rien ne s'accorde mieux.' (866)

The ramifications of the Esther-Nucingen relationship extend in other directions as well. If Nucingen represents the slavish homage 'respectable' society pays to the seductions of the harlot, then Lucien, the dandy and aspiring socialite, represents the pimp who lives off the fruits of that homage. Esther sells herself to Nucingen, whose own fortune is of scandalous origins, to obtain the money necessary to Vautrin's strategy of engineering Lucien's successful marriage into the highly placed Grandlieu family. A fortune, tainted at source, thus circulates via a banker, a prostitute, a criminal and a parvenu into the high echelons of aristocratic society. Until the plan is undone by the machinations of Corentin, a degraded sexuality and a contaminated fortune work to create the initial links and squalid complicities between otherwise radically different milieus. It is, of course, true that the Grandlieu family, in the name of a particular conception of social and moral order, attempt to sever those links (although the Duke's capacity for chicanery will be revealed in another context), but if there is resistance to Lucien in the *haut monde*, there is also accommodation and protection for which the price is again the granting of sexual favours. Lucien's good looks are famed throughout Paris ('la beauté de [Lucien] jouissait d'une célébrité singulière dans les différents mondes qui composent Paris' (v, 919)) and, in the numerous contacts and connections they bring him, constitute a nodal point on which various strands of the narrative converge. Although the text remains obscure on the precise nature of Lucien's relations with Vautrin, the bond between the criminal and the arriviste seems to be founded on the homosexual attraction of the latter to the former. Equally, it is through his beauty that Lucien establishes relations with a variety of women on 'le dernier ou le premier échelon de l'échelle sociale' (669). Above all, it is his entry ticket into high society. If Esther is the prostitute to Nucingen, Lucien is the prostitute to the *grandes dames* of the Faubourg Saint Germain, the comtesse de Sérizy and the duchesse de Maugrigneuse. 'Lucien', we are told, 'cultiva beaucoup la société de madame de Sérizy, avec laquelle il était, au dire des salons, du dernier bien' (715). If Esther markets her body for money, Lucien uses his body to obtain social protection from the women who count, and the analogy is made explicit in the reference to Madame de Sérizy's passion for Lucien as 'un amour semblable à celui du baron de Nucingen pour Esther' (961). Equally insensate and depraved, the source of the 'gigantesques folies de la volupté [qui] rendaient Léontine folle et insatiable' (962), that passion speaks eloquently of the universal vortex of instinct and desire which lies beneath and continually threatens the fragile structure of social differentiation. The animal ferocity with which Léontine reacts to the news of Lucien's death, the abnormal strength with which she tears out the iron bar from the prison grating may strike us as absurdly overwritten but, as François Mauriac reminds us, commenting specifically on this passage in *Splendeurs*,[30] it is precisely at the moment when Balzac seems to be at his most ridiculous, that he is often at his most revealing. Léontine's derangement serves the 'totalizing' vision in that, through the disintegration of the social self, the collapse of those norms and values which, in terms of Balzac's overt ideology, distinguish her as a countess from, say, Esther as a prostitute, it proclaims a level of instinctual reality

common to all, in which the predatory violence of Vautrin and the erotic
compulsions of the society lady are but different manifestations of the
same primordial energy. The point is extended and reinforced in relation to the duchesse de Maufrigneuse. The insight we gain through the
obscene ravings of Mme de Sérizy's delirium ('Il paraît que la pauvre
comtesse dit des choses affreuses. On m'a dit que c'est dégoûtant. . . .
Une femme comme il faut ne devrait pas être sujette à de pareils accès'
(1090)) is paralleled by the sexual content of the correspondence between Lucien and Diane de Maufrigneuse. Once again the social mask
slips to reveal a very different reality. Diane, we learn, keeps Lucien's
letters 'comme certains viellards ont des gravures obscènes, à cause des
éloges hyperboliques donnés à ce qu'elle avait de moins duchesse en
elle. . . . Elle se souvint alors d'avoir, dans l'excès de sa passion, répondu
sur le même ton à Lucien, d'avoir célébré la poésie de l'homme comme
il chantait les gloires de la femme, et par quels dithyrambes!' (1091–2). In
society a duchess, in private a whore—Diane's letters enter into that
'secret history' which yet again subverts the pretences of the 'official
history' and illuminates a levelling process which Vautrin, who will
himself use these letters for his own ends, cynically underscores: 'J'ai le
dossier de madame de Sérizy et celui de la duchesse de Maufrigneuse, et
quelles lettres! Tenez, monsieur le comte: les filles publiques en écrivant
font du style et de beaux sentiments, eh bien, les grandes dames qui font
du style et de grands sentiments toute la journée écrivent comme les
filles agissent. Les philosophes trouveront la raison de ce chassé-croisé'
(1115)

Lucien's body thus circulates throughout the social organism like an
insidious poison generating corruption, excess, madness and death. In
the circuit it travels, it also creates a nexus of interests binding the
underworld and the Faubourg Saint-Germain in such a way that
changes in the fortunes of the one radically affect the situation of the
other. That degree of interdependence emerges clearly in the multiple
reverberations occasioned by Lucien's arrest, imprisonment and interrogation. Furthermore, in this context, the scope of the novel's social
and moral vision widens substantially, the developments of the plot
focusing the pervasive disorders of society in terms not only of sexuality but also of the general issue of justice and its ambiguous, morally
disturbing relation to the sources of power in that society. As Amélie
Camusot remarks, 'De grands personnages sont mêlés à cette déplorable affaire' (v, 1017). Lucien's arrest both adds to and tightens the net of
interlocking destinies; it sets in motion a series of conflicts and struggles
in which passion, self-interest, ambition and expediency, at all levels
from Vautrin upwards, vie with each other in the common pursuit of
interfering with and perverting the due process of law and the course of
justice. At the centre of this storm stands the figure of Camusot, the
examining magistrate, the representative of the theoretical independence and rectitude of the judiciary: 'Aucune puissance humaine, ni
le Roi, ni le Garde-des-sceaux, ni le premier ministre ne peuvent empié-

ter sur le pouvoir d'un juge d'instruction, rien ne l'arrête, rien ne lui commande' (936). Yet it is precisely this principle, vital to the health of the society which, while sustained in the outward show of legal procedure, is systematically attacked and undermined from within by the secret pressures of the various interested parties. Himself prompted by ambition, and ably supported by his scheming wife, Camusot's decisions are dictated not by abstract precepts of legal and moral order, but by a calculation of the relative degrees of power and influence wielded by the highly placed individuals whose conflicting require-ments he is called upon to accommodate. The determining factors in arriving at that decision are not the innocence or guilt of Lucien, objectively established, but rather who stands to gain what according to the outcome of the inquiry. Amélie puts it succinctly when she observes, 'Un homme aimé par la duchesse de Maufrigneuse, par la comtesse de Sérizy, par Clotilde de Grandlieu n'est pas coupable' (945). Lucien's connections with the Faubourg Saint-Germain are a sure guarantee of his ultimate release. Even the Attorney-General, M de Granville, presented elsewhere as the incarnation of high-minded integr-ity, the 'digne successeur des grands magistrats du vieux Parlement' (996), is seen to capitulate, placing the interests of his class before those of his office ('Lui aussi veut donc sauver Lucien, pensa Camusot' (948)). That Camusot, in fact, takes the other course is merely the result of a disastrous error of judgment, a failure to read the signs correctly, and in no sense represents the victory of a commitment to the higher ideals of his profession over the baser imperatives of opportunism.

In undoing society's myth of an impartial justice, situated above the encroachments of private interests, the involved, often tortuous nar-rative of part III of *Splendeurs* serves to enlarge and to redirect that 'total' criticism of society which we have encountered in the elaboration of the novel's sexual themes. The ease with which the institutions and pro-cedures of the law prove malleable under this kind of pressure clearly embodies Balzac's considered judgment of a general collapse of stan-dards. That judgment is further reinforced by the injection into the legal drama of an important political dimension. Camusot learns not only that 'de grands personnages sont mêlés à cette déplorable affaire', but that 'l'Etat avait des intérêts secrets dans ce procès' (941). The exact nature and extent of these 'secret interests' are fully revealed in the final section of the novel, *La Dernière incarnation de Vautrin*, and the key to those secrets, in terms of the narrative, is in the amorous letters which Vautrin has concealed and which he subsequently exploits in an attempt to blackmail the authorities into granting him a pardon. The letters constitute an 'épée de Damoclès suspendue sur le coeur du faubourg Saint-Germain' (1023), a 'canon chargé sur les trois plus considérables familles de la Cour et de la Pairie' (1025). The political implications of that threat for the regime are serious, given the importance to its political stability of an outwardly unblemished aristocracy. It is here that the destiny of a criminal and that of a government become inextricably involved one with the other, and the function of the narrative, in yet another authorial emphasis on the connecting agency of the plot, is to show 'à quel point les actions et les moindres paroles de Jacques Collin . . . intéressaient l'honneur des familles au sein desquelles il avait placé son défunt protégé' (1025). It is here that the major themes of the novel—criminality, prostitution, 'arrivisme', justice and politics—are fully threaded together into one, closely woven fabric. For Lucien's affairs do not simply concern the honour of a few fashionable families; in compromising that honour, they implicate the political credibility of a government, indeed of the King himself; in the words of des Lupeaulx, the Keeper of the Seals, 'Vous avez sagement agi en allant de l'avant, dit des Lupeaulx en donnant une poignée de main au Procureur-général. Le Roi ne veut pas, à la veille de tenter une grande chose, voir la pairie et les grandes familles tympanisées, salies. . . . Ce n'est plus un vil procès criminel, c'est une affaire d'Etat' (1118). The pattern of connection is now complete: the sexual exploits of Lucien will be used by Vautrin to compromise three aristocratic families whose prestige and untarnished reputation are essential to the political objectives and manoeuvres of Charles X. The interests of the underworld and the throne, of a criminal and a king, of the most reviled and the most respected, coincide, and the casualty of that coincidence is, of course, justice itself. In collaborating to prevent a social and political scandal, they are mutual accomplices in the perpetration of an even greater moral scandal. Vautrin will be pardoned, the government secured and the whole sordid tale of corruption and betrayal discreetly swept under the carpet.

The complete obliteration of moral distinctions between the outlaw and 'respectable', organized society engineered by the last section of the narrative may also help to illuminate one of the traditionally more puzzling and intriguing aspects of *Splendeurs*, namely Vautrin's 'conversion' from criminal to policeman. In the light of Vautrin's declaration to M de Granville, 'Je n'ai pas d'autre ambition que d'être un élément d'ordre et de répression, au lieu d'être la corruption même, (1138), it is habitually argued that this change of roles implies a radical and unexpected change in character, a sudden rejection of demonic individualism in favour of the values of social order.[31] However, this is seriously to misread the real significance of the episode in question. For, although the authorial rhetoric frequently presents the conflict between criminal and society in terms of opposing moral categories ('N'était-ce pas l'attaque et la défense? le vol et la propriété? La question terrible de l'état social et de l'état naturel vidée dans le plus étroit espace possible? (1101)), the action of the novel, in continually stressing the moral similarities of protagonists and antagonists, forcefully subverts the patterns of response that the authorial voice attempts to impose. Vautrin experiences no difficulty, undergoes no profound change, in 'joining' society because the real values of that society are qualitatively no different from his own as a criminal. It will be recalled that in *Le Père*

Goriot the lesson Rastignac learns from Mme de Beauséant, that arch representative of the Faubourg Saint-Germain, is virtually identical to that which he learns from Vautrin ('Il m'a dit crûment ce que madame de Beauséant me disait en y mettant des formes' (II, 942)). It will also be recalled that in the same novel Vautrin's ideal is none other than to become a plantation-owner in America, a classic projection of an essentially bourgeois fantasy and no different from the fantasies of wealth and domination that haunt other members of Balzac's world. Despite all the rhetoric of revolt that accompanies the presentation of Vautrin, in his acquisitive dreams, his will to power, his contempt for moral law, he is in fact the quintessential expression of the dominant characteristics of the new society, an extension to the extreme point of its ruthless individualism.

The point is further underlined in the way *Splendeurs* presents the struggle between Vautrin and the police. The police are 'ces génies inconnus chargés de veiller à la sûreté des États' (v, 754); they are the servants of the status quo, protecting and furthering the interests of the ruling class, the necessary instruments with which the establishment does its dirty work, while pretending to keep its hands clean (the revelation of the ineradicable bad faith of that class comes with the duc de Chaulieu's observation on the function of the spy and the policeman, 'tout en les méprisant, on doit s'en servir' (870)). Yet, if they serve the state, in the actual struggle with the enemy there is no accompanying suggestion of any moral superiority on their part. On the contrary, that struggle is continually described as a purely amoral one, for which the shaping image is in the transposition to contemporary Paris of Fenimore Cooper's North American Forests: 'Ainsi, la poésie de terreur que les stratagèmes des tribus ennemies en guerre répandent au sein des forêts de l'Amérique, et dont a tant profité Cooper, s'attachait au plus petits détails de la vie parisienne' (892). To the criminal Paris is 'ce qu'est la forêt vierge pour les animaux féroces' (1047); to the policeman, the criminal is 'ce qu'est le gibier pour le chasseur' (853); Corentin is 'un vrai chasseur' (848), Peyrade est 'le tigre', Vautrin 'le lion' (873), each intent on tracking and devouring 'son gibier'. The insistent recurrence of animal and predatory metaphors effectively undercuts any temptation the reader might have of an easy distribution of moral sympathies. The conflict is not between 'good' and 'bad', but simply 'une lutte où chacun combattit pour sa passion où pour ses intérêts' (770). The opposition between society and outlaw, order and anarchy dissolves into a conflict of morally indistinguishable forces, in which the roles of criminal and ploiceman are, in moral terms, wholly reversible. It is in the perspective furnished by these images and analogies that Vautrin's switch of allegiances becomes fully consistent and intelligible. He himself remarks to Asie, 'Nous étions le gibier, et nous devenons les chasseurs, voilà tout' (1126). Vautrin does not change, and neither does society; as his subsequent activities in *La Cousine Bette* bear witness, both simply recognize that the violence and brutality of Vautrin are exactly what the society requires. Paradoxically (the paradox is of course only superficial), Vautrin's 'dernière incarnation' is at once the last twist in the melodramatic plot of a *roman policier* and, in the implications of the union of criminal and society, the supreme consummation of the 'totalizing' vision, the confirmation of that troubling moral uniformity adumbrated in the opening pages of the novel. In that dual status, it stands therefore as a supreme demonstration of Balzac's ability imaginatively to adapt the conventions of contemporary popular fiction to the aims of significant art.

5 Antithesis and ambiguity

Cette scène comporte avec elle bien des moralités qui sont de plus
d'un genre. Balzac, *La Cousine Bette* (vi, 385)

The argument in the remaining chapters of this book is concerned
essentially with the relation to Balzac's practice of different aspects and
implications of that fundamental convention of melodramatic literature, the stereotype. Every culture possesses stereotypes as part of its
symbolic equipment for ordering reality and, in that broad anthropological sense (the sense in which Gérard Genette can speak of melodrama as being part of 'tout un domaine en quelque sorte ethnologique
de la littérature'[1]) it may therefore be said that every culture possesses
'melodrama'. The stereotype is the basic instrument with which melodrama performs one of its major cultural functions—the reduction of the
complex to the simple, the elimination of ambiguity and anomaly in
favour of maximal clarity. 'Typification', as anthropology and the
sociology of knowledge have shown, is of course a vital operation in
any society's attempt to confer intelligibility upon its reality; the world
must, in some degree, be simplified if one is to make sense of it, and
literature, even where it equivocates and queries in fairly radical ways, is
not exempt from this requirement. The stereotype, however, represents a singularly impoverished, even degenerate form of simplification. The purpose behind the typifying strategies of great literature is to simplify and generalize in a way that incorporates the
largest possible degree of complexity within the constraints of its
sense-making activities. With the melodramatic stereotype the purpose
is, rather, to bypass complexity completely, to pretend, in response to a
comforting fantasy of clarity and mastery, that it simply does not exist.
The convention of the melodramatic stereotype presupposes that
modes of feeling and behaviour are easily named and that they do not
budge from their names. It deals continually in the rapidly identifiable
label, the unproblematical classification. Psychologically, it diligently
serves, to return to Robert Heilman's phrase, the schematic expectations of 'monopathy', defined by Heilman as 'the singleness of feeling
that gives one the sense of wholeness . . . the sensation of wholeness that
is created when one responds with a single impulse or potential which
functions as if it were his whole personality.'[2]

In the melodramatic writing of the nineteenth century, the reductions of experience and the satisfactions of 'monopathy' offered by the stereotype are of a predominantly moral kind; in the familiar melodramatic universe men are either 'good' or 'bad', 'heroes' or 'villains' ('the intimate core of the form is the conflict between heroes and villains'[3]), and the dynamic of the melodramatic plot consists almost entirely in the pressures of the one being met by the resistances, and usually the triumphs, of the other. In more formal terms, the pattern of melodrama is one in which a series of moral stereotypes is distributed and combined within a structure shaped chiefly by the figure of antithesis. Antithesis, as we have previously seen, is the primary rhetorical figure of melodrama; it predominates over all the others, and, in conjunction with the convention of the moral stereotype, it is this which ensures the simplified divisions and classifications which are at the heart of the melodramatic world view.

This easy moral ordering of the world is one that has often been associated with the *Comédie humaine*. Balzac's systematic use of the figure of antithesis has frequently been noted. A sense of sharply defined contrasts (wealth/poverty, success/failure, past/present, etc.) is fundamental to Balzac's imagination, integral to his way of seeing the world, and antithetical categories of opposition, conflict and struggle provide the basic determinants of the structure of many of his novels; thus Félix Davin, acting as Balzac's delegate, speaks of 'la première loi de la littérature' as 'la nécessité des contrastes' (XI, 240). The connection of this general disposition of Balzac's art with nineteenth-century melodrama lies in the way it is often seen as manifesting itself through the grouping of his characters in terms of a set of highly schematic moral polarities. In the words of François Mauriac, 'Les personnages de la *Comédie humaine* sont pour la plupart tout d'une pièce, et appartiennent entièrement au Bien quand ils ne sont pas voués au Mal intégral.'[4] On this view, Balzac's work resembles melodrama therefore in so far as it is the product of a mind apparently unresponsive to nuance and ambiguity in motive and conduct, which, in its commitment to the immediacies of dramatic contrast, either fails to see or chooses to ignore the subtler, more complex modulations of the moral life of both individual and society.

Many of Balzac's major novels would lend themselves in interesting ways to a discussion of the implications of this view, but perhaps none more compellingly than *La Cousine Bette*; indeed partly on external grounds (it was, we recall, the most popular of Balzac's serially published novels), and partly on internal grounds, *La Cousine Bette* is a test case for this approach to Balzac. Among its manifold distinctive qualities, *La Cousine Bette* is an exemplary instance of Balzac's formal use of antithesis in the conception and arrangement of basic narrative design. Despite its improvised composition, its proliferating abundance and variety ('l'un des romans les plus touffus de Balzac'[5]). *La Cousine Bette* is technically one of Balzac's most integrated performances, the structure of the novel being controlled largely by means of a complex though unified network of contrasting patterns. The nature of those patterns varies widely within the text and the axis of contrast frequently shifts according to the angle of vision from which one views the novel. Thus, in the context of the novel's socio-historical themes, Hulot contrasts significantly with Crevel, the one a representative of a declining imperial aristocracy, the other a representative of the bourgeois class in the ascendant. However in relation to the sexual themes of the novel, at one level these two figures fulfil, despite manifold differences, a more or less common role as embodiments of libertine excess, the operative contrasts here being with the prudent Victorin or that 'hoarder' of sexual energy, the old maid Lisbeth. The two Hulot brothers resemble each other as the victims of an historically displaced class, but in terms of public and private morality they are poles apart. The demonic Valérie and the vengeful Lisbeth contrast in an obvious way with the selfless and suffering Adeline. Yet within the framework of this evident antithesis, a number of curious modifications and reversals of the basic pattern take place: the link which unites Valérie and Lisbeth in mutual hostility to Adeline is itself, in a further major emphasis of the novel, founded on a psychologically obscure and disturbing contrast, that of a harsh virile 'masculinity' and a soft, seductive 'femininity'. This in turn suggests another shift in perspective, through which the opposition of Valérie and Adeline is significantly modified: whatever separates the two women in the moral sense, both have physical beauty in common, and in the consciousness of Bette there may well be a strange identification of the two, Bette seeking vicariously to possess and enjoy in Valérie what she herself cannot have and is therefore led to defile and destroy in Adeline.[6] Unquestionably part of the fascination of reading *La Cousine Bette* comes from the ingenuity with which apparently fixed social and psychological configurations are continually manipulated in such a way as to incorporate an increasing complexity of subject matter and to yield richer layers of meaning.

Reduced to their essentials, however, these various patterns can be seen as the diversified projections of a central antithesis which, in thematic terms, holds the coordinates of a fundamental Balzacian preoccupation—the conflict between, on the one hand, the demands of moral and social order and, on the other, the disruptive pressures of the individual ego. In *La Cousine Bette*, as in other novels of the *Comédie humaine*, this struggle finds its concrete narrative shape in the vicissitudes of the Family (often given with a capital in the text as an index of its role as the source and symbol of order in society) attacked and undermined, both from within and without, by the forces of rampant egoism and depravity. Furthermore, the dramatization of this conflict is accompanied by a superstructure of moral and ideological comment which ranges protagonists and antagonists in a straightforward authorial scheme of values: on the one side, prevail the values of love, loyalty, honesty, selflessness; on the other, those of corruption, betrayal, greed, cruelty. At the level both of action and comment, the novel presents a structure of tensions and conflicts in which the issues of guilt and responsibility, and therefore the distribution of moral judgements, appear to present no serious difficulties for the reader. In the words of Philippe Bertault, who in his discussion of the general principle of antithesis in Balzac singles out *La Cousine Bette* for special comment:

> Dans *La Cousine Bette* les personnages incarn [ent] les vices et les vertus contraires. . . . Chacune des vertus est représentée par un personnage différent, mais la troupe des vices, comme un vol d'horribles oiseaux, s'abat sur le héros central, l'infâme baron Hector Hulot. Il a les satellites de sa hideur morale, son affreuse cousine Lisbeth, l'ignoble Crevel et sa femme Valérie Marneffe, créature dépravée. En face d'eux le groupe vertueux fait contraste: la baronne Hulot, ange de bonté, sa fille la comtesse de Steinbock, âme fière et pure, son beau-frère, type de la probité, le maréchal Hulot. . . . Ce roman est comme une vaste synthèse des moyens dramatiques employés par l'écrivain. On peut juger maintenant de l'importance qu'y tient l'antithèse des passions individuelles et des rivalités sociales.[7]

Yet it is in the implications of such a description of the novel that the major critical issue is located. For, on these terms, is it not the case that the moral geometry of the novel's design is just a little too neat and tidy? The degree of narrative control made possible by the author's systematic use of antithetical groupings suggests the imposition on his material of a highly simplistic moral universe, a world in which the questions of good and evil are uncomplicated matters, adapted to the naive 'virtue-villainy' syndrome characteristic of nineteenth-century melodrama. It is, however, precisely this black and white view of the novel that we wish to challenge here. For a close examination of *La Cousine Bette* reveals a whole set of ambiguities and paradoxes which seriously complicate and distort the apparent neatness of the novel's antithetical moral structure. The shifting perspectives we noted in relation to some of the novel's social and psychological themes are also to be seen at work in the moral sphere; polar oppositions curiously converge, as we begin to trace what Jean Hytier has called 'd'horribles équivalences entre la noblesse et le vice';[8] blameless characters find themselves, albeit at times unwillingly or unconsciously, involved in squalid complicities and failures of the moral will; individuals whose entire being seemed to be placed in the service of evil become sympathetic, deeply human. In short,—and it is this that we shall now attempt to demonstrate by focusing in particular upon the character and destiny of Victorin, Adeline and Lisbeth—as the novel progressively deepens in its grasp of the real strains and pressures of living in the contemporary world, there takes place a severe dislocation of the clear-cut manichean or melodramatic world view, making way for a much richer sense of the ambivalent and problematic nature of moral reality. To put it another way, we might say that in *La Cousine Bette* Balzac adopts a primary schema of melodrama for the purposes of a super-ficial ordering of his material, of a kind likely to appeal to the expecta-tions of the reader of the *roman-feuilleton*, only to subvert that schema from within by playing ironically on its basic conventions and devices.

The process of demonstrating these ambiguities in *La Cousine Bette* could be initiated in a number of different ways, but it is perhaps appropriate to begin by examining precisely that section of the novel where the ethical pattern of melodrama is outwardly most strongly articulated—the retribution sequence, in which the play of moral con-trasts is sharpened by the intervention of the *deus ex machina* to restore the declining fortunes of the Hulot family through the dispatch of the ignoble Valérie and her newly acquired husband, Crevel. Although not characteristic of Balzac's general procedure and certainly not consonant with the inner imaginative logic of his vision, the convention of a providential order or 'protector' rescuing the weak and punishing the wicked is one to which Balzac occasionally turned. Indeed in the *Avant-propos*, although the context is essentially a polemical one, it is a principle of declared policy ('Les actions blâmables . . . y trouvent toujours leur punition humaine ou divine' (I, 11)), and, at the level of literary practice, we encounter the convention in works such as *Ursule Mirouët*, *Albert Savarus*, *La Rabouilleuse* as well as in *La Cousine Bette* itself. The reasons why Balzac, at certain moments of the *Comédie*, has recourse to the apparatus of poetic justice remain a matter of some speculation. It could be simply a straight concession, under commercial pressure, to the popular writing of the day. In a more personal sense, the restoration of moral equilibrium has been seen as a kind of instinctive compensatory move generated by a feeling of guilt at his own com-plicity with evil. More importantly perhaps, it could be, as Maurice Bardèche suggests, the expression of Balzac's 'bon gros appétit de justice en présence des "crimes cachés" qu'il découvre partout'.[9] The notion of the 'crime caché' and the 'vol décent', before which the normal machinery of custom, law and justice proves wholly impotent, is central to Balzac's conception of the anarchic nature of modern social reality, and it is all-pervasive in *La Cousine Bette*; confronted with a disease that the 'docteur ès sciences sociales' (VI, 183) finds incurable, horrified by the powerlessness of established moral codes and legal institutions to cope with what, in the text, is described by the police chief, M Chapuzot, as 'certaines monstruosités morales qu'il faudrait pouvoir enlever comme nous enlevons les boues' (464), Balzac seems to have felt impelled to invent his own purely fictional redresser of wrongs. But whatever the motivation behind Balzac's use of the device, objectively and historically, it is rooted in the sub-literary, melo-dramatic idiom of the *roman noir* and *roman-feuilleton*, the classic formula by means of which these forms of writing accommodate that strain in the popular imagination which demands not only a heavy accentuation of the division between good and evil, but also the security of an order which rewards the virtuous and punishes the transgressor.

Yet, in respect of *La Cousine Bette*, it is precisely at the moment when Balzac seems to be at his most crude and naive, when the quality and tone of the writing modulate perceptibly into the schematic and cliché-ridden style of Eugène Sue, that ambiguity intervenes, in relation both to the sources of the punishment visited on Valérie and Crevel and to the difficult decision that Victorin Hulot is called upon to make. The popular convention is unambiguous: retribution is delivered either from an omnipotent and benevolent deity or, where it is delgated to human authority, from a 'protector' whose moral credentials are impeccable. In *La Cousine Bette*, however, the agents of nemesis, Vautrin and Mme Nourrisson ('Nous remplaçons le destin' (462)) and the elemental Brazilian, Montéjanos ('Je serai l'instrument de la colère divine' (496)) belong more appropriately to the Balzacian demonology than to any divine scheme of things. As we know, for Vautrin morality is never an important question, and the shift from criminal to secret policeman should in no way be taken as implying a sudden conversion. As soon as Vautrin and Mme Nourrisson enter the scene, the scheme of right versus wrong immediately dissolves into a purely amoral conflict of different interests and passions, regulated less by a transcendent moral law than by the relative capacity of the different parties for cunning and ruthlessness.

The blurring of moral distinctions that paradoxically results from the introduction of the retributive machinery assumes its full significance in the way it affects the position of Victorin. In the antithetical design of the novel Victorin clearly belongs to the 'groupe vertueux'. Although in the opening section of the novel he is not accorded any particular weight in this respect, the initial stress falling rather on his prudent mediocrity, as the action progresses and as he is increasingly called upon to assume the responsibilities that his father has abrogated, Balzac explicitly invites us to see Victorin's development in terms of a growth in moral stature: 'Victorin Hulot reçut, du malheur acharné sur sa famille cette dernière façon qui perfectionne ou qui démoralise l'homme. Il devint parfait. Dans les grandes tempêtes de la vie, on imite les capitaines qui, par les ouragans, allègent le navire des grosses marchandises. L'avocat perdit son orgueil intérieur, son assurance visible, sa morgue d'orateur et ses prétentions politiques' (441). In the professional sphere, 'Hulot fils, doué d'une parole sage, d'une probité sévère, était écouté par les juges et par les conseillers' (441). In private life, where Hector and Wenceslas succomb, Victorin resists: 'l'avocat puritain avait jusqu'alors trouvé des prétextes pour résister à son père et à son beau-frère. Se montrer chez la femme qui faisait couler les larmes de sa mère lui paraissait un crime' (330). When the possibility of a financially advantageous 'rapprochement' with Crevel becomes poss-

ible, if he will attend the wedding of the latter and Valérie, he refuses 'par
considération d'honneur et de délicatesse' (468). That 'providence'
should intervene on the side of such a high-minded individual is wholly
in accord with the popular convention, but it is just because both the
source and the methods of help are so ambivalent that Victorin's moral
rectitude is in fact fatally compromised by what would normally
enhance it. The aim, in Balzac's terms, is noble, it is a struggle for the
Family and by extension for moral order in society at large; in the words
of Célestine: 'Mon mari tente un effort, il regarde comme un devoir de
venger la société, la famille, et de demander compte à cette femme de
tous ses crimes' (446). But in order to win the battle, Victorin has,
metaphorically, to do a deal with the devil. This surely is the deeper
meaning of the otherwise absurd, extravagantly written episode of
Victorin's encounters with Vautrin and Mme Nourrisson. Victorin
desires the end but is profoundly uncomfortable about the morality of
the means; the initial reaction is a horrified refusal: 'Madame, je
n'accepte pas le secours de votre expérience et de votre activité, si le
succès doit coûter la vie à quelqu'un et si le moindre fait criminel
s'ensuit. Mme Nourrisson, however, offers an arrangement that allows
for a specious reconciliation of interest and conscience, but at the
same time mercilessly underscores the inescapable bad faith of Victorin's position:

> Vous voulez rester probe à vos propres yeux, tout en souhaitant
> que votre ennemi succombe. . . . Oui, vous voulez que cette
> madame Marneffe abandonne la proie qu'elle a dans la gueule. Et
> comment feriez-vous lâcher à un tigre son morceau de boeuf?
> Est-ce en lui passant la main sur le dos et lui disant: *minet, minet*. . . .
> Vous n'êtes pas logique. Vous ordonnez un combat, et vous ne
> voulez pas de blessures. Eh bien, je vais vous faire cadeau de cette
> innocence qui vous tient tant au coeur. J'ai toujours vu dans
> l'honnêteté de l'étoffe à l'hypocrisie (462).

In neither assenting nor dissenting to Mme Nourrisson's proposals,
Victorin effectively gives her carte blanche to do as she sees fit and, as
such, is morally if not physically an accomplice in the business of
murder. The harsh fact of that complicity brooks no facile retrieval into
the reassuring convention of the unequivocal triumph of right over
wrong; it is simply the pursuit and protection of private interests by
means of covert violence and can in no way be recuperated into
the orthodox moral and religious schemes to which Balzac pays lip-
service in the *Avant propos* as elsewhere. The point was not entirely lost
on some of Balzac's own contemporaries; as one critic, Alexandre
Weill, wrote in the left-wing newspaper, *La Démocratie Pacifique*: 'Mais
Monsieur de Balzac, dans notre société catholique que vous trouvez à
merveille, ce brave Brésilien qui remplace la Providence serait traduit

devant le jury et condamné à mort comme empoisonneur; mais Monsieur de Balzac, le fils d'Adeline lui-même serait condamné aux galères et à l'exposition comme complice du Brésilien par l'entremise de Madame de Saint-Estève. Où donc est le triomphe de la vertu catholique?'[10] Weill's observations are of course advanced as a criticism of Balzac, as evidence of a radical confusion and incoherence in Balzac's outlook. We, on the other hand, while acknowledging the pertinence of the critic's rhetorical questions, would turn this round to argue a conscious grasp on Balzac's part of the darker implications of what he is doing in the novel. These implications emerge with even greater clarity in the grim ironies of Valérie's death-bed scene. Confronted with the appalling spectacle of Valérie's rotting body, Adeline and Hortense invoke the comforting myth of divine nemesis. Adeline remarks; 'Le doigt de Dieu est là; as for her daughter, 'Hortense, elle, trouvait Dieu très juste' (vi, 502). That myth collapses, however, before the reactions of Victorin who, alone in possession of the truth, at once suppresses that truth while inwardly acknowledging his own terrible guilt: 'Hulot fils avait le vertige, il regardait sa mère, sa soeur et le docteur alternativement en tremblant qu'on ne devinât ses pensées. Il se considérait comme un assassin' (502). In the ironic juxtaposition of Adeline's innocent reference to the workings of God's justice and Victorin's knowledge of the squalid reality of murder we may perhaps read a conscious parody or subversion on Balzac's part of the usual procedures of popular literature. The operation of poetic justice habitually nourishes a desire for moral reassurance. By taking the demonic Vautrin and Mme Nourrisson as the mediators of vengeance (he could easily have taken another course, by enlarging, for instance, the role of the benevolent 'protector', the Prince de Wissembourg) Balzac turns the device on its head, transforming it to serve a deeper artistic purpose.

The choice that Victorin is called upon to make not only undermines his role in the antithetical structure of the novel as the embodiment of high-minded principle but, in a larger perspective, also evokes in dramatic fashion that zone of ambiguity which calls in question any suggestion there might have been of a tidy, neatly labelled moral universe. For the fact that Victorin is compelled to have recourse to the amoral world of Vautrin embodies a judgement of shatteringly pessimistic proportions on the nature of Balzac's society. Victorin's capitulation speaks eloquently of the tragic impossibility of living in that society according to the values of decency and honour. In order to survive and prosper, one is forced to cross the moral divide; to resist the onslaught of the enemy, one comes to resemble the enemy; under pressure the attempt to sustain moral order yields finally to anarchy and barbarism. It is no accident that Mme Nourrisson's admonition to Victorin is coloured by a series of predatory and military images. The familiar Balzacian conception of society as a jungle in which moral codes and beliefs are helpless and irrelevant constitutes the real centre of the novel. Eat or be eaten, destroy or be destroyed, these are the fundamental imperatives or 'laws', ignorance of which, as everywhere in the *Comédie humaine*, is a recipe for catastrophe and defeat.

Victorin's pact with the devil ('Le diable a une soeur' (463) is his immediate reaction to Mme Nourrisson) is thus a major instance of ambiguity in *La Cousine Bette*, severely fracturing the outwardly unambiguous mould in which the novel is cast. In its implications it is moreover not a purely local affair but evokes a general crisis of values which engulfs the novel as a whole and which consequently leads us to interrogate other dimensions of the text. In particular, it places a question mark over the figure of Adeline. For if, as Victorin's collusion indicates, the necessary price of survival for the Family is the sacrifice of principle, if this is the only way of sustaining some form of order in the face of implacable hostility, how are we meant to react to the one character in the novel who so consistently attempts to meet the dilemmas of life with a firmness of moral resolve and religious belief? Adeline is, in fact, of capital importance for the thesis of ambiguity; for if she is to be found crucially wanting in some way, then the whole system of moral antitheses described by Bertault as the essence of the novel's design and meaning necessarily begins to fall apart.

At one level the role and significance of Adeline are wholly unequivocal: she occupies the moral centre of the novel; where others yield to vice she incarnates the basic Christian values; she is an exemplary being who devotes all her energies to maintaining the cohesion of the family, who resists, through moral example, the forces which threaten the dissolution of vital social bonds and responsibilities. The presentation of this role is accompanied and reinforced by an appropriate authorial rhetoric which, drawing heavily upon the stereotyped formulae of the vocabulary of melodrama, speaks of her 'angélique douceur', of the 'dévouement extraordinaire de cette belle et noble femme', of 'cette sainte femme', 'cette sainte créature' and which reaches its climax in the account of Adeline's superb dismissal of Crevel after the momentary lapse induced by desperation: 'La majesté de la vertu, sa céleste lumière avait balayé l'impureté passagère de cette femme qui, resplendissante de la beauté qui lui était propre, parut grandie à Crevel. Adeline fut en ce moment sublime comme ces figures de la Religion, soutenues par une croix, que les vieux Vénitiens ont peintes' (405). The constant repetition of the epithets 'sublime', 'angélique', 'sainte' clearly tends towards the elevation of Adeline to a point where she seems to be situated wholly outside the critical scope of the novel. Adeline, in short, is perfect, without blemish, unambiguous.

Yet an interpretation of Adeline which allowed itself to be exclusively confined to the emphases of the rhetorical commentary would be profoundly misleading. For the cruel paradox (of which, as we shall see, Balzac himself was fully aware) inherent in the creation of Adeline is that the very idealism which, in the abstract, is the sign of her moral sublimity, at the more concrete level, proves to be an inadequate and even positively disastrous response to the situations in which she finds herself. A clue to that inadequacy is perceptible in the ironic reverberations of her reaction to Valérie's death. Her remark 'Le doigt de Dieu est là' sends us back to an earlier utterance in conversation with Crevel—'Dieu protège les malheureux' (152)—and forward to the homily she delivers to the child-prostitute, Atala: 'Comment veut-tu que Dieu te protège, si tu foules aux pieds les lois divines et humaines? ... Sais-tu que Dieu tient en réserve un paradis pour ceux qui suivent les commandements de son Eglise?' (516). Given the cynical desecration of values enacted by most of the other characters, we may see in Adeline's religiosity and assertions of faith in a moral order Balzac's sense of an alternative way of living characterized by a redeeming spiritual poise and tranquillity. On the other hand, given the actual course of events in the novel, we may be inclined to see her moral and religious piety as the sign of a colossal naivety, a radical failure of comprehension, an inability to cope with the real issues that is almost as damaging in its human consequences as the more obviously disruptive activities of those opposed to her. In the *Avant-propos* Balzac writes that Christianity is the sole means of containing the 'tendances dépravées de l'homme' (I, 8). Yet to the extent that Adeline functions in the novel as the representative of the Christian virtues, *La Cousine Bette* may be read as a grim travesty of what is upheld in the *Avant-propos*. It is not that Adeline, as an incarnation of saintliness, is merely defeated and finally destroyed, for that would simply be a reflection on the strength of the opposing camp. It is rather that Adeline's defeat, and indeed the general collapse of order that occurs in the novel, is in part the direct result of a weakness that springs from the attempt to live by a code of patience, innocence and charity in a struggle that demands other, very different qualities. That weakness, at once a failure of perception and a failure of will, makes itself felt in the context of two closely related themes, both of which receive deep and extended treatment in the novel—sexuality and authority.

Among other things, *La Cousine Bette* is perhaps Balzac's most sustained imaginative inquiry into the forms and pressures of sexuality. As Georges Poulet has observed, the initial moment of the vision that informs the *Comédie humaine* is an intense experience of desire taking shape and direction in a number of different ways.[11] In *La Cousine Bette* desire is explicitly sexual and all-pervasive, a major point of reference for the thematic organization and coherence of the text. The libidinous energies of Hulot, the brutish lechery of Crevel, the corruption of Marneffe, the passionate violence of Montéjanos, the calculating depravity of Valérie, the yielding, almost effeminate *mollesse* of Wenceslas, the strong, imperious sensuality of the youthful Hortense, the repressed and distorted sexuality of the old maid Lisbeth and the disturbing vicarious eroticism of her friendship with Valérie, the atmosphere of licence that reigns over the gathering of the *demi-monde* at the ubiquitous Rocher de Cancale, the insidious and brutalizing corruption that creates the child-prostitute in the lower depths of Parisian slumland—these are some of the fundamental *données* out of which the structure and meaning of the novel are shaped.

The shaping principle, which works these *données* into a coherent conception, is Balzac's awareness of desire as something deeply problematic.[12] In more specific terms, *La Cousine Bette* seeks to chart the catastrophic effects on the fabric of social life wrought by the untrammelled expression and exploitation of sexual passion. Like Laclos's *Les Liaisons dangereuses* (in a conscious echo of Laclos's novel Valérie is significantly described as 'une Madame de Merteuil bourgeoise' (362)), *La Cousine Bette* dramatizes the consequences that ensue from a radical dissociation of sexuality from human feeling and moral responsibility, the collapse of organized life that results from the lack of constraint on the various homages which, in the mythological perspective evoked by Fredric Jameson, the different characters pay to Eros.[13] In this reading of the novel Adeline's significance would seem to be clear: because she is not drawn into the vortex of instinct and desire, because she remains untouched by the aggressive and voracious energies of sexuality, she functions as a point of repose in the novel, as a possible stabilizing and ordering force. Such an approach, however, ignores a great deal, and if the ideologist in Balzac would undoubtedly lend his weight to an approach of this kind, the novelist in him is aware that the problematic nature of desire is a far more complex business altogether. For, as Leo Bersani has shown[14], the central dilemma posed by the tensions between desire and order is not resolved simply by ignoring or repressing desire, but rather involves a difficult and delicate balancing of gratification and repression. If the free expression of desire inaugurates the terrifying possibility of anarchy and chaos, then complete repression leads to suffering, aridity and even, as *Le Lys dans la vallée* illustrates, death. The implicit ideal is a state of equilibrium in which desire is at once gratified and contained, released and yet regulated. Thus, in *La Cousine Bette*, if Hulot's emotional and physical profligacy generates devastation and ruin, repression in Hortense causes neurosis and near hysteria and, more important, accounts in large part for the dangerous and ultimately destructive emotional state of Lisbeth. The imperatives of Eros have to be obeyed, and the problem is therefore to imagine contexts in which desire is not suppressed but both satisfied and yet prevented from breaking the bonds which guarantee order.

It is in this situation that Adeline appears as sadly wanting. When she tries to explain to Hortense why their respective husbands have deserted them for the alluring Valérie, she comments: 'Pour leurs plaisirs, les hommes, mon ange, commettent les plus grandes lâchetés, des infâmies, des crimes; c'est à ce qu'il paraît dans leur nature' (VI, 346). The observation is platitudinous in the extreme and what is absent from it is any sense on Adeline's part that her husband's sexual misdemeanours might be to some degree the result of a particular role she has chosen to play in the marital relationship. Undoubtedly repelled by the all-embracing atmosphere of sexual corruption, Adeline seeks moral sanctuary but does so through a role which seems to be founded on an equally dangerous dissociation of the carnal and the spiritual. An interesting moment in this respect is the one where Adeline greets her husband after his rejection by Valérie: 'Adeline avait dépouillé tout intérêt de femme, la douleur éteignait jusqu'au souvenir. Il n'y avait plus en elle que maternité, honneur de famille et l'attachement le plus pur d'une épouse chrétienne pour un mari fourvoyé, cette sainte tendresse qui survit à tout dans le coeur de la femme' (362). Her moral nobility conceals a lack; all spirituality and saintliness, the innocent, dutiful, virtuous 'épouse chrétienne', Adeline, in the face of the reckless dynamism of appetite and will that suffuses the other creations, seems strangely negative and colourless. Her moral heroism is beyond dispute but there is more than a suggestion of ambiguity in that the price paid is an ignorance of or turning away from the nature of desire and sexuality and, as such, an inability to sustain the kind of relationship necessary for the stability of her husband and therefore of the family as a whole. It might of course be reasonably objected that Hulot's desires are so intense, so monstrously pathological that no marital context could hope to contain them. On the other hand one could at the very least offer the tentative speculation that Hulot's obsessional debauchery is in part the result of a certain poverty in Adeline, that the terrible logic of Hulot's excess is partially shaped by a crucial deficiency in his wife.

On such a highly sensitive question the text is understandably somewhat reticent (we find a similar reticence in *Honorine* and *Une Fille d'Eve*). Yet there are hints, indications, even explicit statements which clearly suggest that this is Balzac's meaning. There is, for example, the highly subtle passage in that magnificently written episode of Adeline's encounter with Josépha, the passage which details Adeline's initial reactions on entering the apartment of the actress:

> La baronne étourdie examinait chaque objet d'art dans un étonnement profond. Elle y trouvait l'explication de ces fortunes au creuset sous lequel le Plaisir et la Vanité attisent un feu dévorant. Cette femme qui depuis vingt-six ans vivait au milieu des froides reliques de luxe impérial, dont les yeux contemplaient des tapis à fleurs éteintes, des bronzes dédorés, des scieries flétries comme son coeur, entrevit la puissance des séductions du Vice en voyant les résultats. . . . Puis elle allait satisfaire cette curiosité qui la poignait, d'étudier le charme que possédaient ces sortes de femmes pour extraire tant d'or des gisements avares du sol parisien. La baronne se regarda pour savoir si elle ne faisait pas tache dans ce luxe (451).

The passage goes on to re-establish Adeline's inner *noblesse* but in an important sense it gives the game away. Adeline's initial bewilderment and astonishment yield a sudden insight into the nature and power of sexual desire and by implication stress a corresponding blindness, even a personal defeat on Adeline's part. Furthermore, given Balzac's propensity for using physical settings as a kind of symbolic language, we might see in her comparison of Josépha's sumptuous apartment with the faded graces of her own salon more than a comparison of material conditions: the terms 'froides reliques', 'fleurs éteintes', 'bronzes dédorés' and above all the more explicit 'flétries comme son coeur' indirectly suggest a corrosive sexual atrophy which, if it does not legitimize Hulot's conduct, at least helps to render it intelligible. In contrast to Adeline Josépha succeeds because, although she manipulates it to serve her own ends, she understands the realities of sexual passion. Similarly, in a more important perspective, Valérie Marneffe, in her oddly erudite remark, 'La Vertu coupe la tête, le Vice ne vous coupe que les cheveux (337), understands, although she too, on an even larger scale of depravity, corrupts and degrades the sexual impulse in pursuit of her mercenary objectives. It is, moreover, in that contrast between ignorance and knowledge, atrophy and vitality that the other form of ambiguity, to which we referred at the beginning, interlocks with the kind of ambiguity at present under discussion—the ambiguity implicit in Taine's celebrated remark 'Balzac aime sa Valérie.'[15] It helps to explain the complicity of the author with his demonic creation, the way in which overt moral condemnation clashes with the evident excited enthusiasm with which, for example, he lingeringly describes the various aspects of Valérie's devastating seductiveness, in contrast with the commensurate lack of emphasis on Adeline's physical presence. At a more explicitly personal level, it contributes to an illumination of the curious letter Balzac wrote to Mme Hanska at the time of writing *La Cousine Bette*: 'je fais pour mon Eve toute les folies qu'un Hulot fait pour une Marneffe, je te donnerai mon sang, mon honneur, ma vie.'[16] The partial identification of Mme Hanska with Valérie in Balzac's imagination must be taken as signalling the importance Balzac attaches to sexual responsiveness and reciprocated desire in a relationship, and by extension it it would seem to carry certain damaging implications in relation to Adeline. It is not of course a question of Balzac 'taking sides' with Valérie against Adeline; it is rather that we have here the spectacle of a mind and imagination split between admiration for Adeline's moral qualities and fascination for Valérie's sensuality, a split which in broader terms could be related to a general cultural and psychological schism of which there are in fact many descriptions and accounts in nineteenth-century thought and literature.

Balzac himself does not put it in quite these terms, but the sense is there in his elaboration of what we might perhaps call his theory of the 'complete' woman, whose completeness consists in uniting the two elements of the carnal and the spiritual in an ideal synthesis. The important texts here would include *La Physiologie du mariage*, *La Maison du Chat-qui-pelotte*, *Petites misères de la vie conjugale*, *Béatrix*. In the latter novel, for instance, in relating the difficulties the virtuous Sabine de Grandlieu encounters in rescuing her husband from the clutches of Béatrix de Rochefide, Balzac has Maxime de Trailles offer the following advice: 'L'on croit qu'Othello, que son cadet Orosmane, que Saint-Preux, René, Werther et autres amoureux en possession de la renommée représentent l'amour! Jamais leurs pères à coeur de verglas n'ont connu ce qu'est un amour absolu, Molière seul s'en est douté. L'amour, madame la duchesse, ce n'est pas d'aimer une noble femme, une Clarisse, le bel effort, ma foi! . . . . L'amour, c'est se dire: "Celle que j'aime est une infâme, elle me trompe, elle me trompera, c'est une rouée, elle sent toutes les fritures de l'enfer . . .". Et d'y courir et d'y trouver le bleu de l'ether, les fleurs du paradis' (II, 591–2). The brutal cynicism with which the advice is offered is typical of Maxime, but its emphasis on sexual strategy is undoubtedly one that Balzac himself would endorse. Indeed in *La Cousine Bette* the necessity of such strategies in the context of love and marriage is explicitly adduced on at least three occasions. Thus Balzac writes; 'On doit avoir toutes les femmes dans la sienne' (VI, 333), a conception that is further amplified later in the novel:

> Beaucoup de femmes mariées, attachées à leurs devoirs et à leurs maris, pourront ici se demander pourquoi ces hommes si forts et si bons, si pitoyables à des madame Marneffe, ne prennent pas leurs femmes, surtout quand elles ressemblent à la baronne Hulot, pour l'objet de leur fantaisie et de leurs passions. Ceci tient aux plus profonds mystères de l'organisation humaine. L'amour, cette immense débauche de la raison, ce mâle et sévère plaisir des grandes âmes, et le plaisir, cette vulgarité vendue sur place, sont deux faces différentes d'un même fait. La femme qui satisfait ces deux vastes appétits est aussi rare, dans le sexe, que le grand général, le grand écrivain, le grand artiste, le grand inventeur, le sont dans une nation. L'homme supérieur comme l'imbécile, un Hulot comme un Crevel, ressentent également le besoin de l'idéal et celui du plaisir; tous vont cherchant ce mystérieux androgyne, cette rareté qui la plupart du temps se trouve être un ouvrage en deux volumes' (385).

The generalized commentary is clearly meant to illuminate the particular limitations of Adeline's relationship with her husband, and if the reader misses the connection, it is again underlined by Josépha who observes with her characteristic brio, 'Dame, ce pauvre homme! il aime les femmes . . . et bien, si vous aviez eu, voyez vous, un peu de notre chique, vous l'auriez empêché de couailler; car vous auriez été ce que nous savons être: toutes les femmes pour un homme' (459). In short, and to adapt Balzac's own somewhat vulgar metaphor of the 'ouvrage en deux volumes', if Adeline had written an element of 'wordlines' into the margins of her personality and conduct, it is conceivable that many of the disasters that befall her and her family could have been averted. In an important sense it is because of Adeline that Valérie is possible, just as it is the high-minded platonism of Henriette de Mortsauf that paves the way for the deadly Arabelle Dudley.

In the context of the novel's engagement with the complex and difficult themes of human sexuality, Adeline's role as the passive 'épouse chrétienne' thus presents itself as a deeply ambiguous one. The implications of that passivity, and the degree of responsibility for misfortune that it carries, may be further traced in relation to another major thematic concern of the novel—the source and legitimacy of social authority. We have already invoked the familiar Balzacian concept of the Family as 'la plus grande chose humaine' (I, 309) and 'le véritable élément social' (I, 9). It enjoys this privileged status in Balzac's mind because he sees its ideal structure as both the microcosm and the concrete basis for that hierarchical and cohesive system which should govern society at large and against which he measures and evaluates the destructive individualism of his own civilization. Within that ideal structure, the figure of the father and husband is necessarily of paramount importance; in accordance with Balzac's essentially feudalistic conception, like God in the creation, the king in the nation, the father in the family is the wielder of power and authority and thereby the guarantor of order; obedience is his due, responsibility his burden. As Louise de Macumer, in *Mémoires de deux jeunes mariées*, puts it, commenting specifically on the obligations of the marital bond and most certainly echoing the considered view of Balzac himself: 'Oui, la femme est un être faible qui doit, en se mariant, faire un entier sacrifice de sa volonté à l'homme qui lui doit en retour le sacrifice de son égoisme' (I, 314).

From beginning to end, Adeline conducts her marriage on the basis of this precept: 'Le baron fut dès l'origine une espèce de Dieu qui ne pouvait faillir. . . . Après s'être bien dit que son mari ne saurait jamais avoir de torts envers elle, elle se fit dans son fort intérieur la servante humble, devouée et aveugle de son créateur' (155). In the abstract, so to speak, there is nothing in this posture that the conservative Balzac would find amiss. However, in the actual relationship itself it becomes ambiguous precisely because the other factor of the social equation (the husband's 'sacrifice de son égoisme') is missing. As the original title of the first section (*Le Père prodigue*) indicates, a central focus in the study of Hulot's sexual obsession is the abdication of familial responsibility, the deleterious social consequences that stem from the betrayal of primary bonds and obligations. By his actions the baron has violated the fundamental principle of the social contract, and consequently the self-effacing reverence and deferential submissiveness, which are the distinctive and constant hall-marks of Adeline's attitude to her husband, are without the justifying rationale which alone can make these integral elements of Balzac's ideal of a stable and harmonious social order. Yet, although she knows that her idol has fallen, and despite the intense suffering, humiliation and even moments of inner revolt these betrayals involve, Adeline nevertheless persists with a code which, because its essential foundations have crumbled, is not only empty and meaningless but leaves her defenceless and ineffectual before the forces which threaten her world: 'Elle savait qu'aucune rivale ne tiendrait deux heures contre un mot de reproche, mais elle fermait les yeux, elle se bouchait les oreilles, elle voulait ignorer la conduite de son mari au dehors. . . . Elle souffrait néanmoins, elle s'abandonnait secrètement à des rages affreuses; mais en revoyant son Hector, elle . . . perdait la force d'articuler une seule plainte' (156). That inability to utter 'une seule plainte' dictates the basic pattern of the relationship throughout the novel and points to Adeline's fatal weakness. At various junctures the action is punctuated by the return to the family of the 'prodigal father' seeking consolation at moments of distress, and on each occasion Adeline never abandons the part she has chosen. Thus, when early in the novel, Hector, with that blind, self-absorbed egocentricity that characterizes his mania, complains bitterly of the financial difficulties of keeping his mistresses, Adeline not only accepts the humiliation of listening to his confession, but actively commiserates ('Pauvre ami', 'Ne te tourmente pas, Hector'); she offers him her diamonds and sees his refusal as 'sublime', and finally capitulates completely ('Il est le maître, il peut tout prendre ici' (177)). Again, when Hulot abandons Adeline to live with Valérie, her only response is, 'Il me veut ainsi; que sa volonté soit faite' (279). When Hulot, summarily dismissed by Valérie, crawls home like a wounded animal, Adeline hovers on the verge of plain speaking but, 'Elle n'osa poursuivre, elle sentit que chaque mot serait un blâme' (vi, 363). Finally, when the baron reaches the depths of disgrace, dismissed from public life and responsible for the deaths of his brother and uncle, Adeline is presented as 'ne sentant plus, de tous les sentiments qui lui remplissaient le coeur, qu'une pitié profonde' (426). This inexhaustible capacity for 'Christian' forgiveness, the continual inability to adopt a more active and challenging role ultimately tend to arouse irritation rather than admiration. Zola described Adeline as a 'mouton sublime'[17] and this has been a habitual response of criticism ever since. The imperative 'courage et silence' which Adeline enjoins upon Hortense as the sole means of coping with adversity, though it indicates a truly heroic martyrdom (Balzac refers to 'un père si héroiquement protégé par un sublime silence' (348)), represents nonetheless a wholly inadequate reaction, which not only condemns Adeline to inertia but actually aggravates and intensifies the situation; the extremity of her moral effort and the very qualities of her moral greatness paradoxically and tragically end up as a form of indulgence which Hector exploits and which therefore make her partially responsible for what happens. The critical perspective in which we must inevitably see Adeline is in fact suggested by Balzac himself; echoing and expanding the view expressed in *La Fille aux yeux d'or* that 'les extrêmes se touchent' (v, 308), Balzac writes in *La Cousine Bette:* 'Les sentiments nobles poussés à l'absolu produisent des résultats semblables à ceux des grands vices' (202). Morally Adeline is perfect, tactically she is pathetic, and it is in the disjunction between motive and result that the eminently 'pragmatic' mind of Balzac locates the source of her ambiguity. Furthermore—and this is the supreme sign of the novel's unrelenting pessimism—the fatal indulgence she grants her husband inexorably makes her an accomplice, albeit an unwilling one, in the very corruption to which she was supposed to act as a moral corrective. Since she has decided against overt and active resistance, since she rigorously eschews any expression of anger and defiance, she is compelled, by the logic of her self-imposed inertia, to compromise with her husband's abject moral squalor. This is the only way that we can interpret, for example, that excruciating moment when Adeline meekly suggests to her husband that he abandon his mistresses but that he keeps them within the limits of the family purse: 'Mon ami . . . s'il te faut absolument des maîtresses, pourquoi ne prends-tu pas, comme Crevel, des femmes qui ne soient pas chères et dans une classe à se trouver longtemps heureuses de peu' (202). Here Adeline approaches the issue on her husband's terms and is thereby trapped into acceptance and compromise. More degrading still—perhaps more degrading than the oft-quoted episode of her attempted self-prostitution—is the sudden reflection, in the midst of anguish and despair, that her husband's frequentation of the *demi-monde* might at least yield a husband for Hortense. We recall that she has just learnt from Crevel, to her horror and disgust, that the marriage of Victorin and Celestine (to her the emblem of decency and respectability) has its origins in the ignoble depravity of the two fathers: 'Elle entrevoyait dans les discours grossiers de l'ancien parfumeur irrité le compérage odieux auquel était dû le mariage du jeune avocat. Deux filles perdues avaient été les prêtresses de cet hymen proposé dans quelque orgie au milieu des dégradantes familiarités de deux vieillards ivres'. Yet this shocking and painful realization is immediately followed by the thought, 'Il oublie donc Hortense . . . il la voit cependant tous les jours, lui cherchera-t-il donc un mari chez ces vauriennes?' (158). It is a thought induced by the desperation of a mother but, objectively viewed, it is the index of an insidious contamination, a coming to terms with evil and what it has to offer.

It is this that makes a reading of *La Cousine Bette* such a disconcerting experience—the realization that in the end nothing is or remains innocent; that what is thought of as pure turns out to have its roots in corruption and decay; that the attempt to stand by certain standards and values leads only further into the morass. The motif of disease, so vividly rendered in the putrefying body of Marneffe and the physical decomposition of Valérie, extends metaphorically across the text, breaking up the antithetical patterns, blurring the outlines of moral differentiation until everything and everybody is finally entangled in the web.

To recognize the ambiguous and disabling aspects of Adeline as the embodiment of pure goodness is already to engage in a reading of the novel that transcends a simplistic approach to the moral experience it dramatizes. However, to complete the argument, to shatter finally the sentimental-melodramatic scheme, we must turn to the figure whose apparent function is the incarnation of pure evil—Lisbeth Fischer. Bette is generally and rightly acknowledged as one of Balzac's most terrifying creations: 'l'atroce Bette' is Balzac's description of her, 'dont le caractère infernal se donnait pleine carrière (442); a seething mass of irrational and violent emotions, an 'abstraction active' (278) of hatred and jealousy, possessed by a neurotic and compulsive will to destruction, the primary image we are given of Bette is that of the 'araignée au centre de sa toile' (284), silently and remorselessly organizing the ruin of those closest to her. The motivation of this role is constructed essentially out of two motifs which, in a broader focus, act as one of the points of intersection for the social and sexual themes of the novel in general. Firstly, Bette is given as representing what Balzac, within the assumptions of his highly personal social psychology, sees as the endemic primitive wildness of the peasant mentality: Bette is 'la sauvage Lorraine . . . qui, bien observée, eût présenté le côté féroce de la classe paysanne', whose instinctual violence illustrates 'la différence qui sépare l'homme naturel de l'homme civilisé' (165). That potentiality for violence is added to and strengthened with the tensions and energies engendered by the ungratified sexuality of the old maid, whose virginity, Balzac tells us, is the source of 'une force diabolique ou la magie noire de la volonté' (230). The combination of peasant and virgin is explosive and lethal, 'comme un germe de peste qui peut éclore et ravager une ville, si l'on ouvre le fatal ballot de laine où il est comprimé', (161) and, as we progressively witness the depths of malicious cruelty with which Bette pursues and accomplishes her strategies of destruction, we may well feel that the only possible response to her is one of unmitigated fear and revulsion.

Such a response, based on a view of Lisbeth as evil incarnate, clearly lends support to the dualistic view of the novel we have been here attempting to call in question. Yet, once again, it proves on examination to be an inadequate response, passing over important areas of the novel which, if fully considered, demand a richer and more intricate interpretation. Lisbeth is in fact an unusually complex creation. If Hulot sometimes strikes us as acting in excess of the motives he is given (perhaps the reason for the frequently encountered charge of 'exaggeration')[18], with Lisbeth it is the converse; that is, she is provided with an excess of motivation for the relatively simple, single-minded course of action she follows. The sexual jealousy and frustration of the old maid would, for instance, have sufficed to explain her hatred of Adeline. Balzac however complicates the moral and psychological pattern, and thereby our own response, by injecting another, crucially important factor—the feelings of resentment caused by her status as a 'parente pauvre'. This indeed was the central idea in the original conception of the novel and it is interesting to note the specific terms Balzac uses in outlining that conception to Mme Hanska: '*Le Vieux musicien* est le parent pauvre, accablé d'injures, plein de coeur. *La Cousine Bette* est la parente pauvre, accablée d'injures, vivant dans l'intérieur de trois et quatre familles, et prenant vengeance de toutes ses douleurs.'[19] 'Accablée d'injures, prenant vengeance de toutes ses doubleurs'—these terms require a very different perspective, a recognition that, however monstrous Bette's actions, they are rooted in an experience of suffering and humiliation for which her relatives must be held in large part responsible. It is this experience which serves to humanize Bette, which, in enabling us to break through the simplified view of her as a mere abstract cipher of pure evil, elicits a sympathetic understanding of her as the victim of certain unmistakable class attitudes and values.

Ugly, deprived, sacrificed from the beginning to the beautiful and successful Adeline, Lisbeth occupies a position in the Hulot household that is a continual and insulting reminder of her inferior and dependent role as a poor relation. Our very first glimpse of Bette furnishes immediate confirmation of that role. On Crevel's arrival, Adeline peremptorily dismisses Hortense and Bette from the drawing-room, and Balzac describes Bette as leaving 'sans paraître offensée de la façon dont la baronne s'y prenait pour les renvoyer, en la comptant pour presque rien' (137). Implicit in Adeline's gesture is a particular definition of Lisbeth, conformity to which is evidently the tacit foundation of her place in the family. That definition is summarized in the recurring phrase 'la bonne Bette' 'C'est une bonne et brave fille, était le mot de tout le monde sur elle' (163)) with all the overtones of patronizing condescension that it carries. There are of course individual acts of generosity on the material level, but its moral ambiguity—the kind of ambiguity so sharply presented by Baudelaire in the *Petits poèmes en prose*—lies in the fact that it is the generosity offered *de haut en bas*, depending for its expression on the humility of the recipient, reinforcing rather than diminishing a fundamental inequality, a constant testimony, as Michel Butor has pointed out,[20] to the social distance travelled by the rest of the family. Thus Lisbeth is made welcome in the house but 'elle se refusait elle-même à venir aux grands dîners, en préférant l'intimité qui lui permettait d'avoir sa valeur et d'éviter des souffrances d'amour-propre' (163); she is quick to grasp the implications of a required subservience: 'Sa complaisance... était d'ailleurs... une nécessité de sa position. Elle avait fini par comprendre la vie en se voyant à la merci de tout le monde; et voulant plaire à tout le monde, elle riait avec les jeunes gens... elle paraissait être une bonne confidente, car elle n'avait pas le droit de les gronder' (163).

Apart from Butor's brief but perceptive essay, critical writing on *La Cousine Bette* has never fully come to terms with this complicating element.[21] André Lorant, for instance, has argued (though with very little textual evidence by way of his comparison of the available variants) that Balzac modified his original intentions as set out in the letter to Mme Hanska, that in contrast to the very real humiliations suffered by Pons, Lisbeth's wounds are self-inflicted ones, the obsessional imaginings of a mind that uses them to justify a hatred governed by entirely different and much deeper motives.[22] It is true that Balzac generally presents Lisbeth's grievances as seen through her eyes, through a consciousness that is unquestionably dominated by a complex of feelings that cannot be exhaustively defined by the attitudes towards her of her relatives. It is also true that the authorial rhetoric tends in places to adopt an uncritical posture on those attitudes, emphasizing the 'generosity' of the family in a manner that seems to be unconscious of the patronizing element: 'Mais tous les ans, à sa fête et au jour de l'an, Lisbeth recevait des cadeaux de la baronne et du baron; le baron, excellent pour elle, lui payait son bois pour l'hiver; le vieux général Hulot la recevait un jour à dîner, son couvert était toujours mis chez sa cousine. On se moquait bien d'elle mais on n'en rougissait jamais. On lui avait enfin procuré son indepéndance à Paris, où elle vivait à sa guise' (162). The 'on se moquait bien d'elle' strikes a discordant note, but the general bearing of the passage is clearly favourable to the family, and by implication, therefore, lends weight to the view that Lisbeth's resentment is a baseless, purely subjective projection. We should however by now be fully alive to the limitations of the Balzacian commentary, its frequent inadequacy in relation to the whole emotional and moral significance of a given narrative situation. Balzac is one of those novelists whose right hand is often unaware of what the left hand is doing, whose conscious valuations cannot always be said to express the full range of meaning contained in the totality of the work. Lisbeth is a classic example of that disparity, a creation whose abundant and varied life demands a level of understanding that cannot possibly be accommodated within the restricted frame of reference made available by the author's commentary.

Any truly objective analysis has to acknowledge the assaults on Lisbeth's sense of pride and dignity which she has to endure within a situation shaped by definite class attitudes and values. Above all, this is the case in relation to the unforgivable, scandalous behaviour of the family over her young 'protegé', Wenceslas Steinbock. For Lisbeth, the discovery and salvation of Wenceslas provide the one context in which she can satisfy her real emotional needs and, if the relationship is in part marked by a domineering and tyrannical possessiveness, it also releases in Bette deep reserves of compassion and maternal solicitude. It is therefore the point at which she is both at her most sensitive and her most vulnerable. Yet the Hulot family manifest a total disregard for that sensitivity. In the scene where Bette tentatively and defensively reveals her secret, Adeline and Hortense, in blithe ignorance of or indifference to what this means to Bette, respond with a display of mocking disbelief and callous ridicule. In the course of their conversation Adeline sanctimoniously remarks, 'il y a des femmes qui aiment et qui restent égoistes, et c'est ton cas' (167). But with regard to Wenceslas, the charge is more appropriately levelled against the conduct of the family, for the real egoism is in the unconscious assumption (all the more cruel for being unconscious) that the feelings of 'la bonne Bette' are of no consequence, that almost by definition the 'poor relation' is not entitled to or is incapable of experiencing the human needs and aspirations of others. It is on that assumption that Hortense, with 'la profonde adresse des jeunes filles agitées par l'instinct' (209), perpetrates, with the willing connivance of her family, what must be literally described as an act of theft. Just as the greedy Camusot steal from Pons his precious art collection, so the 'generous' Hulot unashamedly steal from Lisbeth the only thing she really treasures. However, the real injury is not simply in the deprivation of Bette, but in the accompanying lack of awareness that any serious injury has been done. Probably Bette's most painful and humiliating moment comes when Adeline remarks, 'Cousine Bette, le baron et moi, nous avons une dette envers toi, nous l'acquitterons' and the magnitude of the debt is then precisely quantified at 'six cents francs de rente' (249). *La Cousine Bette* is saturated in images of people treated as 'commodities' to be bought and sold subject to the terms of a commercial transaction (Crevel is given a special language all of his own for this purpose). That the 'noble' Adeline should play the same game, assuming that Lisbeth has her price, that the theft can be redeemed by transforming it in to a purchase is perhaps the novel's bitterest comment on the all-embracing presence of the acquisitive ethic. What is beyond doubt is that the behaviour of the family helps us to comprehend the ferocity of Bette's famous outburst of hatred in front of Valérie (224), and it may well also invite us to see the terrible vengeance Lisbeth wreaks unnoticed upon the family as a not altogether unjustified nemesis. There is, moreover, a deep and satisfying irony in the fact that Bette goes about her work of destruction unheeded. Why does the family never perceive Bette's machinations? Part of the answer stems from Lisbeth's capacity for dissimulation, but it springs also from a general blindness and insensitivity on the family's part where Bette's desires and emotions are concerned. Lisbeth as destroyer goes unnoticed because she goes unnoticed in all other contexts. Since they never see her as a full human being to be credited with ordinary needs and feelings, they can never grasp the hatred and vindictiveness generated by the frustration of those needs and feelings. For them, quite simply, Lisbeth is unimaginable as an enemy, since in their eyes she has no conceivable motive for becoming one.

All this calls for an important realignment of the reader's sympathies, transgressing once again the schematic demarcation of the characters into categories of 'good' and 'bad'. In this connection, one of the greatest triumphs of the novel is the scene in which Lisbeth confronts Wenceslas in the knowledge that he is about to desert her. As one might expect, the reader's attention is drawn initially to the interplay of furious anger and hysterical possessiveness. Towards the end of the scene, however, Balzac effects a sudden and startling shift in direction: quite unexpectedly we are given a glimpse of a broken, lonely, suffering woman, crushed with grief and faced with solitude, and yet who, in her moment of supreme loss, is capable of a genuine act of forgiveness:

> Lisbeth s'assit, contempla d'un air sombre cette jeunesse, cette beauté distinguée, ce front d'artiste, cette belle chevelure, tout ce qui sollicitait en elle les instincts comprimés de la femme, et de petites larmes aussitôt sechées mouillèrent pour un moment ses yeux. . . . Je ne te maudis pas, toi, dit-elle en se levant brusquement, tu n'est qu'un enfant. Que Dieu te protège. Elle descendit et s'enferma dans son appartement (vi, 245).

For a novelist so frequently accused of abusing the hyperbolic resources of language, that last sentence represents a masterly use of *litotes*, strong in its suggestive evocation of contained sorrow and tragic resignation. It is a very fine moment indeed, and bears witness to the intelligence and humanity of a novelist capable, at the important points, of rising above and going beyond narrow and limiting moral definitions of his characters. Criticsm has traditionally saluted *La Cousine Bette* as one of Balzac's most outstanding achievements. It has stressed the author's fluent virtuosity of creative inspiration, his technical control and sophistication, the range of subject matter and theme. What has not been sufficiently emphasized is its subtle and disorientating sense of ambiguity at the heart of human affairs. Yet, as the often glib and platitudinous moral certainties of the conventional narrator begin to break down before different kinds of suffering, weakness and failure, as the novel plunges deeper into the complexity of moral experience, *La Cousine Bette* stands as perhaps Balzac's most accomplished refutation of that schematic 'obviousness'[23] for which he has been often criticized.

6 Surface and depth

> En effet, parfois un geste développe tout un drame, l'accent d'une
> parole déchire toute une vie, l'indifférence d'un regard tue la plus
> heureuse passion. Balzac (ii, 841)

Lubbock's remark that Balzac's 'obviousness' is the major characteristic of his work (an emphasis which Lubbock himself subsequently modifies[1]) can be examined and questioned in other ways that are equally relevant to the topic of Balzac's relation to the melodramatic stereotype. One line of inquiry that could be profitably pursued is through a concern with what we might call the technique of the 'surface'. 'Amelia', the name given by James Smith to the eponymous heroine of nineteenth-century melodrama, throws up her hands as she cries 'Protect me from this villain', and it is the external, physical gesture that is supposed to guarantee the emotional reality of her distress (Frédérick Lemaître's phenomenal success in convincing the boulevard audiences of the reality of his performances depended vitally on his remarkable powers of bodily and facial expression[2]). A corollary of this was the increasing attention paid to the details of scene setting. An important part of the history of stage melodrama was its progressive movement towards a peculiarly intricate kind of scenic naturalism, culminating in the amazingly elaborate stage directions and scenic constructions of Boucicault's plays. The growth of this technical realism in the melodramatic theatre was not accidental, but a logical extension of the form. Lacking any sense of 'depth', melodrama could work only at the 'surface' of things, and its only scope for development therefore was in extending and refining the possibilities of surface naturalism. The result was not a gain in any qualitative sense. Its minutely detailed simulacrae of landscape and artefact ('when he needed a tenement room for *The Easiest Way*, Belasco stripped a real slum of its doors, windows and even wall-paper'[3]), its technologically ingenious but purely mechanical arrangement of external effects, did not serve the purposes of 'realism' in any of the deeper senses of that term; they merely intensified the form's endemic theatricality, providing essentially a scenic complement to the surface gestures and movements through which the character stereotypes of melodrama typically functioned.

This peculiar relationship between melodrama and 'naturalism' has a direct counterpart in nineteenth-century fiction. In terms of the role played by melodrama in the work of serious novelists, it has been strongly focused, for example, by Leo Levy in his study of Henry James. Levy suggests that the elements of melodrama present in many of the early texts of the Jamesian *oeuvre* derive to a large extent from the adoption by James of a particular naturalistic method, according to which 'the naive dependence upon the "factual" served largely as a means for evoking the intensified dramatic postures' of the stereotype.[4] Thus, the 'external melodrama of gestures, movement and response'[5] which Levy discerns in *Roderick Hudson*, for instance, has to be seen as the fictional equivalent of melodramatic theatricality, illustrating a certain staginess of presentation which prevents the text from penetrating the 'surface', from 'going behind', in James's famous phrase, to the rich, implied life beneath the surface.

James was, of course, subsequently to adapt the crude technique of the surface to aims of a much subtler, consciously equivocating nature—the force of a novel such as *What Maisie Knew* depends crucially on the child's interpretation of the implications of surfaces. For this reason his example is a useful one, especially when we recall that his early involvement with the strategies of melodrama has often been specifically ascribed to the 'lesson of Balzac'. James knew better than his critics what he learnt from the master. The general emphasis nevertheless persists; discussing the relation between James and Balzac, John Bayley has recently remarked: 'Balzac's great effects are always on the surface. His very energy and flamboyance make him the most obvious of writers: he has no buried riches for the critic to harvest and for the modern reader to rediscover.'[6] One concedes that there are legitimate grounds for this view. Take, for example, the following passage from *Gobseck*, which gives us the reactions of the Comte de Restaud to the discovery of his wife's ultimate perfidy:

> —Ah! ah! s'écria le comte, qui, ayant ouvert la porte, se montra tout à coup presque nu, déjà même aussi sec, aussi décharné qu'un squelette. Ce cri sourd produisit un effet terrible sur la comtesse, qui resta immobile et comme frappée de stupeur. Son mari était si frêle et si pâle, qu'il semblait sortir de la tombe.—Vous avez abreuvé ma vie de chagrins, et vous voulez troubler ma mort, pervertir la raison de mon fils, en faire un homme vicieux, cria-t-il d'une voix rauque. La comtesse alla se jeter au pied de ce mourant que les dernières émotions de la vie rendaient presque hideux et y versa un torrent de larmes.—Grâce! grâce! s'ecria-t-elle.— Avez-vous eu de la pitié pour moi! demanda-t-il. Je vous ai laissée dévorer votre fortune, voulez-vous maintenant dévorer la mienne, ruiner mon fils!—Eh! bien, oui, pas de pitié pour moi, soyez inflexible, dit-elle, mais les enfants! Condamnez votre veuve à vivre dans un couvent, j'obéirai; je ferai pour expier mes fautes envers vous, tout ce qu'il vous plaira de m'ordonner; mais

que les enfants soient heureux! Oh! les enfants! les enfants!—Je
n'ai qu'un enfant, répondit le comte en tendant, par un geste
désespéré, son bras décharné, vers son fils.—Pardon! repentie,
repentie! . . . cria la comtesse en embrassant les pieds humides de
son mari. Les sanglots l'empêchaient de parler et des mots vagues,
incohérents sortaient de son gosier brûlant.—Après ce que vous
disiez à Ernest, vous oser parler de repentir! dit le moribond qui
renversa la comtesse en agitant le pied.—Vous me glacez!
ajouta-t-il avec une indifférence qui eut quelque chose d'effrayant.
Vous avez été mauvaise fille, vous avez été mauvaise femme, vous
serez mauvaise mère. La malheureuse femme tomba évanouie. Le
mourant regagna son lit, s'y coucha, et perdit connaissance quelques heures après. Le prêtres vinrent lui administrer les sac-
rements. Il était minuit quand il expira. La scène du matin avait
épuisé le reste de ses forces (ii, 665).

Clearly there are no 'buried riches' here. It is pure melodrama in the
sense that the encounter between the Count and the Countess is completely 'on the surface', held within the stereotyped verbal and gestural
rhetoric of the erring wife and the wronged husband. As an account of
the agony and death of a man, the scene carries no force of conviction
whatsoever, precisely because we are not given any opportunity to
'know' Restaud, or rather because what we know of Restaud, his
suffering, his grief, his anger, is presented entirely at the level of surface
gestures and attitudes, which instead of realizing the intended emotional and moral crisis, actually squeeze it out of existence. Generalizing
from this example, we might then say that Balzac's creations resemble
the stereotype of melodrama in that they hardly ever give us any sense
of implied life. Another way of putting this would be to claim that not
only is there very little to know, in a psychological sense, about Balzac's
characters, but that all there is to know is immediately available on the
surface of the text. On this view, Balzac, the insistently, indeed aggressively, omniscient narrator ('le narrateur est tout' (xi, 180)), tells us
everything ('who has ever known so much about his creations',
remarks Lubbock, 'as Balzac'?[7]); everything the text has 'to say' is
explicitly stated, all the enigmas satisfactorily resolved and all the
recesses illuminated.

   Nevertheless, the generalization will not hold, and it breaks down,
paradoxically, in the very area from which it springs, namely Balzac's
handling of 'surfaces'. The point was made superbly by Proust, in the
essay 'Saint-Beuve et Balzac': 'Il ne cache rien . . . il dit tout. Aussi est-on
étonné de voir que cependant il y a de beaux effets de silence dans son
oeuvre. Goncourt s'étonnait pour *L'Education*, moi, je m'étonne bien
plus des dessous de Balzac. Vous connaissez Rastignac? Vrai?'[8] Proust's
crucial insight is that surfaces are rarely merely superficial in Balzac,
that there is often the suggestion of something more, beyond that
which is immediately present. The insight would gain support from a

number of observations within the *Comédie humaine* itself; for example, in the course of describing Nicola's passion for 'la Péchina' in *Les Paysans*, the text offers the following generalization: 'Les dérèglements de l'homme sont des abîmes gardés par des sphinx, ils commencent et se terminent presque tous par des questions sans réponses' (VIII, 176). The implications of the remark are highly interesting: in the emphasis on enigma ('sphinx'), depth ('abîme') and impenetrability ('questions sans réponse'), it effectively dramatizes Proust's feeling about the Balzacian text, its abiding sense of the opaqueness of life, its awareness of areas of reality which are not available to immediate scrutiny, but which remain half submerged, veiled in the mists, only occasionally glimpsed through, while at the same time evoked by, the play of surfaces and appearances. Commenting on the last line of *Sarrasine* ('Et la marquise resta pensive'), Roland Barthes has observed[8] (though in context he is making a somewhat different point) that one of the major effects generated by the Balzacian text is, precisely, that it leaves the reader 'pensif', in a quizzical and questioning frame of mind, having imaginatively to fill in the gaps and silences before which the narrator either presents himself as helpless or from which he has deliberately withdrawn. For, although the hermeneutic code (in Barthes's sense of the term as the unravelling of mysteries, the laying bare, the bringing to the 'surface', of a final and defining truth) is strongly present in the Balzac text, although the imperious gesture of a Godlike omniscience is a familiar aspect of Balzac's procedure, that gesture is in fact frequently refused in the effort to sustain both the reader's and the author's sense of the irreducible opacity of things, of those hidden, implied dimensions of life suggested by, but not immediately accessible on, the surface of the text.

Proust's injunction to listen closely to the Balzac text in order to capture its deeper rhythms and resonances, and exemplified in the marvellous subtlety of his reading of the closing pages of *Illusions perdues*, is one that should be constantly heeded in approaching the *Comédie humaine*. Numerous examples spring readily to mind, in particular, the various studies grouped under the heading *Scenes de la vie privée*, of which Balzac was himself significantly to write: 'Il s'est flatté que les bons esprits ne lui reprocheraient point d'avoir parfois présenté le tableau vrai de moeurs que les familles *ensevelissent aujourd'hui dans l'ombre et que l'observateur a quelquefois de la peine à deviner*' (XI, 163). Take, for instance, the short narrative, *Honorine*: the reasons which account for the central drama of the story, the separation of Honorine from her husband, Octave de Bauvan, remain shrouded in obscurity; we suspect that in the hidden recesses of Honorine's being there is a deep physical aversion from her husband, but the point that needs stressing is that we are never sure as to what exactly is involved. The narrator whom Balzac interposes between reader and events, Maurice de l'Hostal, enjoys only a limited and incomplete perspective on the crucial matters; the major protagonists themselves appear to be relatively ignorant of, or incapable of expressing, the real nature of their own feelings ('We suspect that Honorine may not be able to say more, lacking the vocabulary of her secret aversions'[9]). In short, the whole narrative is a masterpiece of understatement and allusion, constantly hinting at possibilities that are never explicitly formulated and which remain therefore in the penumbra of the novel, leaving the reader to play an extended game of imaginative guesswork, to exercise his capacities for what Balzac, in a famous passage from *Facino Cane*, himself called 'observation intuitive' (VI, 66).

In taking *Honorine* as an example, we are interested not so much in the substance of what is half submerged in the narrative (in this case, sexual antipathy), but in the method by which it is conveyed. More specifically, the important point is the partial abdication here of the privileges of authorial omniscience. It is not of course that Balzac himself does not 'know' the hidden depths of his own characters, although this could indeed be tentatively speculated;[10] it is rather that Balzac, to adopt the phrase from Henry James, does not always 'go behind', taking the reader with him into a detailed scrutiny of individual consciousness, but deliberately elaborates, as it were, a strategy of significant 'silence', thus at once sustaining a sense of the enigmatic and the impenetrable and allowing the reader room for imaginative manoeuvre of his own. In a passage at the beginning of *La Muse du département*, another novel in which a marital relationship is painted in colours that are almost wholly opaque, Balzac refers to this method of elucidating 'les coins les plus obscurs du coeur' in terms of applying to the tissue of private life 'l'avide scalpel du Dix-Neuvième Siècle' (IV, 67). The metaphor of the 'scalpel' is both characteristic and helpful, but it remains an imperfect one in that it tends to imply an analytic dissection that exposes everything to the light of day. It would perhaps be more appropriate to speak of Balzac's technique as in a way analogous to the activity of a 'divining-rod' which, from above the ground, detects subterranean movements and disturbances without systematically unearthing them. And indeed we will find exactly this kind of comparison in the extended metaphor that Balzac, or rather the narrator, uses in *Honorine* to evoke the concealed sorrow and suffering of the Comte de Bauvan:

> en pratiquant cet homme . . . je sentis de vastes profondeurs sous ces travaux, sous les actes de sa politesse, sous son masque de bienveillance, sous son attitude resignée qui ressemblait tant au calme qu'on pouvait s'y tromper. De même qu'en marchant dans les forêts, certains terrains laissent deviner par le son qu'ils rendent sous les pas de grandes masses de terre ou le vide; de même l'égoisme en bloc caché sous les fleurs de la politesse et les souterrains minés par le malheur sonnent creux au contact perpétuel de la vie intime (II, 261).

Like Maurice, the reader has to proceed in the dark, gropingly, attempting to reconstruct a domain of psychological and emotional reality, the fundamental coordinates of which are only hinted at and never fully clarified by the author. Like a door that opens and shuts in quick succession, the work affords an occasional, rapid insight into its deeper secrets, only to distance the reader immediately afterwards; the mists disperse only instantly to reform, as the author discreetly draws a veil over the spectacle we have momentarily and confusedly witnessed. We are left to fill in for ourselves, through an effort of imagination that snatches at, deciphers and rearranges as best it can a number of clues and indications scattered with deliberate carelessness throughout the text. The process is of course—this is its literary justification and its artistic triumph—akin to the ways in which we perceive others in actual life; as Hugo von Hofmannsthal put it in his brilliant, and unfortunately neglected, essay on Balzac: 'Elles [verités] nous sont offertes comme s'offre à nous la vie même: à la faveur de rencontres, de drames soudains, au cours de l'évolution des passions, au hasard d'aperçus ou de vues pénétrantes à l'instant fugitif òu s'ouvrent des brèches dans l'immense forêt des phénomènes.'[11]

The literary tactics which sustain a strategy of this kind are various. The interrogative statement (e.g. 'Quel acide avait dépouillé cette créature de ses formes féminines? . . . était-ce le vice, le chagrin, la cupidité? (II, 855)), the hypothesizing 'peut-être' and 'sans doute' in the presentation of motive, are recurrent stylistic devices which imply an element of ambiguity or uncertainty on the part of the author. More important, however, such a strategy, by refusing the advantages of 'going behind', must of necessity rely heavily on the suggestive value of externals. In presenting his characters largely from the outside, the novelist is committed to exploiting the evocative potential of the material reality and physical presence of his creations to provide the hints and allusions which at once reinforce the mysteriousness of character and yet furnish the fleeting, fragmentary glimpses into their elusive inner life. We are wholly familiar now with Balzac's manner of using externals as a form of symbolic and metaphorical shorthand to resume the deeper patterns of human and social reality: it is the 'yeux fatigués', the 'crasseux abat-jour en taffetas vert', the 'châle à franges maigres et pleurardes', 'son regard blanc', 'sa figure rabougrie' which lead to the formulation of the questions about the character and past of Mlle Michonneau quoted above. We have here an example of what Henry James called in 'The Art of Fiction' 'the power to guess the unseen from the seen, to trace the implications of things',[12] a process in which descriptive materials exist not simply as neutral informants, but have a distinct semantic function as integral, signifying components of the general thematic structure of the novel. Externals constitute a kind of language, a series of 'hieroglyphs', a network of signs which have to be deciphered by the reader if he is to detect the deeper realities of the novel. In the work of Balzac, 'historien, sociologue, romancier du signe', as Roger Kempf has described him,[13] everything signifies, everything has to be translated: streets, interiors, clothes, faces, gestures, smiles, intonations—all contribute to an interplay of surfaces which, rich in allusive meaning, continually refer the reader to something beyond themselves; to return again to Proust's essay, where he is commenting on the role of surface particulars in the closing pages of *Illusions perdues*: 'chaque mot, chaque geste a ainsi des dessous dont Balzac n'avertit pas le lecteur et qui sont d'une profondeur admirable.'[14] One could of course illustrate the procedure almost at random, but, as an example, let us take—since it leads directly into our central analysis—the following passage from *L'Interdiction* which relates the arrival of Popinot and Bianchon at the house of Mme d'Espard:

> En apercevant Popinot qui s'arrêta sur la porte comme un animal effrayé, tendant le cou, la main gauche dans son gousset, la droite armée d'un chapeau dont la coiffe était crasseuse, la marquise jeta sur Rastignac un regard dans lequel la moquerie était en germe. L'aspect un peu niais du bonhomme s'accordait si bien avec sa grotesque tournure, avec son air effaré, qu'en voyant la figure contristée de Bianchon, qui se sentait humilié dans son oncle, Rastignac ne put s'empêcher de rire en détournant la tête. La marquise salua par un geste de tete, et fit un effort pour se soulever dans son fauteuil où elle retomba non sans grâce, en paraissant s'excuser de son impolitesse sur une débilité jouée (II, 46).

In its counterpoint of feigned politeness and scarcely dissembled impertinence, the passage represents a masterly illustration of the Proustian formula of 'les dessous de l'oeuvre de Balzac'. Enacted entirely at the level of externals—a handful of glances, gestures, movements—the scene nevertheless captures, through those very externals, a whole range of underlying psychological and social attitudes—fear, contempt, ridicule, humiliation. The social comedy of polite conversation will be quickly resumed, but already a kind of 'sous conversation' (the phrase is Nathalie Sarraute's and we shall return to it later) has been engaged, the tensions and undercurrents of which will be held and expressed, throughout the rest of the episode, by precisely this kind of external detail.

The text I wish to take as my central example is that of *Béatrix*, a novel whose impact depends on a particularly fertile relationship between an awareness of hidden depths and the expressive possibilities of gesture and appearance. In a strict sense, *Béatrix* in fact does not stand in a particularly close relation to the conventions of nineteenth-century melodrama, and to a certain extent the analysis which follows is essentially of a strategic kind, opening on to some of the issues discussed in the final two chapters. *Béatrix* is however a novel that has been generally underrated or ignored by criticism, often on grounds similar, if not identical, to those informing traditional responses to the great 'melodramatic' fictions of the *Comédie humaine*. That the novel is an uneven performance with a number of blatant faults cannot be denied. Balzac himself indicated a certain uneasiness about it when he wrote to Mme Hanska, 'Non, je n'étais pas heureux en faisant *Béatrix*.'[15] The weaknesses are obvious: excessive indulgence in the sentimental rhetoric of romantic love and the wearisome clichés of *la femme française*; the intrusive didacticism of conservative ideology; the embarrassing pathos of Camille's withdrawal to the convent; the absurd imbroglio by means of which Calyste is finally extricated from the clutches of Béatrix. There are, however, a number of other criticisms that have been levelled against the novel, whose general assumptions and criteria need perhaps to be called in question. Thus Maurice Bardèche, in an otherwise sensitive and perceptive essay, writes, 'Cette comédie féminine est savoureuse, bien qu'elle soit parfois un peu énigmatique.'[16] That 'bien que', implying, as it does, an adverse judgment, seems to rest on the view that absolute clarity should be a *sine qua non* of the novelist's art. Similarly, H. J. Hunt writes of *Béatrix* that it lacks 'clarity and consistency', that there are 'uncertainties of motivation', that 'it is the part played by Camille Maupin that is ambiguous; it is her motivation that is hesitant.'[17] We, however, would turn these criticisms on their head, transforming apparent faults into virtues by arguing that it is precisely the elements of hesitancy, ambiguity and enigma that comprise an essential dimension of the novel's achievement. It is certainly true, for example, that the motives behind Camille Maupin's behaviour are unclear: in trying to help Calyste win Béatrix, she could be prompted by a disinterested and self-effacing affection, by the need to play the role of substitute mother, by a desire to avenge herself for the previous loss of Conti to Béatrix, or even perhaps by the artist's 'curiousity' to see what will result from intervening in and altering a particular configuration of relationships, or—in the perspective of the Freudian concept of 'overdetermination'—by a combination of all four. However, this does not mean incoherence on Balzac's part; what is of importance, what is of value, is the absence of a categorical and reductive statement by the author as to which is the definitive motive, and a corresponding implicit respect for the irreducible and multiform complexity of the character's inner life. The instructive analogy is perhaps with Proust; confronted with Camille, the reader is left to speculate on a variety of available possibilities in much the same way as he is free to speculate about the motives of a Proustian character.

Nearly the whole of *Béatrix*, and in particular the first instalment, 'Béatrix ou les amours forcées, is bathed in a similar atmosphere of uncertainty and obscurity, constituting, in Bardèche's words, 'un assez long cryptogramme'[18] which the intelligent and discriminating reader has to decipher for himself. In presenting the tangled web of relationships that draws together Calyste, Camille, Vignon, Conti and Béatrix, the novel persistently emphasizes that it is taking us into dark

corners, into 'l'ombre et le mystère de la vie privée' (II, 395) where we
are to witness 'la tragédie intime de tant de passions contrariées' (504).
Shadow, mystery, darkness, secretiveness, depth, dissimulation—these
are recurrent terms in the vocabulary of the novel, establishing a narrative tone resonant with the suggestion of levels of reality which
require a sustained and sensitive attention if they are to be caught at all.
The initial *donnée* of nearly all the characters is, precisely, their almost
impenetrable opaqueness: Vignon 'offre des mystères à deviner' and
Camille says of Conti, 'il faut vivre longtemps avec lui pour avoir le
secret de cette fausse bonhomie et connaître le stylet invisible de ses
mystifications' (404). Béatrix, we are told at a crucial stage in the drama,
'fut impénétrable' (466), and subsequently, 'jamais Calyste ne devait
voir la femme vraie qui était en Béatrix' (493); through his involvement
with Camille and Béatrix, Calyste is thrown into an emotional world
which Balzac describes in terms of that metaphor of the 'abyss' we
encountered in the earlier quotation from *Les paysans*: 'le jeune Breton
. . . demeura comme un voyageur à qui, dans les Alpes, un guide a
démontré la profondeur d'un abîme en y jetant une pierre' (429); as for
the struggle between Camille and Béatrix, 'Rien n'était plus bizarre que
le combat moral et sourd de ces deux amies, se cachant l'une à l'autre un
secret' (475). On the surface, all is calm, orderly, civilized, sending
scarcely a ripple across the tranquil life of Guérande; underneath, however, 'au fond des coeurs', 'un drame tragique se déroula dans toute son
étendue' (501), a drama compounded of anxiety, desire, jealousy, possessiveness and hatred.

Balzac's task— to which he devotes all his considerable technical
skills—is therefore of a twofold nature. On the one hand, he has to make
the 'secret tragedy' intelligible by clarifying motives and passions, and
here the most obvious weapon is that of explicit authorial analysis.
Excessive reliance on the insights provided by omniscient comment,
however, would militate against the solution of the second problem.
For, if Balzac is to remain true to the psychological movement and
texture of the narrative, he must attempt to evoke and maintain a sense
of the opaque and an atmosphere of mystery. First and foremost,
characters must be seen as opaque, in part to themselves (unsure or
ignorant of their own motives) and, more especially, to each other
(since they constantly disguise their true feelings). At this level, of
course, there is no major technical problem, since the third person
narrator, situated outside the drama, is free to tell the reader that of
which the protagonists themselves may be unaware. But it is also
crucial to the effect the writing seeks to create that the reader, too, be left
partly in the dark, that is, that he be made to experience, in its immediacy, something of the obscurity, the difficulties of interpretation and
understanding that confront the actors themselves. Although the
reader's perspective will be more spacious and comprehensive than
that of any individual participant, his immediate perception of any
given situation must remain relatively incomplete in order to enable

him to experience events as the characters experience them, with all the limitations, errors, the fumbling attempts at comprehending the scarcely perceptible undercurrents of feeling and tension. In short, it is essential that the narrator does not tell everything, that he steer a course, so to speak, between the Charybdis of absolute clarity and the Scylla of complete confusion and chaos.

That middle course Balzac finds in the exploitation of the mystery and the expressiveness of the human face and, in particular, of the glance. For Balzac, the face and the eyes constitute an almost inexhaustible source of artistic inspiration; they nearly always present themselves as a 'text' to be read (in *La Peau de Chagrin*, Raphael's scrutiny of Foedora's outward appearance leads him to remark significantly, 'C'était plus qu'une femme, c'etait un roman' (IX, 105)), a text simultaneously obscure and revelatory, concealing secrets and yet, to the trained observer, obliquely expressing them. There is, of course, a quasi-theoretical backdrop to this procedure; early in *Béatrix* Balzac generalizes, 'Il est dans toute figure humaine une place où les secrets mouvements du coeur se trahissent' (II, 355), and again, 'Ces mignons détails de leur changeante physionomie correspondent aux délicatesses, aux mille agitations de leurs âmes. Il y a du sentiment dans toutes ces expressions' (425). The tendency to codify a specifically literary technique into a scientific 'law' (the operative reference here is to Lavater's theory of physiognomy) and to apply it backwards to ratify the technique is characteristically Balzacian, and, in having thrust upon him the assumption of a necessary, mechanistically causal relation between outer forms and the inner life, the reader is more likely to respond with mild irritation than with any spirited enthusiasm. Yet the schematizing scientific-determinist emphasis is not one that the critic should take too seriously; above all, it should not be allowed to inhibit our response, at the immediate level of the writing itself (in fact untrammelled by pseudo-scientific preconceptions), to the extraordinarily subtle modulations of feeling realized through the artistic manipulation of the glance-motif.

I have already claimed that the technique is all-pervasive in *Béatrix*; indeed it could be said to saturate the text, being present, in one form or another, on almost every page of the novel. Such a claim, however, must remain largely at the level of assertion, since to elucidate this saturation fully would involve a degree of textual analysis and an abundance of lengthy quotation that could not possibly be accommodated here. Narrowing the focus radically therefore, I shall concentrate on an examination of merely one sequence of the narrative. What follows is therefore to be seen as a preliminary and preparatory analysis to be worked through in detail elsewhere.

The sequence in question—the *soirée* at the maison des Touches which brings together for the first time Béatrix, Conti, Vignon, Camille and Calyste (421–8)—is relatively brief, but one in which the informing structure of feeling is extremely complex. It will be recalled that Béatrix and Conti, who have just arrived from Italy, are at the tail-end of a liaison whose defiance of social norms is but a hollow mockery of what it originally was; Béatrix would like nothing more than to be rid of Conti, but cannot risk another affair, since society will not tolerate the same lapse twice; as for Conti, he is bound to Béatrix solely by the pride of possession. Similarly, the relationship between the eccentric Camille and the cynical, cerebral Vignon has exhausted itself; Camille is half in love with Calyste, but Vignon, for reasons of male vanity, is still capable of jealousy. Finally, Calyste, previously in love with Camille, is now intoxicated with Béatrix, or rather, since he has not yet seen her, with the image of Béatrix that Camille has painted for him. The initial situation is therefore a complicated one, rife with potential suspicion, jealousy and hatred. It is further complicated by two other shaping factors; the first is a radical uncertainty on everyone's part as to the feelings of the others (Conti is uncertain as to how Béatrix will react to Calyste; Vignon is unsure of Camille; Calyste is wholly in the dark over the responses he will arouse in Béatrix); the second is the need each character experiences to suppress and to hide his or her desires and anxieties (Calyste has to contain his ardent admiration for Béatrix; Vignon and Conti have to dissemble any sign of jealousy; Béatrix must feign total indifference to the handsome and adoring Calyste; Camille has to sustain the facade of the good hostess). Since therefore the unspoken imperative which binds the characters is that of disguising their real emotions, since the drama of desire and antagonism is essentially a mute, silent drama or one in which it is the job of words to conceal, in which language is an instrument of treachery and deceit, the burden of conveying the scarcely perceptible, yet powerful emotional patterns falls largely on a series of allusions and innuendoes, and, more specifically, on an elaborate play of glances.

The tone is set by the brief descriptive passage that accompanies Calyste's arrival from du Guénic: 'Le jeune Breton trouva la compagnie dans le petit salon de l'appartement de Camille. Il était environ six heures: le soleil en tombant répandait par la fenêtre ses teintes rouges, brisées dans les arbres; l'air était calme, il y avait dans le salon cette pénombre que les femmes aiment tant' (421). The atmosphere of stillness speaks of a deceptive outward calm masking the ominous threat of an impending storm, while the gathering darkness is the natural correlative of the hidden drama of gestures and glances about to unfold. That unfolding begins the moment Calyste crosses the threshold:

Voici le député de la Bretagne, dit en souriant Camille Maupin. . . .
    Vous avez reconnu son pas, dit Claude Vignon à mademoiselle des Touches.
    Calyste s'inclina devant la marquise qui le salua par un geste de tête, il ne l'avait pas regardée; il prit la main que lui tendait Claude Vignon et la serra.

> Voici le grand homme de qui nous vous avons tant parlé,
> Gennaro Conti, lui dit Camille sans répondre à Vignon. (421–2)

There are clearly two levels of discourse here: on the one hand, the ordinary formulae of an introduction, on the other, the level implicit in Vignon's remark, apparently innocuous, but in fact loaded with innuendo, suggesting a regularity in Calyste's visits which, to the jealous mind, cannot be regarded with anything other than suspicion. A set of underlying tensions has thus already been established, and the atmosphere thickens as the focus of the scene shifts from Camille and Vignon to Béatrix and Conti. Calyste, compelled by the presence of Conti to restrain his passionate interest in Béatrix, finds an outlet only in a secretive glance: 'Il s'assit dans un fauteuil et jeta sur la marquise quelques regards à la derobée (422). As Conti becomes aware of the significance of these furtive glances, and as Calyste himself registers Conti's reactions, suppressed currents of envy and menace develop between the two: 'Le jeune Breton sentait en lui-même s'élever une force à tout vaincre, à ne rien respecter. Aussi jeta-t-il sur Conti le regard envieux, haineux, sombre et craintif de la rivalité' (423). The tensions threaten to erupt in an angry outburst, and it is once again the function of a glance, the silent but imperious command conveyed by Béatrix's eyes, to contain the antagonisms and preserve the superficial and fragile appearance of decorous and civilized behaviour: 'Ce fougueux ouragan s'apaisait dès que les yeux de Béatrix s'abaissaient sur lui . . . déjà le pauvre enfant la redoutait à l'égal de Dieu' (423).

The interchange of glances, cutting across the interchange of words, thus establishes a network of relationships, a submerged drama of communication, reception and response which we glimpse and comprehend only obliquely, and yet which is vibrantly present beneath the formal set of relationships instituted by a conventional gathering at a supperparty. This process of contrast and interaction intensifies as they sit down to table:

> Aux regards de Félicité, Béatrix devina l'adoration intérieure qu'elle inspirait à son voisin et qu'il était indigne d'elle d'encourager, elle jeta donc sur Calyste en temps opportun un ou deux regards répressifs qui tombèrent sur lui comme des avalanches de neige. L'infortuné se plaignit à mademoiselle des Touches par un regard où se devinaient des larmes gardées sur le coeur avec une énergie surhumaine, et Félicité lui demanda d'une voix amicale pourquoi il ne mangeait rien (425).

The passage is a beautiful example of the novel's dialectic of surface and depth, and typical of the continually shifting and interacting two-level movement of the scene as a whole. Félicité's glances yield meanings detected by the observant Béatrix; she in turn generates a change in the emotional situation by the 'repressive glance' she bestows upon Calyste, who himself communicates, by a mute appeal of the eyes, his inward pain to Félicité, while finally there is a resurfacing to the banal domain of ordinary conversation, as Félicité brightly enquires why Calyste is not eating. A similar movement (only this time in the reverse direction, from surface to depth) follows almost immediately, when Claude Vignon, having perceptively picked up the secret threads, proceeds to translate them into the barbed irony of conventional platitudes:

> Vous qui admirez tant la poésie, dit Claude Vignon à la marquise, comment l'acceuillez-vous si mal? Ces naives admirations si jolies dans leur expression, sans arrière-pensée et si dévouées, n'est-ce pas la poésie du coeur? Avouez-le, elles vous laissent un sentiment de plaisir et de bien-être.
>
> Certes, dit-elle; mais nous serions bien indignes, si nous cédions à toutes les passions que nous inspirons.
>
> Si vous ne choisissez pas, dit Conti, nous ne serions pas si fiers d'aimer.
>
> Quand serai-je choisi et distingué par une femme? se demanda Calyste qui réprima difficilement une émotion cruelle. Il rougit alors comme un malade sur la plaie duquel un doigt s'est par mégarde appuyé. Mademoiselle des Touches fut frappée de l'expression qui se peignit sur la figure de Calyste, et tâcha de le consoler par un regard plein de sympathie. Ce regard, Claude Vignon le surprit. Dès ce moment, l'écrivain devint d'une gaieté qu'il répandit en sarcasmes . . .
>
> Tenez-vous-en aux livres, ne critiquez pas nos sentiments dit Camille en lui lançant un regard impérieux.
>
> Le dîner cessa d'être gai. Les moqueries de Claude Vignon avaient rendu les deux femmes pensives. Calyste sentait une souffrance horrible au milieu du bonheur que lui causait la vue de Béatrix. Conti cherchait dans les yeux de la marquise à deviner ses pensées (426).

The cardinal opposition here is between spoken words and unspoken thoughts, some of which are revealed to us by authorial analysis (for instance, Calyste's), some of which remain wholly opaque ('les femmes pensives'); the crucial shift in the development of the passage is that from Conti's trite remark to Calyste's inner state, his revealing blush, Camille's sympathetic glance, Vignon's detection of the glance and his return, in an emotionally altered situation, to the witty cynicism of his verbal performance, this in turn bringing about a further withdrawal of the characters into their private worlds, surrounded with an aura of impenetrability and suspicion ('Conti cherchait dans les yeux de la marquise à deviner ses pensées'). Once again, we are confronted with two levels of narrative and psychological action, with a continual movement from one to the other: one that is the overt level of small-talk, though fraught with dishonesty and play acting, another that is half buried, where the characters anxiously watch their own and each other's deepening involvement in a potentially explosive situation which the clever small-talk can paper over but cannot obliterate.

Finally, let us consider a passage from towards the end of the scene, where the tensions appear to have been momentarily relieved and stabilized by Conti's singing:

> Mademoiselle des Touches regarda Calyste en dissimulant une vague inquiétude. Béatrix, ne voyant point Calyste, tourna la tête comme pour savoir quel effet cette musique lui faisait éprouver, moins par intérêt pour lui que pour la satisfaction de Conti: elle aperçut dans l'embrasure un visage blanc couvert de grosses larmes. A cet aspect, comme si quelque vive douleur l'eût atteinte, elle détourna promptement la tête et regarda Gennaro (427).

Again the organizing terms that shape the passage are 'regarda', 'tourna la tête', 'aperçut', 'à cet aspect', 'détourna la tête', and again a complex range of feelings (anxiety, indifference, vanity, suffering) is mediated by the physical gestures. There is, however, something else here which needs stressing. When Béatrix looks at Calyste to see what effect the music is having upon him and when she sees his face covered with tears, she turns away 'comme si quelque vive douleur l'eût atteinte'. Joachim Merlant has shown that this phrase was an addition made in the final stages of revision.[19] It therefore comes into being at precisely the moment when Balzac is at his most careful and scrupulous. And yet, what does it mean? Why does the sight of Calyste's tears cause Béatrix pain and force her to turn her eyes away? What in the exchange of glances has been communicated? Merlant speaks of 'ces mots si importants pour la psychologie de Béatrix', but makes no attempt to elaborate that importance. Is it that Béatrix, with her defences suddenly down, shows an element of tenderness that the hard and sophisticated exterior conceals? Is the spectacle of Calyste's anguished love a bitter reminder of the emotionally exhausted state of her relationship with Conti? In a phrase, the novel provides us with a sudden insight into a hidden recess of Béatrix's personality, which yet remains opaque, unexplained. To adapt Proust's question to the present context: 'Vous connaisez Béatrix de Rochefide? Vrai?' Like Proust confronted with Rastignac, we are left questioning, with almost unlimited possibilities of interrogation. To try and resolve the enigma would, however, be to react in the wrong way; it would be to engage in a reductive, explanatory exercise in violation of the spirit of the writing itself, which momentarily suggests something of the irreducible mystery of human personality. It is a moment that we simply experience and whose integral opaqueness we must respect. The narrative proceeds, and all that the reader can do is to go along with it, thinking what he will.

The analysis I have just given of this single episode from *Béatrix* will, hopefully, have revealed something of the scope and complexity of psychological experience captured in the interplay of surfaces and depths. If space allowed, that analysis could and should be extended to the rest of the novel, in particular to the sustained 'duel de tromperies' entered into by Camille and Béatrix. I should like to conclude, however, by widening the perspective a little, and introducing a stress that will be more fully developed in the final chapter, through a few suggestions on the relationship of this technique of Balzac's to certain developments in the modern novel, and in particular to the work of Nathalie Sarraute. Since the publication of Robbe-Grillet's essays, it has become a commonplace of avant-garde criticism to see Balzac's work as constituting the classic fictional model against which new experiments in the novel in part define themselves.[20] However, it is possible that, beneath the breaks and discontinuities, a certain line of continuity can be discerned, to which the mode of writing exemplified by *Béatrix* provides a clue. If such an assertion at first sight appears as something of a heresy, we might perhaps approach the connection through the middle ground of a novelist, who faces both ways and whose name has already figured centrally in the argument—Proust.

To explore in detail the precise nature of Proust's relation to Balzac would, of course, be full-scale critical topic in itself, but one area in which Proust undoubtedly learnt from Balzac was in the exploitation of externals as an instrument of psychological inquiry. One thinks, for example, of the web of psychological speculation that the narrator weaves around the simple matter of the way Saint-Loup wears his cap at Doncières or, more pertinently, of the manner in which Proust's own reading of the role of physical details in the Vautrin-Lucien encounter is rewritten into the pages which relate the meeting of the narrator and Charlus. Since, however, we are dealing here specifically with the function of the glance as an indicator of inner realities, we could not better than cite the passage, rich in psychological and social reference, that describes Legrandin's reaction when, in the company of a society lady, he meets the narrator's family:

> Nous croisâmes pres de l'église Legrandin qui venait en sens inverse conduisant la même dame à sa voiture. Il passa contre nous, ne s'interrompit pas de parler à sa voisine, et nous fit du coin de son oeil bleu un petit signe en quelque sorte intérieur aux paupières et qui, n'intéressant pas les muscles de son visage, put passer parfaitement inaperçu de son interlocutrice; mais, cherchant à compenser par l'intensivité du sentiment le champ un peu étroit òu il en circonscrivait l'expression, dans ce coin d'azur qui nous était affecté il fit pétiller tout l'entrain de la bonne grâce qui dépassa l'enjouement, frisa la malice; il subtilisa les finesses de l'amabilité jusqu'aux clignements de la connivence, aux demi-mots, aux sous-entendus, aux mystères de la complicité; et finalement exalta les assurances d'amitié jusqu'aux protestations

de tendresse, jusqu'à la déclaration d'amour, illuminant alors pour nous seuls, d'une langueur secrète et invisible à la châtelaine, une prunelle enamourée dans un visage de glace ... Elle (l'attitude de Legrandin) était comme toute attitude ou action ou se révèle le caractère profond et caché de quelqu'un.[21]

From Balzac to Proust . . . to Nathalie Sarraute? It is through the example of Proust and its similarity to what we find in Balzac that we may suggest a point of connection between the latter and the practice of Nathalie Sarraute. While insisting on her attempts to go beyond him, Nathalie Sarraute has explicitly acknowledged her debt to Proust's work, the nature of the debt being in the attempt to refine and extend the techniques of a psychological realism (she has described her work as 'un petit pas plus avant dans l'exploration psychologique: là où de grands écrivains comme Dostoevski, Proust et Joyce ont fait des pas de géant.'[22]). The central focus of that 'exploration psychologique' is, of course, situated in the related concepts of 'le tropisme' and 'la sous-conversation', the assumption of a hidden psychological domain of violent 'tropistic' movement at once masked and yet generated by the banal surface of the encounters and conversations of everyday life. And the opposition here between surface and depth, may well remind us not only of Proust, but of the kind of opposition we have been investigating in Balzac's *Béatrix*. To illustrate the parallel in a more concrete way, we might consider the following passage from *Portrait d'un inconnu* where, once again, it is through a play of the eyes that the deep psychological drama is projected:

> Je la regarde: il me semble qu'elle m'observe d'un regard grave et pénétrant que je ne lui ai encore jamais vu; elle détourne les yeux, elle a l'air de fixer quelque chose au loin, mais je sens que c'est en elle-même qu'elle regarde, et elle sourit doucement—un de ces sourires gênés, amusés et attendris qu'ont parfois les gens quand on évoque devant eux des souvenirs intimes, un peu ridicules, de leur petit enfance. Je me sens soulevé tout à coup dans un élan de reconnaissance, d'espoir . . . cette lueur timide et tendre, ce rayon caressant dans son regard, je le vois qui se pose, qui s'attarde avec complaisance sur une image en elle, celle que je vois en moi, celle qu'elle a aperçue, sans doute, reconnue en moi tout à l'heure quand elle me m'observait si attentivement.[23]

This does not, of course, mean that we should read Nathalie Sarraute as we read Balzac. The differences are manifold and profound; in particular, it would have to be emphasized that whereas in Balzac the buried psychological tensions articulated by external details generally operate in a context where 'character' is sharply individualized and differentiated, in Nathalie Sarraute's work 'this individuality is seen as no more than a flimsy envelope covering the automatic flow of impersonal, anonymous tropistic movement, common to all men',[24] the undoing of the solid Balzacian 'character' being precisely one of the major objectives of her fiction. Yet, all the differences and proportions observed, it remains possible to conclude that the Balzacian text, if read closely and without preconceptions, contains many lessons for the modern novelist, to conclude, indeed, with Michel Butor that:

> L'oeuvre de Balzac est incomparablement plus révolutionnaire qu'il n'apparait à une lecture superficielle et fragmentaire; parmi les nouveautés qu'elle apporte, certaines ont été exploitées systématiquement au cours du XIXe siècle, d'autres n'ont trouvé d'échos que dans les oeuvres les plus originales du XXe, et cette fécondité est bien loin d'être encore epuisée.[25]

7 *Beyond pastoral*

The strategy of silence that accompanies the presentation of Béatrix's moment of pain introduces into the text a kind of 'gap', an element of discontinuity, in which assumptions of the absolute knowability and predictability of a fictional creation are suddenly brought into question. Pursuing this further, we might say that it is a technique which succeeds in pushing the text beyond the limits of 'pastoral'. The term 'pastoral' is used here in the sense in which it is adapted (from William Empson) by John Bayley, in *Tolstoy and the Novel*, to describe that literary mode in which the main emphasis falls on the principles of fixity and predictability in the elaboration of character, an emphasis which, in a broader focus, derives from an insistent literary concern with the 'characteristic' or the 'typical'. 'By pastoral', writes Bayley, 'I understand the process of making everything in a work of literature characteristic'; pastoral, in this sense, embodies a 'process of enclosure, of caging' in which 'there is no play between the fixity of character and the freedom of consciousness.'[1]

Evidently, as both a descriptive term and an evaluative criterion, Bayley's application of the concept of pastoral to the novel raises many difficulties. But even if we take it as it stands (and despite its difficulties as a critical concept, it does crystallize a number of significant issues), there seems to be in Bayley's argument the curious implication that it is only Tolstoy, in the whole tradition of the European novel, who properly transcends the limits of pastoral. If, as Bayley's general remarks suggest, the essence of pastoral is to be found in the process of 'enclosure' and the principle of 'fixity', than one can think of very many important novelists whose work, in major ways, escapes those restrictions—in the nineteenth century, supremely, Stendhal and Dostoyevsky. Balzac however might seem a relatively unproblematical case. Not surprisingly, Bayley sees the *Comédie humaine*, which has the theory and practice of typicality at its very centre, as a massive example of pastoral art: 'The *Comédie humaine* is the most gigantic pastoral enterprise ever undertaken by a novelist.'[2] The Balzacian 'type', because it is structured according to a set of assumed psychological and social norms, a set of preconceived schemas and definitions, is the fictional character par excellence that is always known in advance of the realization of its particular destiny, the character who, like Eugénie Grandet (one of Bayley's examples), can always be guaranteed to do the 'right thing'.[3]

Predictability is, therefore, of the essence of pastoral art and it is also, of course, one of the fundamental aspects of the characters of melodrama—'the whole men who can be guaranteed to think, speak and act exactly as you would expect'.[4] At no point in his discussion of pastoral in general and Balzac in particular does Bayley in fact introduce the notion of melodrama (the context of his argument is rather that of Lukács's theory of realism and types), but it would not be implausible to infer that it is perpetually hovering in the wings of the argument. Realism, at least as defined by its major theoreticians such as Lukács, skirts very close, we sense Bayley to be saying, to the schematic reductions of melodrama; the implied closeness of the two comes out strongly in Bayley's discussion of the role of pastoral stereotypes in Socialist Realism which, in formal terms, is of course a modern variant of the idiom of melodrama. Or to put it another way, 'pastoral' represents an axis of schematization along which one can move very rapidly from the type to the stereotype, that is, to the moral and psychological abstractions of melodrama. The idea that Balzac holds his characters within the straitjacket of abstraction is a very familiar one; as Ramon Fernandez put it, in perhaps still the most intelligent and persuasive advocacy of this particular approach, Balzac's characters 'ont été des idées avant d'être des individus vivants ... l'individu déterminé n'ajoute rien par lui-même aux lignes abstraites dont il est le recoupement ... sa détermination est si rigoureuse qu'il ne saurait échapper à sa dèfinition.'[5] In these terms, for all its variety and abundance, Balzac's world is recurrently experienced, from an artistic point of view, as a relatively stable one; its relentless focus on the 'characteristic', on the synthesizing of experience into a set of known and knowable patterns, means that it contains very little room for surprise, for any feel for the autonomy and indeterminacy of individual consciousness.

However, the example of *Béatrix* suggests, if only fleetingly, that this way of seeing Balzac's creations is not entirely satisfactory. One could multiply the examples; several have been examined, in an explicit critique of Fernandez's account, by Samuel Rogers, in his perceptive short study of Balzac.[6] Where the suggestion might be felt to break new ground is in its extension to a text that, on most external criteria, seems to be totally controlled by the conventions of pastoral representation, to function entirely within a system of very crude melodramatic reductions and stereotypes—namely, *La Femme de trente ans*. A critical argument built around *La Femme de trente ans* is inevitably a perilously exposed one. Faguet thought it quite appalling, and critical opinion since has not shown much inclination to revise that judgment. Clearly, it would be absurd to argue that, as a whole, *La Femme de trente ans* lays claim to our attention as a major work of fiction. Indeed, as Faguet's merciless inventory of its indebtedness to the clichés of Romantic melodrama demonstrates, *La Femme de trente ans* is, for our purposes, an almost exemplary text; in an ostensibly quite unreconstructed way, it displays all those devices and conventions of melodramatic writing we have been considering so far—naive antithetical orderings, cheap sensationalism, mystery, coincidence, poetic justice and so on. The picture is hardly an encouraging one. As Faguet drily remarked, after his own synopsis of the grosser absurdities of the novel, 'Voilà ce que Balzac considérait, très sérieusement peut-être, comme un roman de moeurs',[7] and on the evidence perhaps the wisest, certainly the safest, course would be to accept this acid comment as the last word on the matter.

But to do so is to miss a great deal of the underlying force and meaning of the text. Clumsy, regressive, at times embarrassingly silly and naive, *La Femme de trente ans* nevertheless solicits from the reader a response more complex and demanding than its surface features would appear to support. And, once again, it is by means of a certain work of transformation on what is apparently the text's greatest liability that this response is possible. The crux of the matter lies in a paradox, in a paradoxical relationship between 'pastoral' and 'melodrama'. I have suggested that melodrama embodies an extreme form of the pastoral mode, and in many respects the melodrama of *La Femme de trente ans* does just that. Yet there is an area of the text where it does the opposite, in which 'melodrama' serves to free the text from, rather than imprison it within, the restrictive strategies of pastoral. To argue this point of view I shall concentrate chiefly on one episode of what is unquestionably the most crudely melodramatic section of the whole novel—Hélène's departure with the mysterious criminal in *Les Deux rencontres*.

To all outward appearances, *La Femme de trente ans* is firmly anchored within the framework of pastoral representation. The characters appear before us wearing schematic labels, from which their personality and conduct are never, or rarely, allowed to deviate—dominating husband, erring wife, noble lover, worldly seducer, etc. A prime example is furnished by the figure of Lord Grenville. Grenville, the silent, self-effacing wooer of Julie d'Aiglemont, recalls similar figures from both Balzac's *oeuvres de jeunesse* (in particular *Annette et le criminel* and *Wann-Chlore*) and the popular literature of the period generally, and he does little in the text to escape from or modify that unfortunate resemblance. Grenville in fact is pure pastoral, unalloyed stereotype. Grenville is noble, and always behaves in the way we expect noble lovers in fiction to behave. He enters the narrative silently and exits silently, while in between murmuring utterances such as 'je dois mourir, mais mourir sans vous avoir vue . . . quelle mort!' (II, 732). Grenville is someone who, quite emphatically, is always found doing the 'right thing', who, so to speak, never puts a foot wrong, even in the heroic leap on to the window sill where he dies from pneumonia but saves his beloved's honour.

Grenville is, of course, an extreme case of melodramatic stereotype, but for most of the time all the other major protagonists talk and behave within a similar system of constraints. Yet within that system, certain movements and shifts of perspective can be detected. One notices, for example, the way in which the text often presents a certain disjunction between the perception of a character by others, in terms of expectations derived from a stereotypic literary or social model, and the actual situation of that character. Julie's unhappiness, for instance, is twice misinterpreted by her aunt, Mme de Listomère, on quite plausible grounds. On the first occasion, Julie's distress is, reasonably, attributed by Mme de Listomère to the enforced absence of her husband ('la pâleur et la tristesse lui parurent causées par cette séparation forcée' (692)). When knowledge of the facts brings her to abandon that assumption, she immediately latches onto another, equally plausible yet equally erroneous hypothesis: 'elle pensa joyeusement que sa nièce allait être réjouie par quelque secret d'amour, car sa nièce lui parut avoir quelque intrigue amusante à conduire' (693). In terms of Mme de Listomère's 'pastoral' constructions of the social world, both these explanations of Julie's sorrow are rational ones and, to the extent that Julie does not fit them, she is an anomaly, located outside her framework of expectations, and a source, therefore, of considerable surprise and unpredictability: '[elle] fut stupéfaite en découvrant qu'elle n'aimait personne' (696).

Allied to this kind of disjunction in point of view are certain effects of mobility and indeterminacy generated, perhaps unintentionally, by the circumstances of the composition and publication of the novel. *La Femme de trente ans* was originally written and published as a series of separate stories, with different names for the major characters, and only later, along with some additions and revisions, brought together as rather loosely related episodes of a continuous narrative.[8] For a criticism that places a high value on the virtues of continuity and linear coherence, the gaps and discontinuities entailed by this open, episodic manner of composition are necessarily a serious blemish. They can, however, be seen in a different way. Certainly if they do constitute a flaw, Balzac had the means at hand to have done something about it. For in the shift from one episode to the next, Balzac could easily have filled in the gaps and ironed out the inconsistencies by means of his characteristic devices of the explanatory *exposition* and the summarizing *retour en arrière*, one of whose chief functions is to provide background information on stretches of time relevant to, but not covered by, the narrative proper. But, as Maurice Bardèche has pointed out,[9] *La Femme de trente ans* is conspicuous by the near total absence of the familiar expository method. As we move from one episode to the next, we learn virtually nothing about the often substantial intervening periods of time. The result of this residue of the original composition is a curious effect of temporal ellipsis, the sense of an openness in the characters to changes which, because they go unexplained, because they take place, as it were, in the interstices of the text, carry with them the force of the unexpected and the indeterminate; although in the revised version, the characters are nominally the 'same' from one episode to the next (the continuity of proper names being the mark of the identity of the narrative as 'une même histoire')[10], in a deeper and more important sense they are not the 'same'. Thus, the innocent and inexperienced Julie of *Premières fautes* withdraws from the world in *Souffrances inconnues*, only to reappear some years later in *A trente ans* as a very worldly lady indeed, equipped for her encounter with the subtle Vandenesse with all the conversational gambits of the seduction game. The changes are important; why and how they have occurred is not elucidated. A similar switch in perspective across time occurs in connection with the relationship between Julie and her husband, Victor. In *Premières fautes* the failure of the marriage leads to an 'élégant divorce' (727) in which the couple go their separate ways, sleep in separate rooms, with the tacit proviso that Julie remain technically 'loyal' to Victor ('Si Victor croyait avoir le droit de ne plus m'estimer, je n'ose prétendre ce qui pourrait arriver; car il est violent, plein d'amour-propre et de vanité surtout' (729)). The first episode thus generates and reinforces two relatively stable assumptions—that, sexually and emotionally, the marriage is effectively over; but that, for the outer shell of the relationship to remain intact, the vanity and egoism of Victor have to be accommodated through the chastity of Julie. In the event, facts prove quite otherwise; not only does the relationship remain intact, despite a lover and illegitimate children but, from the evidence of *Les Deux rencontres* which is placed many years later, it has been sexually restored and there are now more children born of the marriage. Again, important changes have taken place over time, but since they are not prepared or explained by the narrator, they are changes which take us by surprise, which unsettle fixed assumptions and expectations. One should of course avoid the temptation of overinvesting in these examples. In themselves they obviously do not provide sufficient justification for a full-scale critical revaluation of the novel. They do, however, suggest that there is room in the text for a certain play; the discrepancies, ellipses, unelaborated transitions create a substantial margin of uncertainty in an otherwise highly schematic narrative, opening up areas of indeterminacy from which the unexpected emerges to trouble patterns of stereotypic fixity.

This dimension of *La Femme de trente ans* can be somewhat more extensively illustrated by an inquiry into the events surrounding the flight of Hélène in the episode entitled *Les Deux rencontres*. The episode opens with the evocation of one of the classic stereotypes of nineteenth-century melodramatic fiction, that of the happy family. The father sitting 'au coin de la cheminée' in a pose 'dont l'indolence peignait un calme parfait, un doux épanouissement de joie'; the glances

exchanged between husband and wife expressing 'de muettes jouis-
sances'; the elder son absorbed in *The Thousand and One Nights*; the elder
daughter busy with her sewing; the younger children laughing and
playing by the fire—all the initial signs proferred by the text combine to
present the d'Aiglemont household in an image of almost Dickensian
domestic bliss (788–90). Yet in relation to what both precedes and
follows this moment in the text, the image is of course a sentimental
fiction. For all his ideological commitment to the principle of the
integrated family unit, Balzac the novelist rarely deals in the idiom of
cosy domesticity. Balzac's families—it is one of his profoundest
themes—are generally divided, conflict-ridden bodies, torn and dismembered by intra-familial warfare. And it is here, in the explosion of
this stereotype, that not only do we encounter the deeper thematic
configurations of *La Femme de trente ans*, but also, and interrelatedly, can
ascribe a new and positive function to some of the ostensibly most
recalcitrant elements of the 'melodrama' of the text. In respect of the full
ramifications of the family theme in *La Femme de trente ans*, interpretative criticism has said remarkably little. To the extent that
interpretation has concerned itself at all with this novel, it has been
almost entirely on extremely narrow doctrinal and polemical grounds.
La Femme de trente ans is of interest primarily as a crude dramatization of
Balzac's position in the 'feminist' debate of the 1830s; although worth-
less as a novel, it has some interest as a document, as a source for
Balzac's views on marriage, adultery, the oppression of women and so
forth.[11] Thus, like many of the *Scènes de la vie privée*, it is easily read as a
moral tale, articulating the twin themes of the *mal mariée* and the *femme
adultère* and advocating the familiar Balzacian hard line on the matter of
wifely duties, marital responsibilities and the like. On this view, the
meaning of the narrative is entirely didactic; the multiple disasters that
befall Julie and her family are the inevitable consequences of, and a
salutary warning against, violating the marriage vows. Alternatively,
one can read it in the contrary way, as surreptitiously criticising the
paternalistic and reactionary ideology which it appears to be defending;
Julie, although outwardly condemned by Balzac for transgressing 'les
lois de sagesse, les principes de vertu sur lesquels la société repose'
(707), nevertheless elicits his covert sympathies; as elsewhere in the
Comédie, empathy with individual passion and the spirit of revolt
ultimately wins out over official didactic purpose; secretly it speaks for
the liberation of women rather than their subjugation; Julie's grand
declamation to the priest in *Souffrances inconnues*, which exposes the
exploitation and abuse of woman by man, is the real core of the novel,
and so on.

Both these views are arguable. But the relative claims of each are not
our concern here, although the idea that the novel is, at some level,
ideologically radical rather than conservative has some bearing on the
argument I wish to develop. To restrict the concerns of *La Femme de
trente ans* to the terms of a particular nineteenth-century polemic is,

however, to overlook a great deal. At a deeper level, the sense of the novel is not polemical at all; it resides not so much in admonitions on 'les dangers de l'inconduite', nor in a plea on behalf of the subjugated female estate, as in an articulation of the ancestral tensions and conflicts of the family. The central subject of *La Femme de trente ans* is a powerful drama of the conflicts between kinship obligations and sexual desire, authority and individuality, repression and violence, enacted at various levels of familial relationships—husband and wife, parent and child, brother and sister. A precise thematic analysis of the text could doubt-less yield a coherent schema within which the major characters and their actions might be classified in terms of an interplay between the authoritarian pressures of the family (those mediated variously by father, mother, husband) and movements of rebellion and transgression in which individuals (Julie, Hélène, Moina) seek, often in the most dramatic and desperate ways, to affirm their own autonomy against those pressures. Fathers and husbands assert an aggressive dominion over wives and children; Julie's father forbids her to marry Victor d'Aiglemont; the prohibition is made on grounds of an ostensibly disinterested wisdom, but is also tinged with feelings of a quasi-sexual jealousy and possessiveness; sexual relations between husband and wife are marked by brutishness and disgust; three of the major peripeteia of the narrative hinge on the daughters' rejection of the tyranny of parental authority over the choice of a sexual partner; mother loathes daughter (fruit of the legitimate but detested relationship) and adores son (fruit of the illicit relationship); daughter reciprocates hatred and externalizes her feelings in the act of fratricide; another daughter (Moina, offspring of the adulterous relationship with Vandenesse) resists her mother's efforts to prevent her embarking on a liaison with Vandenesse's son, and is hence involved in incest. The novel ends, as it were, by loyally keeping sex in the family but, if one is tempted to be flip here, it is precisely because the very meaning of 'family', as Balzac the ideologist was fond of describing it, has undergone a huge devaluation.

The specific details of this broad thematic design could be examined from a variety of angles, but the important point here is its general bearing on the question of melodrama and 'pastoral'. Its relevance becomes clear if we now return to the image of domestic harmony offered in the opening pages of *Les Deux rencontres*. Evidently, in the context of the central themes of the novel, the status of that image is ironic; it is set up only to be subverted by what happens in the rest of the episode, where the facade of unity is suddenly and dramatically cracked wide open. However, the interesting question is the way in which it is subverted, for on the surface the literary means employed by Balzac partake of the crassest form of low melodrama. The essence of the matter lies in Hélène's extraordinary decision to leave her home with the mysterious stranger who arrives unexpectedly seeking sanctuary from the pursuit of the law. The critical question is, why does Hélène leave? What is the motive and the meaning of her act? To put it mildly, it is odd; more strongly, it is preposterously implausible, an instance of the wildest form of Romantic extravagance; on any reasonable criteria, abandoning home and hearth with a complete stranger who turns up in the middle of the night, declares himself an assassin and finally takes off for a life of piracy on the high seas, is not likely to command serious attention from the reader. It is easily said that Hélène's action disrupts 'expectations', confounds assumptions about the ways in which young women 'of her sort'[12] typically behave, but this is hardly likely to carry much weight in an argument about the capacity of a text to escape the constraints of pastoral. This is how the moment of decision is represented in the text:

> Vous ici! s'écria le général . . . Un assassin couvert de sang ici. Vous souillez ce tableau! Sortez! ajouta-t-il avec un accent de fureur.
> Au mot d'assassin, la marquise jeta un cri. Quant à Hélène, ce mot sembla décider de sa vie, son visage n'accusa pas le moindre étonnement. Elle semblait avoir attendu cet homme. Ses pensées si vastes eurent un sens. La punition que le ciel réservait à ses fautes éclatait. Se croyant aussi criminelle que l'était cet homme, la jeune fille le regarda d'un oeil serein: elle était sa compagne, sa soeur. Pour elle, un commandement de Dieu se manifestait dans cette circonstance (804).

Naturally, the reader winces, or simply yawns, reminded of the frequency with which young girls elope sensationally with criminals and outlaws in the popular literature of the period. Even Balzac himself, hardly the most self-critical of writers, appears to have winced. In 1843 he wrote to Mme Hanska, 'Combien de fautes n'ai-je pas laissées! sans compter qu'entrainé par la rapidité de l'impression, j'ai maintenu une oeuvre indigne de cette oeuvre (*Le capitaine parisien* dans *Les deux rencontres*) qui est à remplacer par autre chose, je l'ai vu. Mais il fallait paraître, et je n'ai pas eu le temps de refaire ce mélodrame indigne de moi. Mon coeur d'honnête homme de lettres en saigne encore.'[13] What offends even Balzac, therefore, is precisely the 'melodrama' of the episode. More specifically, the key issue for Balzac is that of motivation and verisimilitude and, on these terms, in later revisions of the text for subsequent editions, definite attempts were made to remedy matters. Thus, in another letter to Mme Hanska, concerning revisions made for the forthcoming reprint of the 1834 Werdet edition, he speaks explicitly of the efforts he has made to render the episode of Hélène's flight more plausible: 'Nous réimprimons en ce moment le quatrième volume des *Scènes de la vie privée*, où j'ai fait de grands changements par rapport au sens général de *Même histoire*. Ainsi la fuite d'Hélène avec le meutrier est rendue presque vraisemblable; il a fallu longtemps pour trouver ces derniers noeuds.'[14] The most important modification to the earlier version was the interpolation of the long passage dealing with Hélène's reaction to reading Schiller's *Wilhelm Tell* and the 'ravage causé par cette lecture dans l'âme d'Hélène [qui] venait de la scène où le poète établit une sorte de fraternité entre Guillaume Tell, qui verse le sang d'un homme pour sauver tout un peuple, et Jean-le-Parricide' (II, 792). The intention therefore is clear—to create a psychological climate that assures a plausible motive for Hélène's departure; identifying herself with the criminal is at once an expression of guilt and an act of expiation for the earlier deed of fratricide. Evidently anxious to reinforce this emphasis, Balzac returned to the point, in a paragraph added by hand to his own copy of the preface he wrote for the 1834 edition, this time explicitly drawing out the idea of remorse and self-immolation as the basic motive for Hélène's otherwise quite incomprehensible act: 'Chargée d'un fratricide, elle succombe sous le remords; elle ne se croit digne de personne; elle se voit en pensée la camarade des forçats' (XI, 168).

Here, then, we find Balzac demonstrating a readily understandable anxiety about the motivation of his narrative, and urgently trying to redeem its apparent extravagance by accommodating it to the elementary requirements of *vraisemblance*. In an important sense, however, he was actually doing a disservice to his work. For the essential force of Hélène's act—and it is here that the 'melodrama' of the text acquires a radically different significance—lies in its fundamental indeterminacy, its opaque resistance to rational structures of motivation and conventional systems of plausibility. And in fact, despite the attempt in the preface to identify a specific psychological cause for Hélène's behaviour, elsewhere in the same document Balzac himself seems to have perceived this quality of indeterminacy, in the sense of a spontaneously unpredictable act irreducible to the terms of rational analysis, as the decisive feature of the episode:

> D'autres reproches ont été adressés à l'auteur, relativement à la brusque disparition de la jeune fille dans *Les Deux rencontres*. Il existerait dans l'oeuvre entière de plus fortes incohérences si l'auteur était tenu d'avoir plus de logique que n'en ont les événements de la vie. Il pourrait dire ici que les déterminations les plus importantes se prennent toujours en un moment; qu'il a voulu représenter les passions rapidement conçues, qui soumettent toute l'existence à quelque pensée d'un jour; mais pourquoi tenterait-il d'expliquer par la logique ce qui doit être compris par le sentiment. . . . Quoique la vie sociale ait, aussi bien que la vie physique, des lois en apparence immuables, vous ne trouverez nulle part ni le corps ni le coeur réguliers comme la trigonométrie de Legendre. (XI, 167).

From a writer who saw the intelligibility of the human world in terms of explanatory models derived from the natural sciences, who was so strongly wedded to the concepts of system, law, causality, this is an exceptionally interesting passage. It hints at an idea that will later exercise a seminal influence in twentieth-century thinking about the novel (much favoured by Gide, for instance, who, it will be recalled, objected to Balzac's work on the grounds of its imprisonment in a systematic determinism[15])—the idea that, at certain crucial moments, 'life' defies 'system', at both the social and fictive levels, as both a set of social determinations and generic expectations. This idea is a difficult and complicated one, whose manifold implications cannot be fully rehearsed here.[16] But, in relation to the special uses to which the conventions of melodrama are put by Balzac, its importance may be helpfully clarified if we briefly consider the passage from the preface alongside the one from *Splendeurs et misères des courtisanes*, cited earlier in connection with the role played by 'chance' in the *Comédie humaine*:

> Une des obligations auxquelles ne doit jamais manquer l'historien des moeurs, c'est de ne point gâter le vrai par des arrangements en apparence dramatiques, surtout quand le vrai a pris la peine de devenir romanesque. La nature sociale, à Paris surtout, comporte de tels hasards, des enchevêtrements de conjectures si capricieuses, que l'imagination des inventeurs est à tout moment dépassée.

From this juxtaposition, one might say that the preface to *La Femme de trente ans* expresses the subjective equivalent of the emphasis placed, in the other extract, on the significance of the unpredictable in the external social world; the spontaneous welling up of latent regions of the inner world parallels, in its disruption of stable models of personality, the disruption by the agencies of chance of the principles of causality taken for granted as regulating the outer world. In both cases, 'melodrama' thus serves to liberate the text from the grip of a quasi-mathematical system of programmed and predictable regularities.

The negative reference to 'trigonométrie' in the passage from the preface is indeed instructive. Fernandez, in his strictures on what he saw as the artificially schematic nature of Balzac's art, remarked that its operations often struck him as analogous to the working out of a mathematical problem;[17] nothing in Balzac escapes the 'system', and the system is like the kiss of death, trapping the fictional creations in an abstract, formulaic order of discourse in which they have no room to breathe, to develop, above all to surprise us. The method of *La Femme de trente ans*, however, calls upon us to question and modify that judgment. It might also remind us, although the analogy should obviously not be pressed too hard, of the practice of that supremely 'anti-pastoral' novelist, Stendhal. Stendhal as is well known, liked to hold up mathematics as a model for both dealing with the world and writing about it; like the famous *logique*, it provided a pattern of shape and intelligibility, a means of prediction and control; he admires a certain style of art because he finds in it 'une science exacte de même nature que l'arithmétique, la géométrie, la trigonométrie'.[18] His own novelistic world in action is, however, a quite different affair where, as Michael Wood has remarked, his 'delight in patterns' is being continually outplayed by 'his fidelity to a bewildering world'.[19] 'Je me tromperai toujours lorsque je croirai un homme totalement d'un caractère', he writes in the *Journal*,[20] and it is this perception that underlies many of the most compelling effects of his fictional world. Stendhal's creativity is the very reverse of a fixed 'pastoral contemplation'[21] of unchanging essences; rather it is founded on an ineradicable sense of mobility and discontinuity. At their most important moments, Stendhal's characters are hardly ever found doing the 'right thing', the expected thing, in either the psychological or generic sense of expectation. As has often been remarked, what distinguishes Stendhal's creations is their inexhaustible capacity for the *imprévu*, their constant ability to surprise themselves, the reader and perhaps even their creator himself. Radically indeterminate beings, they produce and inhabit a universe of latency and uncertainty in which the sudden decision of an instant can switch the whole direction of a novel, and impose upon us the strenuous task of completely rewriting the system of expectations, the 'internalized probability system',[22] we bring to it. Some of course are not prepared, or are unable, to rise to the challenge. Of Mathilde de la Mole, Jules Janin wrote, echoing the impressions of many nineteenth-century readers, 'On n'a jamais imaginé une fille comme cela.'[23] For Janin, Mathilde is unacceptable, unintelligible even, because she eludes and defeats the categories we habitually bring to the reading of fictions. Her bewilderingly unpredictable behaviour not only contravenes the standards of social conduct of her class, but also—the two are related—places a severe strain on the credence a certain kind of reader can give to the text; it puts pressure on the generic and social codes that inform our established models of *vraisemblance*. But this is precisely one of the marks of the strength and vitality of Mathilde as a literary creation.

Naturally, we cannot simply elbow the example of Stendhal into speaking on behalf of Balzac. The comparison is not however entirely inapposite, especially when we remember that in his last, though uncompleted, novel, *Lamiel*, the projected finale for perhaps his most splendidly outrageous heroine (in both senses of outraging conventional moral attitudes and generic expectations) was to elope with a criminal; the *poncif* of popular Romantic melodrama thus reappears but, in the context of the whole of Stendhal's work, it becomes invested with a new and sophisticated meaning. Stendhal draws on the materials of a particular stereotype to undo a more fundamental stereotype; as Simone de Beauvoir recognized,[24] the audacious mobility and elusiveness of Stendhal's heroines is at bottom a matter of shattering the 'pastoral' mould in which the nineteenth-century consciousness typically cast its image of woman as such, that ideological image, repeated and naturalized a thousand times in the fiction of the period, of the very reality of 'woman' as the passive, inert creature of the domestic world of the nineteenth-century family. Clearly it would be extravagant to place quite that weight of meaning on Hélène in *La Femme de trente ans*. But beneath its outwardly flamboyant theatricality, it does seem to me that it is this kind of insight that the text is trying to articulate. Hélène's sudden decision becomes the occasion for the breaking of a self-image embedded in the safe, secure world represented by the fiction (lie) and the fictions (novels) of the united family. It is the moment at which the claims on her, both as individual person and fictional character, exercised by 'normal' reality are lifted. Interestingly, the whole episode occurs as though in a dream. The evocation of dream-like states at moments when characters behave in unusual and unexpected ways is a feature of the work of many major novelists. The most spontaneous and indeterminate actions in Dostoyevsky's novels, for instance, often take place when the characters retreat into an almost somnambulistic condition over which social convention and rational determinations have no hold. In the most famous example of Stendhalian indeterminacy, Julien Sorel sets off on his wild journey across France to kill Mme de Rênal as if he were in some kind of trance. In *La Femme de trente ans* the pretext or mechanism of this shift in narrative atmosphere is provided by the presence of the stranger. Once again, with the arrival of the stranger the novel appears to collapse into the worst kind of Gothic sensationalism. Hélène's first encounter with him is described in the following terms:

> Quoique son ouïe fut très fine, il resta presque collé sur le mur, immobile et comme perdu dans ses pensées. Le cercle de lumière projeté par la lanterne l'éclairait faiblement, et il ressemblait, dans cette zone de clair-obscur, à ces sombres statues de chevaliers, toujours debout à l'encoignure de quelque tombe noire sous les chapelles gothiques. Des gouttes de sueur froide sillonnaient son front jaune et large. Une audace incroyable brillait sur ce visage fortement contracté. Ses yeux de feu, fixes et secs, semblaient contempler un combat dans l'obscurité qui était devant lui. Ses pensées tumultueuses passaient rapidement sur cette face, dont l'expression ferme et précise indiquait une âme supérieure. Son corps, son attitude, ses proportions, s'accordaient avec son génie sauvage. Cet homme était tout force et tout puissance, et il envisageait les ténèbres comme une visible image de son avenir.... Hélène fut saisie par le mélange de lumière et d'ombre, de grandiose et de passion, par un poétique chaos qui donnait à l'inconnu l'apparence de Lucifer se relevant de sa chute (801–2).

There seems very little we can do with this, except to acknowledge its obvious source in the popular literature of the times. The overblown rhetoric points unmistakeably to a reincarnation of Balzac's Argow and, more widely, to the figure of the Romantic brigand popularized by Byron's *Corsair*, Scott's *The Pirate*, Cooper's *Red Rover*, not to mention their countless imitators (Sue's *Kernok le Pirate* had just come out at the time Balzac published *Les Deux rencontres*). But what makes the presence of the stranger more than simply a repeat performance of a hackneyed melodramatic theme is its effect on the d'Aiglemont household. At one level, that effect derives once more from a highly conventional Gothic motif—the power of the demonic glance. The stranger almost literally hypnotizes the whole family: 'ils étaient soumis à une torpeur inexplicable; et leur raison engourdie les aidait mal à repousser la puissance surnaturelle sous laquelle ils succombaient. Pour eux l'air était devenu lourd, et ils respiraient difficilement, sans pouvoir accuser celui qui les opprimait ainsi, quoiqu'une voix intérieure ne leur laissât pas ignorer que cet homme magique était le principe de leur impuissance' (807). Hélène succumbs to the 'pouvoir magnétique de ce regard', 'un regard de serpent [qui] remua dans le coeur de cette singulière jeune fille un monde de pensées encore endormi chez elle' (803). Monsieur d'Aiglemont is the victim of 'un regard dont la vive clarté pénétra l'âme du général. Ce jet d'intelligence et de volonté ressemblait à un éclair, et fut écrasant comme la foudre'(796); when he tries to resist by force Hélène's departure with the stranger, he is paralysed by 'un regard qui versait la stupeur, et le dépouilla de son énergie' (806).

It is, of course, all rather like the 'regard magnétique' of Argow, and later Vautrin. But, as with the manipulation of the glance-motif in *Béatrix*, it can also be interpreted in a more interesting and complex way. In the narrative the stranger in fact operates essentially as a device, a convenience even, as the alien element which catalyses the unfolding of the deeper drama of awakening and dissolution within the family itself. The hypnotic gaze of the intruder produces a temporary slackening in the grip of the normal and normative structures of reality, represented primarily by the authority and control of the father. It pushes the narrative into a realm of dreamlike indeterminacy in which almost anything might happen. 'Rêve', 'rêverie', 'rêveux', 'rêveuse' are recurrent terms in the vocabulary of the book as a whole; at key points the characters withdraw from the pressures and demands of the external world into an unfathomable inner meditation ('j'avais surpris sur le visage de la petite fille rêveuse et taciturne les traces d'une pensée plus profonde que ne le comportait son âge' (II, 777); 'elle s'engourdit dans une rêverie' (712); 'chaque phrase amenait de longues rêveries' (696)). This kind of psychological withdrawal is often the preparatory stage for a decisive turn in the narrative. Here the gaze of the stranger effects a sudden suspension of the rhythms of daily life. After the departure of Hélène the exigencies of ordinary reality will immediately reassert themselves; the father awakens as from a dream to re-enter the external world of decision and action: 'En prononçant ce nom [Hélène], le général rompit, comme par enchantement, le charme auquel une puissance diabolique l'avait soumis' (810). The whole episode is built around a series of abrupt transitions, from the cosy normality of the opening scene, to the nightmarish unreality of the central sequence, back into the familiar world of deed and control. In the dreamlike atmosphere produced by the intruder, however, the father yields to a form of spell, in which his traditional role as arbiter of behaviour, as source of what is known and accepted as 'reality', are momentarily eclipsed. For Hélène, on the other hand, that eclipse is the occasion of an inner awakening, for the release of 'un monde de pensées encore endormi chez elle' (803), a nexus of obscure, latent energies repressed in the structure of familial relationships, but now brought into the open. Her mother appeals to her in the name of the values of 'society', the 'family'; Hélène responds with cool contempt: 'Hélène, vous mentez à tous les principes d'honneur, de modestie, de vertu, que j'ai tâché de développer dans votre coeur. . . . Je vous estime trop pour supposer. . . . Oh! supposez tout, madame, répondit Hélène d'un ton froid' (806). Psychologically, what surfaces here are feelings of hatred and rejection, loathing for the mother who has shown preference for the son born of adultery and secret aversion for the child born of the marriage. More broadly, Hélène's rejection, less an act of guilty self-immolation than an act of revolt, explodes the myths and pretences embodied in the stereotype of the ordered family and unquestioning filial submission as a 'natural' component of that order. In this respect, there is quite a crucial exchange between daughter and father, in which the latter attempts to prevent Hélène's departure through an explicit appeal not simply to a notion of 'correct' behaviour, but, more interestingly, to a notion of 'natural' behaviour:

> —Hélène, demanda-t-il d'une voix altérée par un tremblement convulsif, est-ce la première fois que vous avez vu cet homme?
> —Oui, mon père
> —Il n'est pas alors naturel que vous ayez le dessein de . . .
> —Si cela n'est pas naturel, au moins cela est vrai, père (806)

In Hélène's opposition to what her father views as 'natural' or rational conduct there lies the whole hidden drama of the text: the eruption of that uncontrollable part of Hélène's being over which the norms of social rationality, represented by the ideology of the family and the authority of the father, have no power. In terms of these norms, her act is indeed irrational, mad ('un mouvement de folie' (808)), incomprehensible, 'unnatural'; yet for Hélène it is the irrevocable 'truth' of her being that is in question.

The point to be remarked on, however, concerns less the thematic and psychological aspects of the opposition between the terms 'vrai' and 'naturel', than its formal and literary implications. The refusal by Hélène of the prohibiting and sanctioning authority of the father is, at the level of the functioning of the novel itself, a refusal by the text of the permitting and constraining authority of the codes of *vraisemblance*. The two, the law of the father and the logic of verisimilitude, authoritarian control of reality and authoritative versions of reality, are almost certainly interrelated, to the extent that the actual and symbolic power of the former is central to the security of the established, normative culture from which the rules and conventions of the latter to a large extent inevitably flow. For—to open briefly a perspective that will be more fully explored in the final chapter—what is deemed 'probable' in literature is often intimately related to what is seen as 'rational' or 'natural' in society at large; it is that which meets the expectations enshrined in socially constructed models of rationality and normality, generally as these are mediated by those who organize and control the values and institutions of the social universe in question. Hence the significance of the fundamental indeterminacy of Hélène's action: her defiance of the family, of their expectations as to how she ought to behave, is also a defiance of a set of literary expectations about 'character' in fiction, a moment at which the autonomy of the inner life bursts spontaneously into the text to subvert definitions which are taken for granted, to push the text decisively beyond the limits of pastoral modes of representation. Hence therefore the significance of the 'melodrama' of Hélène's action; it is indeed appropriate to describe it as 'melodramatic', in the sense of implausible, but precisely because its function is to outplay causal and logical descriptions of behaviour and to call in question the assumptions underlying the social and analytic 'trigonometry' which regulates our habitual conceptions of plausibility.

The reader is, of course, free to speculate about the reasons for Hélène's departure, to rationalize and reduce its indeterminate quality. A more appropriate response, however, would be to see it as an example of what elsewhere Balzac refers to as 'ces mouvements instinctifs que l'homme ne sait pas toujours expliquer' (796). Certainly, in response to her father's plea 'explique-moi les raisons qui te poussent à laisser ta famille' (808), Hélène herself makes remarkably little effort to give any explicit and intelligible account of those reasons. There is a suggestion that she does not really know, that her action springs from a level of being that cannot be articulated ('il existe des pensées auxquelles nous obéissons sans les connaître: elles sont en nous à notre insu' (761). More significantly, the narrator himself behaves in a not dissimilar fashion. For, despite the anxiety shown by Balzac over the motivation of the narrative, despite the additions and modifications to later editions of the text, the narrator in effect tells us very little. Rather, as in *Honorine* and *Béatrix*, the drama is played out at the level of the unspoken and the half said, the oblique gesture and the enigmatic glance. In the repeated exchange of looks between mother and daughter, for instance, a whole range of feeling and meaning is implied, but never explicated.

> Dites tout, ma fille, je suis mère. Ici la fille regarda la mère, et ce regard fit faire une pause à la marquise. (808)

> Elle resta silencieuse, et baissa les yeux après avoir interrogé la marquise par un coup d'oeil éloquent. (807)

> Une seule fois, sans se défier mutuellement, ses yeux et ceux de la

marquise se heurtèrent. Ces deux femmes se comprirent alors par un regard terne, froid, respectueux pour Hélène, sombre et menaçant chez la mère. Hélène baissa promptement sa vue sur le métier, tira l'aiguille avec prestesse, et de longtemps ne releva sa tête, qui semblait lui être devenue trop lourde à porter. La mère était-elle trop sévère pour sa fille, et jugeait-elle cette sévérité nécessaire? Etait-elle jalouse de la beauté d'Hélène, avec qui elle pouvait rivaliser encore, mais en déployant tous les prestiges de la toilette? Ou la fille avait-elle surpris, comme beaucoup de filles quand elles deviennent clairvoyantes, des secrets que cette femme, en apparence, si religieusement fidèle à ses devoirs, croyait avoir enseveli dans son coeur aussi profondément que dans une tombe? (792)

This last passage merits special attention, as it contains in concentrated form the distinctive features of Balzac's method. The glance is susceptible of many interpretations; but it produces from the narrator a set of questions which however remain unanswered. Here the text, like the reader, speculates, but does not conclude; it opens up a range of possibilities but decides in favour of none. The essential stress is on the opacity and impenetrability of the exchange, before which the narrator declares his own helplessness ('Nul homme n'aurait eu l'oeil assez perspicace pour sonder la profondeur de ces deux âmes féminines' (793)).

Balzac himself emphasized in the preface to La Femme de trente ans that Hélènes act is beyond the reach of 'la logique', that it could not be reduced to the categories of rational, discursive language. As Martin Kanes has argued,[25] there is in La Femme de trente ans, as in many other texts of the Comédie humaine, a certain problematic of language which implicates not only the characters and their ability to communicate their feelings, but also the narrator himself. It may be exaggerated to speak, as does Kanes, of an experience of 'linguistic despair' in La Femme de trente ans, but there is considerable evidence in the text of a certain unease before language, the feeling of a gulf between the explanatory operations of rational discourse and the enigmas and indeterminacies of what is going on in the mind of the characters. Over and over again the narrator confesses to a sense of what, in the text, is called 'l'impuissance des discours': 'je ne sais quel trait indéfinissable' (689), 'une indéfinissable appréhension' (699); 'des pensées si vagues, si indécises, qu'elle n'eût pas trouvé de langage pour les rendre' (710) 'le langage ne suffirait pas à exprimer le torrent de pensées' (712); 'la nature de douleurs qu'il engendre se refuse à l'analyse et aux couleurs de l'art' (746); 'ce monologue dont les mille pensées contradictoires, inachevées, confuses, sont intraduisibles' (756); 'une de ces sensations pour lesquelles il manque un langage' (765); 'un moment où le langage des yeux suppléa complètement à l'impuissance des discours' (770); 'Horribles souffrances, incroyables, sans langage' (841).

In many of these examples there is of course a certain element of rhetorical flourish and vacuous hyperbole. When Balzac says that something is 'inexpressible', we do not necessarily take this very seriously. We may be even less inclined to do so when we recall that some of these disclaimers of linguistic competence occur in contexts of otherwise quite uninhibited garrulity, as the familiar Balzacian voice goes about it business of naming, generalizing, classifying with characteristic gusto. The narrator may well claim, for instance, that Julie's suffering 'se refuse à l'analyse et aux couleurs de l'art', but this in no way restrains Balzac from producing a formidable array of analytical generalizations in his presentation of her, above all in the famous set of propositions organized around the concept of 'la femme de trente ans'.

Yet for all its demiurgic exuberance, its self-confident drive towards mastery and intelligibility, the narrative voice is not omnipotent. In the text there are gaps, lacunae which the voice does not seek to fill; moments before which it retreats, falls silent. The word 'silence' recurs with insistent regularity in *La Femme de trente ans* and, above all in relation to Hélène's decision, the ultimate strategy adopted by the narrator is the strategy of silence. Maurice Bardèche, commenting on the technique of the dénouement in *La Femme de trente ans*, has remarked that Balzac's most felicitous device lies in what he calls the 'refus de conter';[26] at the end of the first section, for example, the narrative simply fades, disappears into the penumbra of the unsaid. It is a technique that Balzac used on various occasions in, for example, the ending of *Ferragus* and *La Duchesse de Langeais*. Stendhal too was fond of the fading device, as in the closing lines of 'Vanina Vanini'; there is much there that we would like to know, but Stendhal prefers to leave us guessing, prefers the opaque to the explicit. This preference is, moreover, not just a matter of endings; it appears elsewhere, notoriously of course in the presentation of Julien Sorel's crime. Criticism has speculated endlessly about Julien's 'motives'. The crucial literary point, however, is that, whatever the critic's speculations, they get no support whatever from the narrative voice in the text; by way of psychological analysis, the voice says virtually nothing; it respects the mysterious indeterminacy of the act. In his remarks on this episode of *Le Rouge et le Noir*, Michael Wood contrasts Stendhal's method with that of Balzac: 'Julien's decision is abrupt, and the shooting described with an extreme terseness where Balzac or Dickens would have gone richly to town.'[27] Of course, but this is not invariably the case. In his review of *La Chartreuse de Parme*, Balzac remarked of Stendhal that '[il] laisse beaucoup à deviner' and in the same article identified the maxim 'malheur en amour, comme dans les arts, à qui dit tout'[28] as one of the fundamental 'beyliste' principles. It is a principle that Balzac himself followed in some of his own fictions. Balzac too often leaves us guessing, withdraws into silence. Hélène is a case in point, and the ostensibly melodramatic 'improbability' of her action is, in part at least, a function of the narrator's refusal to analyse it, to recuperate it into the terms of a conventional intelligibility, just as this is the case with Julien Sorel's crime. Indeed, on a certain reading, what could be more 'melodramatic' than Julien's incredible escapade? In his account of *Le Rouge et le Noir*, Faguet, although he does not use the term 'melodrama', as he does in connection with *La Femme de trente ans*, found Julien Sorel's crime quite implausible.[29] Yet it is arguable that, in its very implausibility, in the fissure it introduces into the language of common sense and the expectations of verisimilitude, it is the very cornerstone of the meaning of the novel as a whole.

I have already noted, and the point doubtless bears repetition, that it would be straining the legitimacy of literary comparison to imply that *Le Rouge et le Noir* and *La Femme de trente ans* occupy the same space of creative achievement (some would say it is a breach of elementary decorum even to speak of them in the same breath). Certainly, to put it no stronger, it would be intellectually disingenuous to use the comparison to try to obscure the faults of the latter; of all the Balzac novels I have discussed in this book, *La Femme de trente ans* is beyond doubt the weakest. Yet, when all the necessary caveats have been entered, the comparison still remains, I believe, a fruitful one. The 'melodrama' of *La Femme de trente ans*, one might perhaps say, taught Balzac a lesson, but not simply, as the familiar critical tradition would have it, a penitential one. In its primitive disdain for the customary procedures of motivation and *vraisemblance*, its brash commitment to the 'implausible' as a category of life itself, it may well be linked not only to Balzac's capacity to read sympathetically his great contemporary but, more importantly, to some of the central effects of his later fictions—those effects which critical custom has tended to lump together under the heading 'exaggeration' and which we must now go on to discuss in the next chapter.

8 Type and transgression

Notre société a besoin du mythe du 'roman'. . . . Le roman est la manière dont cette société se parle . . . quelle parole échapperait à cette parole insidieuse, incessante, et qui semble toujours être là avant que nous y pensions. Philippe Sollers, *Logiques*[1]

La vie humaine ne peut en aucun cas être limitée aux systèmes fermés qui lui sont assignés dans des conceptions raisonnables. L'immense travail d'abandon, d'écoulement et d'orage qui la constitue pourrait être exprimé en disant qu'elle ne commence qu'avec le déficit de ces systèmes. G. Bataille, *La Notion de dépense*[2]

In most definitions or descriptions of melodrama, one almost invariably encounters the term 'exaggeration' ('Melodrama thrives solely upon exaggeration'[3]), and it is a term, along with its various synonyms, habitually invoked by criticism in relation to many of Balzac's major creations: 'exaggerated beyond the limits of verisimilitude'; 'énormes, excessifs, presque inadmissibles'; 'l'exagération de quelques caractères'; 'passions excessives'; 'démesurément amplifiés' 'pas des êtres réels'.[4] One could enumerate at length, but the essential point is that the terms 'exaggeration' and 'excess' have occupied a relatively stable place in the vocabulary of a central, often dominating critical approach to Balzac, generally to designate what is seen as the tendency of the Balzacian imagination to run out of control, to sacrifice the 'real' to the hyperbolic imagery of melodrama. There have, of course, been various resistances to such a description of Balzac's work. One can attempt, for instance, to recuperate the 'être excessif' of the *Comédie* by stressing the dense historical or physical particularity with which he or she is surrounded (the emphasis of Lanson), but this still leaves a 'gap', a dimension which, despite Balzac's own explicit theories of historical and environmental causation, cannot be adequately reduced to these positivist forms of determination. Alternatively, while acknowledging that these creations do appear to transcend the codes of narrative 'realism', one can make the rather helpless gesture towards the notion of the 'mystery' of the creative process in Balzac; despite all the critical evidence to the contrary, Balzac, by means of an arcane procedure of the imagination, 'somehow' (a favourite verbal refuge for the critical mind defeated by the ostensibly intractable) manages to convince us of the 'reality' of his creations: 'Balzac's capacity for compelling us to believe in his monomaniacs is a mystery hard to explain.'[5] Neither the reductive determinism of the first approach, nor the unsupported impressionism of the second is satisfactory; the problem still remains, and if the attempt to negotiate it remains held within the terms of either of these two alternatives, then the door is left wide open for the familiar view of the ineradicable presence of a melodrama of 'exaggeration' in the *Comédie humaine* to reappear relatively unscathed.

In this respect, perhaps the most instructive example of the kind of criticism we are here dealing with (instructive partly because it is historically contemporary with Balzac himself—the importance of this will emerge later—and partly because of the specific terms in which it is cast) is that offered by the critic Hippolyte Castille, in the review of Balzac published in 1846. In this review Castille observed: 'A l'opposé des grands maîtres qui tous ont pris leurs types à la généralité, M de Balzac procède par l'exception. . . . Voilà où il cesse d'appartenir à cette école réaliste. . . . Dans tous les romans de M de Balzac le héros et plusieurs comparses n'appartiennent jamais à l'humanité.'[6] The key emphasis in this critical comment is in the opposition between 'type' and 'exception': the great types of literature embody the representative patterns of human and social experience, whereas Balzac's productions are strictly unrepresentative, deviant, aberrant, the productions of a literary mind that has failed to connect with the 'typical' forms of reality; in short, they are *invraisemblables*, to be unhesitatingly excommunicated from the canonic text of representational writing. Castille's observations can be responded to in a number of ways, but the main issue which they compel us to confront—and it is, fundamentally, a major problem of general critical theory—is the basis on which the discourse of criticism uses the terms 'exaggeration', 'excess', 'exception' as value terms. Put in another, more properly focused way, the question concerns firstly, the foundations of the *vraisemblable* and its relation to the elaboration of the fictional type, that is, the general system of intelligibility within which are held, at a given historical moment, the conventions of *vraisemblance* and typicality; and secondly, the complex and often ambivalent relationship of serious literature to that system. I want to look at this question in the context of a number of general reflections on the nature of the *vraisemblable* and in terms of an analysis of the figure of Hulot in *La Cousine Bette*; in respect of the latter I shall attempt to show that, if indeed it is 'melodrama' that we are faced with here, it is melodrama of a peculiar kind, of an original and essentially revolutionary order.

The critical and theoretical space opened up by the long history of the concept of the *vraisemblable* from Aristotelian poetics onwards is not one that can or need be fully explored here. The crucial point for our purposes is that with the rise of the novel and, more particularly, with the growth of the idea of 'realism' in the course of the nineteenth century, the *vraisemblable* of the literary text is increasingly assimilated to the notion of a direct, immediate fidelity to the world 'out there', a function of that 'reproduction rigoureuse' of reality of which Balzac speaks in the *Avant-propos* (I, 3). Whereas seventeenth-century classical poetics, following Aristotle's distinction between 'convincing impossibilities' and 'unconvincing possibilities', often identifies and defends the *vraisemblable* in terms of an openly recognized set of specifically literary and social conventions (Chimène's marriage to Rodrigue in *Le Cid* is historically true but *invraisemblable* because it transgresses both the rules of tragedy and of the social *bienséances*), in the nineteenth century the recognition of the conventional basis, the coded nature of the *vraisemblable*, tends to disappear behind the assumption of the text as standing in a relation of complete immediacy and transparency to reality. Yet although, in this context, it frequently offers itself in grand epistemological terms, as a direct reflection of the 'truth' of reality, the *vraisemblable* of the nineteenth-century novel is in fact founded, like all forms of the *vraisemblable*, on a body of specifically social and cultural transactions with the notion of 'reality'.

This repression or concealment of the cultural is, of course, by no means unique to the conventions of literary *vraisemblance*. In their book, *The Social Construction of Reality*, Peter Berger and Thomas Luckmann comment extensively on the tendency inherent in all societies to 'naturalize' the reality they have historically constructed —the tendency to convert a world dynamically produced by a specific socio-historical praxis into the World *tout court*, permanent, unalterable, natural. Thus, in the words of Berger and Luckmann, although 'social order is not part of the "nature of things" and . . . cannot be derived from the "laws of nature"', nevertheless the social world is habitually experienced by its inhabitants 'in the sense of a comprehensive and given reality confronting the individual in a manner analogous to the reality of the natural world'.[7] The processes of naturalization at work within a given society are necessarily complex and varied, but one of the essential strategies through which a socially constructed reality is internalized and maintained in consciousness as a taken-for-granted, 'natural' reality is in the creation and transmission of a stock of 'social knowledge', the consolidation of a 'socially shared universe of meaning'.[8] This knowledge is not primarily theoretical knowledge, although it can ramify into this sphere, but essentially pragmatic or 'recipe' knowledge, a generally shared body of norms, attitudes, beliefs, values, a diffuse ideology whose main function is to stabilize and legitimate a network of social practices and customs as a natural condition of man ('it is the sum total of "what everybody knows" about a social world, an assemblage of maxims, morals, proverbial nuggets of wisdom, values and beliefs, myths and so forth'[9]).

The relations that literature, and criticism, can sustain with this corpus of social knowledge are various. A dominant type of relationship, brilliantly explored by Lukács in *Theory of the Novel*, is that of irony; witness, for example, the ironic relation to the cultural text of chivalry sustained by Cervantes's *Don Quixote* or the ironic mode of Flaubert in relation to the *idée reçue*, the whole activity of Flaubert's writing lying, precisely, in the ferocious outplaying and deconstruction of the codes of nineteenth-century social knowledge. There can, however, also be a relation of pure repetition, where the assumptions controlling the discourse of the novel derive directly from the text of an established social wisdom, where, as Kenneth Burke has put it, even the most complex and sophisticated work of art may be considered in part as 'proverbs writ large'.[10] And it is here, in this kind of relationship, that we find one of the most basic contexts of the *vraisemblable* in literature. The *vraisemblable* inscribes itself in the space of the prevailing stock of social knowledge and, as such, marks one of the vital points at which literary studies connect with the sociology of knowledge and of symbolic articulations. The *vraisemblable* both reflects and participates in the processes whereby a particular social construction of reality is transformed into the natural order of things. It is one example among many of what, at a given historical moment, is constituted as 'commonsense' knowledge, the structures of the *vraisemblable* being therefore regulated by the implicit norms and conventions of that diffuse social text. In the words of Gérard Genette, 'ce qui définit le vraisemblable, c'est le principe formel de respect de la norme, c'est-à-dire l'existence d'un rapport d'implication entre la conduite particulière attribuée à tel personnage, et telle maxime générale implicite et reçue.'[11] An event or a character is, thus, received as *vraisemblable* if it conforms to the norms implicit in a society's general representation of its own reality, and as *invraisemblable* if it deviates from those norms.[12] In other words, the *vraisemblable* is fundamentally a matter of 'general opinion', what the consensus of a particular society generally assumes and receives as 'reality', a culturally regulated construction that goes, however, unrecognized as construction, but is rather hypostasized in what Husserl called the 'natural attitude' of a given social order.

The relationship between the *vraisemblable* and 'common opinion' (between, in Aristotle's terms, 'eikos' and 'endoxon') has been a major point of reflection for contemporary literary theory in France. Thus, for example, Todorov writes in *Qu'est-ce que le structuralisme?*: 'Aristote ... avait déjà clairement dit qu'il ne s'agissait pas d'une relation entre le discours et son référent (relation de vérité), mais entre le discours et ce que les lecteurs croient vrai. La relation s'établit donc ici entre l'oeuvre et un discours diffus qui appartient en partie à chacun des individus d'une société, mais dont aucun ne peut réclamer la propriété; en d'autres mots, à l'opinion commune.'[13] The claim to the authority of Aristotle is in fact somewhat problematical,[14] although, in any case, such illustrious paternity is not essential to the validity of the argument itself. The connection is, however, unequivocally present in seventeenth-century poetics. The critic Rapin describes the *vraisemblable* explicitly as 'tout ce qui est conforme à l'opinion du public',[15] and it is in the sense of an appeal to common opinion that we should also read Scudéry's remark concerning *Le Cid*, 'Il est vrai que Chimène épouse le Cid, mais il n'est point vraisemblable qu'une fille d'honneur épouse le meurtrier de son père'.[16] In short, it is an appeal to what society construes as 'typical' behaviour (although significantly, in the seventeenth century there is a marked tendency, in accounts of the *vraisemblable*, for the cognitive and prescriptive elements of 'common opinion' to shade into each other: Chimène's marriage is both an ethical transgression—what young women of honour should not do, and a logical failure—what young women of honour do not, normally, do). Observing all obvious differences in the transition from the seventeenth to the nineteenth century, it is in this general sense of an appeal to consensus that we should also interpret Castille's strictures on Balzac. What makes Castille's document such an important one is that through it speaks the voice of the nineteenth-century *vraisemblable*; when we read Castille's description of Balzac's characters as 'exceptions', as not 'belonging to humanity', what we are witnessing is Balzac being brought to trial before the authority of nineteenth-century common opinion, being judged according to the assumptions of the nineteenth-century 'endoxal' text, assumptions occulted as self-evident truths of nature (in this particular case, human nature).

One way of approaching the question of 'exaggeration' in Balzac is, therefore, by seeing it in relation to the constructions of reality hypostasized in the 'natural attitude' of the early nineteenth century. Yet—and it is this that makes the question such an instructively ambiguous one—there is in fact a vast level of Balzac's own writing that is held within the very codes of *vraisemblance* from which Castille sees Balzac's work, at its decisive moments, as radically departing. The paradox becomes apparent if, for example, we consider some of Balzac's own statements on the nature of the *vraisemblable*. There is no fully articulated theory of *vraisemblance* to be found in Balzac's diverse writings on literature and art; it is, rather, a question of reconstituting a more or less coherent approach from a number of relatively undeveloped and scattered observations. Broadly speaking, as we have seen in a previous chapter, Balzac follows the Aristotelian distinction between the 'probable' and the 'true': 'Le vrai souvent ne serait pas vraisemblable, de même que le vrai littéraire ne saurait être le vrai de la nature.' (XI, 366-7); 'L'historien des moeurs . . . doit rendre tout probable, même le vrai' (VIII, 154); 'Je ne cesserai de répéter que le vrai de la nature ne peut être, ne sera jamais le vrai de l'art.'[17] The distinction between the 'vrai' and the 'vraisemblable', between the 'vrai de la nature' and the 'vrai de l'art' is confidently, indeed emphatically affirmed. But what, for Balzac, are the foundations of the latter, what, in specific terms, is the 'logic', the system of rules that regulates the creation and the functioning of the 'vrai de l'art'? In a continuation of one of the above remarks, Balzac, following another major emphasis of Aristotle's *Poetics*, suggests that it is primarily a matter of establishing the internal logic of the narrative, of elaborating an inner coherence from which all elements of the random and the fortuitous are rigorously excluded (at the level of plot we have already seen the kinds of tension between different narrative demands that this can involve): 'Je ne cesserai de répéter que le vrai de l'art ne peut être, ne sera jamais le vrai de l'art. . . . Le génie de l'artiste consiste à choisir les circonstances naturelles qui deviennent les éléments du Vrai littéraire et, *s'il ne les soude pas bien*.... l'oeuvre est manquée.'[18] However, a created coherence can, theoretically at least, be a purely arbitrary one. What therefore validates it as a form of 'truth', as a significantly representative arrangement of experience, as distinct from a purely arbitrary one? Here Balzac is strikingly explicit in his recognition of the social and cultural basis of such a validation; the narrative achieves the status of 'truth' precisely in the degree to which it coincides with the assumptions of 'common opinion', with what people generally regard as true: 'La vérité littéraire consiste à choisir des faits et des caractères, à les élever à un point de vue où chacun les croie vrais en les apercevant.'[19] It is therefore a matter of appeal to consensus, to common-sense knowledge. In his review of Hugo's *Hernani*, Balzac dismisses the play as *invraisemblable* on the grounds that 'la conduite des personnages' is 'contraire au bon sens';[20] in a letter to Mme Hanska, he states that 'notre pays est fanatique du vrai, c'est le pays du bon sens'.[21] Here the idea of the 'true' is fully assimilated into the space of common-sense, the space of the 'natural attitude' ('the natural attitude is the attitude of common-sense consciousness'[22]), and the implications of this for the art of fiction are further clarified in his *Lettres sur la littérature*: 'Les personnages d'un roman sont tenus à déployer plus de raison que les personnages historiques. Ceux-ci demandent à vivre, ceux-là ont vécu. L'existence des uns n'a pas besoin de preuves, quelque bizarres qu'aient été leurs actes, tandis que l'existence des autres doit être appuyée par *un consentement unanime*.'[23] The 'raison', the logic of the fiction, is therefore rooted in and assured by the 'consentement unanime' of the readers, the credibility (*vraisemblance*) of the characters being directly dependent on a common assent and on common assumptions shared by author and reader concerning the nature of 'reality'.

In Balzac's reflections there is, therefore, a fairly clear connection between the conventions of *vraisemblance* and the endoxal text of social knowledge. This social knowledge (what Roland Barthes in his analysis of *Sarrasine* has called the 'codes culturels' or 'codes référentiels')*

---

*Because of its extremely fruitful possibilities as an analytical tool, I have used Barthes's concept of the 'cultural code' throughout this chapter as if it were relatively unproblematical. There are, however, a number of difficulties attaching to it, some of which should perhaps be briefly commented on here. The first and most fundamental problem concerns the basis on which we can justifiably identify certain items of the Balzac text as direct citations from the social text of common opinion. Quite simply, how do we know that a given generalization in the text derives from the existing stock of a collective wisdom? To approach the issue at this level is to encounter the often intractable requirements and constraints of empirical verification; legitimate use of the concept of the cultural code to describe certain operations of Balzac's novels would seem therefore to entail a detailed archeology of the belief-systems and discursive practices of the early nineteenth century. But this raises all the problems inherent in attempts at historical reconstruction of a 'collective consciousness'; at what point, for example, are we entitled to stop our researches and claim that we have a satisfactory number of empirical correlations; alternatively (often a problem for historical sociology), what if there is a shortage of the relevant material from which to construct such correlations? This is a difficult issue, but it is in fact something of a red-herring. For the important point about the cultural code in the *Comédie humaine* is that Balzac repeats not so much the content of the nineteenth-century *doxa* as its underlying forms (the maxim, proverb, tautology, enthymeme, etc.). What matters is that he deploys not so much the specific 'utterances' of nineteenth-century consensus-knowledge (what people in society generally held to be the case) as its underlying 'grammar', a syntax rather than a stock of wisdom; to pursue further the analogy from linguistics, Balzac exploits less the specific 'performances' of the endoxal text that its regulative 'competence' which, once its basic rules and strategies have been mastered, is of course capable of generating a theoretically infinite set of 'new' (though formally similar) utterances. In fact many of Balzac's typifications and generalizations are almost certainly invented by him and are not drawn from a pre-existing corpus of norms and beliefs (for example, the code of 'la femme de trente ans' is probably to a large extent Balzac's own creation, itself in turn entering into and modifying the public *doxa*). It is in this sense that we can speak of Balzac as inventing his own *doxa*; with a quite staggeringly imperturbable self confidence and formidable persuasive power, he generates a system of knowledge and meaning entirely from within the *Comédie humaine* itself and to which, in a circular gesture of self-validation, appeal is continually made to vouchsafe the *vraisemblance* of his narrative.

To see Balzac as inventing, rather than repeating, an endoxal text may help to illuminate and resolve another problem associated with Barthes's account of the workings of the cultural code in Balzac: namely, the insistently explicit nature of the social 'knowledge' offered by the text. In Barthes's analysis, the cultural code designates the area of knowledge and understanding assumed by the text as being in the possession of the reader and, as such, the analysis seems to imply the existence in both Balzac's work and the culture to which it belongs of a high degree of cultural and ideological homogeneity, of a universally shared *sagesse* speaking univocally through the text. Yet, as Genette has pointed out, the prime feature of a truly homogeneous culture is the essentially implicit or 'silent' nature of the relationship that obtains between the naturalized consensus of that culture and its works of literature. The 'truths' of the constructions of 'common opinion' are so taken for granted that they do not even have to be named by the text; they are simply assumed: 'Le récit vraisemblable est donc un récit dont les actions répondent, comme autant d'applications ou de cas particuliers, à un corps de maximes reçues comme vraies par le public auquel il s'adresse; mais ces maximes, du fait même qu'elles sont admises, restent le plus souvent implicites. Le rapport entre le récit vraisemblable et le système de vraisemblance auquel il s'astreint est donc essentiellement muet.' (*Figures*, p. 17) But how much do Balzac's fictions actually assume? Very often what is assumed is the reverse, namely, an absence of the knowledge vital to the intelligibility of the narrative and which therefore has to be explicitly developed for the reader by the narrator. This may simply be a matter of empirical ignorance arising out of geographical separation or regional difference as, for example, in *Eugénie Grandet* where the detailed account of the manners of provincial life is offered on the grounds that such knowledge may not be available to the Parisian reader (*Eugénie Grandet*, p. 483). The question, however, becomes more problematical at the level of the generalizing rhetoric, as distinct from the purely descriptive or documentary explanations. Genette suggests that the function of the more or less proverbial generalizations is to create a 'vraisemblable artificiel', to provide pragmatic 'motivators' for narrative sequences whose motivation is otherwise uncertain or absent. In a more sociological perspective, however, it might be suggested that the very explicitness of the text signifies the beginnings of a breakdown of cultural homogeneity. It is as if Balzac can no longer take everything for granted; as if he had to remind the reader of a 'truth' that he might have forgotten, or to persuade the reader of a 'truth' he might not automatically hold to or have even heard of. Paradoxically, the energetic insistence of the Balzacian *discours* speaks perhaps of the lack of that complete poise and confidence which a culture based on implicit recognitions enjoys; of an opening up within the society of division, specialization, fragmentation in the sphere of 'knowledge', which the rhetoric tries to cover up and pull together. Such a reading would doubtless gain support from the point made by Berger and Luckmann that in a society (such as Balzac's) based on the increasing division of labour, ideological and cultural unity tends to give way to the saturates the *Comédie humaine* at almost every point. Take, for instance, the following passage from *Gambara*:

> Après un tour de galerie, le jeune homme regarda tour à tour le ciel et sa montre, fit un geste d'impatience, entra dans un bureau de tabac, y alluma un cigare, se posa devant une glace, et jeta un regard sur son costume, un peu plus riche que ne le permettent en France les lois du goût. Il rajusta son col et son gilet de velours noir sur lequel se croisait plusieurs fois une de ces grosses chaînes d'or fabriquées à Gênes; puis après avoir jeté par un seul mouvement sur son épaule gauche son manteau doublé de velours en le drapant avec élégance, il reprit sa promenade sans se laisser distraire par les oeillades bourgeoises qu'il recevait. Quand les boutiques commencèrent à s'illuminer et que la nuit parut assez noire, il se dirigea vers la place du Palais-Royal en homme qui craignait d'être reconnu, car il côtoya la place jusqu' à la fontaine, pour gagner à l'abri des fiacres l'entrée de la rue Froidmanteau (xı, 416).

This passage constitutes a particularly interesting example because it is precisely this extract that the linguist Emile Benveniste has adduced as evidence of the exact reverse of what is being argued here. In his *Problèmes de linguistique générale*, Benveniste, in a specific consideration of the language of narrative, makes a fundamental distinction between what he calls 'discours' and 'histoire'. By 'histoire' Benveniste understands 'la présentation des faits survenus à un certain moment du temps sans aucune intervention du locuteur dans le récit', while 'discours' is defined as 'toute énonciation supposant un locuteur et un auditeur, et chez le premier l'intention d'influencer l'autre en quelque manière'.[24] As an illustration of 'énonciation historique', Benveniste cites the passage from Balzac's *Gambara* of which he writes: 'A vrai dire, il n'y a même plus alors de narrateur. Les événements sont posés comme ils se sont produits à mesure qu'ils apparaissent à l'horizon de l'histoire. Personne ne parle ici; les événements semblent se raconter eux-mêmes. Le temps fondamental est l'aoriste, qui est le temps de l'événement hors de la

emergence of variations in the social distribution of knowledge, to 'socially segrated sub-universes of meaning . . . It goes without saying that the multiplication of perpectives greatly increases the problem of establishing a stable symbolic canopy for the entire society' (p. 102). This explanation might also help to account for the many instances of contradiction in the Balzacian *discours*, the contradictions springing to a certain extent from the plurality of competing codes at work in a society that finds itself in a radically unsettled state of division and transition. Thus, in *La Cousine Bette* the behaviour of Adeline vis-à-vis her husband is described and evaluated in terms of two quite contradictory codes. On the one hand, the *discours* draws upon the emphases of the Christian text, presenting Adeline's conduct admiringly as 'sainte', 'sublime', 'héroique', etc. On the other hand, it is also described critically in terms of the values of the prudential Bourgeois text: 'Les sentiments nobles poussés à l'absolu produisent des résultats semblables à ceux des grands vices.' There is clearly an uncertainty of stance here, and this may well be directly connected to our main concern—the ambiguity of Hulot, the way he is able, as it were, to 'slip through' the endoxal constraints of the text.

personne d'un narrateur.'[25] In terms of the specifically linguistic criteria that Benveniste uses, in particular, his view of the status of the pronoun and the significance of the different tenses of the verb, the passage from *Gambara* (with the exception of one phrase which Benveniste acknowledges) would seem fully to exemplify the notion of an 'histoire pure'. Yet, as Genette has pointed out,[26] through the use of other categories and criteria it can easily be shown that Benveniste's analysis is extremely oversimplified and that the passage in question is in fact impregnated with the discursive mode. Benveniste himself recognizes that the phrase 'son costume un plus riche que ne le permettent pas en France les lois du goût' is an 'authorial' reflection to be situated at the level of 'discours' and not of 'histoire'. There are, however, other items of the passage that would have to be classified in a similar way: thus, 'avec élégance' and 'oeillades bourgeoises' contain interpretations or judgments as distinct from a purely objective presentation of facts and, as such, must necessarily refer back to the subjective source of a narrator ('subjectivity' here must not be misinterpreted—the voice that speaks is the anonymous, diffuse voice that issues from and is organized by that body of texts through which the culture to which Balzac belongs articulates and naturalizes its reality); again, 'une de ces chaînes fabriquées à Gênes' and 'en homme qui craignait' are instances of authorial intrusion in that they refer beyond the specifics of the particular episode to an extraneous body of knowledge (the kind of chains made at Genoa) and to a set of general psychological assumptions (what constitutes a man in a state of fear), references, that is, which can be accounted for only in terms of an implied address by a narrator to his readers.

If we have picked up the limitations in Benveniste's reading of this extract from *Gambara*, it is because it is instructive in at least three respects. In the first place, it shows the extent to which, even in a passage scrupulously chosen by Benveniste for its narrative 'objectivity', Balzac's work is strongly marked by the presence of an authorial 'rhetoric' (using the term 'rhetoric' here in Wayne Booth's sense of the term). Secondly it reveals something of the great variety of stylistic forms through which that presence makes itself felt, running from the choice of a single epithet to a fuller and more explicit intrusion. Thirdly, it yields a precise illustration of the general nature and function of Balzac's rhetoric, for what the various discursive elements in the passage have in common is the assumption they make of a common area, of a community of knowledge, understanding and feeling shared by narrator and reader. The 'discours' assumes that the reader is aware of 'les lois du goût en France', that he know the kind of 'chaînes fabriquées à Gênes', that he understands the implications of the social concepts 'avec élégance' and 'bourgeoises', and so on.

The operations of 'discours' are in fact virtually omnipresent in the *Comédie humaine*, their essential function being to found, guarantee and demonstrate the intelligibility of the 'histoire'; they furnish the general system of understanding without which the particular actions and situations of the narrative would not be fully comprehensible. Basically, two types of 'knowledge' are involved here, although any schematic distinction is blurred by a good deal of actual overlap between the two. Firstly, there are references to knowledge of a purely empirical or factual order, such as the mass of historical and topographical detail that is such a regular feature of the novels. This knowledge can either be assumed, as in ('Adeline . . . pouvait être comparée à la fameuse Mme du Barry' (VI, 154), and 'Réunis par la catastrophe de Fontainbleau, les trois frères Fischer. . . .'(VI, 161), where it is assumed that the reader grasps the historical allusions; or alternatively, it can be explicitly elaborated (generally in the context of Balzac's celebrated 'expositions'), and asserted as vital to a proper understanding of the story: thus, the long topographical survey of Issoudun in *La Rabouilleuse* is prefaced by the remark: 'Sans cette peinture, on comprendrait difficilement l'héroisme que déployait Mme Hochon, en secourant sa filleul et l'étrange situation de Jean-Jacques Rouget' (III, 934); or again, in *Illusions perdues*, 'Il est d'autant plus nécessaire d'entrer ici dans quelques explications sur Angoûleme qu'elles feront comprendre . . . Mme de Bargeton, l'un des personnages les plus importants de cette histoire' (VI, 490). Secondly—and, for our purposes, far more important—there are the references to what we would call social 'knowledge' proper, that is, collective opinion socially objectivated as knowledge, that tissue of accumulated experiences, common attitudes and consolidated beliefs which form the corporate 'wisdom' of society and which enters in a decisive way into that society's construction of its own intelligibility. It is here that we can locate the significance of all those clichés, proverbs, generalizations of a psychological, social or moral bearing with which the Balzacian text is so liberally furnished: 'Quand il s'agit de se précipiter dans les abîmes, les jeunes gens font preuve d'une adresse, d'une habileté singulières' (IV, 390); 'En toute situation, les femmes ont plus de causes de douleur que n'en a l'homme' (III, 597); 'Enfin, né gracieux, comme presque tous les enfants de l'amour'(III, 957); 'l'avarice commence où la pauvreté cesse' (IV, 466); 'Il est un âge où la femme pardonne des vices à qui lui évite des contrariétés' (III, 105); 'les séducteurs à petits motifs ne comprennent jamais les grandes âmes' (VI, 143); 'la paresse, état normal à tous les artistes' (VI, 323); 'en ceci consiste peut-être toute la différence qui sépare l'homme naturel de l'homme civilisé' (VI, 165). In context, all these comments refer out from the particular situation or character, at a given moment in the novels in question, to a principle of psychological reality or social conduct whose normative status is taken for granted; through the activity of the 'discours', the particular is generalized into a 'law' of being or behaviour to whose validity it is assumed the reader will subscribe. In more precise terms, the process here is a two-way one: the general law, itself validated by the consensus of received opinion, renders the particular act intelligible, assures its *vraisemblance*, while the particular is offered as a purely empirical notation which serves to illustrate and to 'prove' the validity of the general law—a strategy that we might describe as the literary equivalent of tautology (all the more marked in the case of the nineteenth-century novel, the history of whose empirical 'realism' has not only reflected but, at certain levels, actively modelled the *vraisemblable* of our culture; it is in this sense that Sollers's reference to 'le mythe du roman' in the remark cited at the beginning of this chapter is to be understood).

The 'discours' thus serves to establish the *vraisemblable* of the text in that, by continually affirming its drawing rights upon the socially available fund of endoxal 'truths', it focuses and emphasizes the representative value of the particular elements of the fiction and, more globally, of their combination into a whole. In other words, the social language, the cultural paradigms which structure the *vraisemblable* are above all reflected in the elaboration of the type—which at once returns us to the terms of Castille's criticism and simultaneously brings us to the very heart of Balzac's own conception of his literary enterprise. For Balzac the notion of 'typicality', the production of a comprehensive fictional typology of contemporary society, was the cornerstone of the *Comédie humaine*; in the words of the *Avant-propos*, 'en composant des types par la réunion des traits de plusieurs caractères homogènes, peut-être pouvais-je arriver à écrire l'histoire oubliée par tant d'autres historiens, celle des moeurs' (I, 7). But where do these typical configurations come from, what are the criteria and the rules which determine that one pattern can be seen as typical and another as atypical? To a very large extent, the answer lies in a restatement of precisely the argument we have been considering in relation to the nature of the *vraisemblable*. In the preface to *La Femme supérieure* Balzac writes concerning a particular problem of characterization, 'que faire d'un notaire vertueux et joli garçon dans un roman? Vertueux et joli garçon, ce ne serait pas littéraire [i.e. *vraisemblable*], les deux qualités se contrariant' (XI, 362). In strictly formal terms, there is of course no logical reason whatsoever for the necessary incompatibility of good looks and moral virtue; equally, in purely empirical terms, one would be certain of finding actual cases where the two qualities coexist. On both logical and empirical grounds Balzac's statement is therefore a nonsense. It does make sense, however, if we relate it to the existence of a socially conventionalized typology, to the production by a consensus of received opinion of a set of opposed types (*homme vertueux/joli garçon*), naturalized, in the form of an implicit proverb, as an eternal law of nature ('handsome young men are rarely virtuous'). Berger and Luckmann have indeed explicitly stressed both the role of typification in the way we constitute and apprehend our social reality as Reality ('the social reality of everyday life is apprehended in a continuum of typifications'), and also the importance of the various forms of social knowledge, especially its linguistic forms such as the proverb and the maxim, as the prime source of the typificatory schemes a given culture uses ('Language typifies experience, allowing us to subsume them under broad categories in terms of which they have meaning not only to myself but also to my fellow-men. . . . The social stock of knowledge supplies me therefore with the typificatory schemes required for the major routines of everyday life.')[27]. In the specific case of literature, this connection between the verbal forms of social knowledge and the constitution of the typical may be further glossed by reference to the link suggested by Kenneth Burke between literary texts and the proverb; in his essay *Literature as Equipment for Living*, Burke writes: '[Proverbs] name typical recurrent situations. That is, people find a certain social relationship recurring so frequently that they must "have a word for it". . . . Social structures give rise to "type" situations. . . . Why not extend such analysis of proverbs to encompass the whole field of literature?'[28] There can, of course, be no question of extending the significance of the proverb 'to encompass the whole field of literature', but Burke's remarks are certainly relevant to the quasi-proverbial generalizations enunciated by the 'discours' of the Balzacian text. The most characteristic of these are, precisely, so many linguistic typifications: 'comme toutes les Parisiennes' (VI, 276); 'un de ces gens qui' (173); 'une de ces toilettes que les Parisiennes inventent' (382); 'douée d'une finesse devenue profonde, comme chez tous les gens voués à un célibat réel' (162); 'Crevel, incapable de comprendre les arts, comme tous les bourgeois' (427); 'elle était envahie par un amour que toutes les jeunes filles ont subi' (172); 'ce naturel de l'Amérique, logique comme le sont tous les hommes nés dans la nature' (295); 'les coquets mensonges que débitent presque toutes les femmes dans la situation où se trouvait Valérie' (262); 'le type de ces ambitieuses courtisanes mariées' (265); 'l'esprit diabolique de ces sortes de femmes' (270); 'les avantages que le sang donne à tous les vrais gentilshommes' (283); 'Marneffe appartenait à cette nature d'employés . . . le type que chacun' (181); 'l'appartement, occupé par ce ménage, type de beaucoup de ménages parisiens' (181); 'il fumait comme tous les gens qui ont ou des chagrins ou de l'énergie à endormir' (192); 'comme toutes les belles âmes, le pauvre garçon oubliait le mal' (195); 'un de ces héroiques efforts dont sont capables les grandes mères' (345). All these examples, taken from the single text of *La Cousine Bette*, refer to a whole range of individual experiences, feelings, actions, personalities, environments, practices, objects, with the sole purpose of rescuing them from their isolated contingency in order to invest them with typical or paradigmatic significance, the validity of the paradigms resting in turn on an appeal to common-sense knowledge, on what, in *Le Père Goriot*, Balzac claims that 'un homme de bon sens' (II, 948) would accept as the normal and the characteristic.

We have, then, three principles—*vraisemblance*, typicality and social knowledge (the first two are virtually synonymous and together can be subsumed under the general umbrella of the third) which indicate the extent to which the 'representation' of 'reality' in the *Comédie humaine* is shaped by the assumptions or the 'grammar' of the nineteenth-century endoxal text. In other words, in a number of vital respects, Balzac seems to conform to the attitudes of his contemporary critic, Hippolyte Castille, and it should therefore come as no surprise to find Balzac elsewhere expressing a view about fiction which is virtually identical to that of Castille: 'Les exceptions ne doivent jamais jouer dans l'action d'un roman qu'un rôle accessoire. Les héros doivent être des généralités.'[29] We are faced, therefore, with something of a paradox: that of a novelist endorsing, in both theory and practice, a view of 'realistic' fiction held by a critic who describes crucial areas of that very novelist's work as deviations from that view, thus laying the ground for the charges of 'exaggeration' that will reappear as such a constant feature of later Balzac criticism. Clearly, the paradox suggests the presence of a radical tension between different levels of writing in the *Comédie*. On the one hand, there is the level that is deeply implicated in the conventions and constraints of literary 'representation' prescribed by the *vraisemblable* of the early nineteenth century (precisely that level which Castille, whose review is not in fact entirely negative, can accept as 'realistic'). On the other hand, there is the level which conflicts violently with that *vraisemblable*, which cannot be accounted for or named by the typifying enunciations of the Balzacian 'discours'. And could it perhaps be that it is just this level which forms the most radical, subversive, 'modern' dimension of Balzac's work? 'Le narrateur est tout' (XI, 180) is the confident comment of the preface to the *Scènes de la vie parisienne* and, identifying 'narrateur' in Benveniste's sense of 'discours', one can perhaps construe this as signifying, among other things, the triumphant hegemony of the endoxal over the whole of the *Comédie humaine*. Yet against that comment, one should set the remark in *Sarrasine*, 'l'aventure a des passages dangereux pour le narrateur' (VI, 92), a sense of 'danger' which Barthes has linked to what he calls a certain 'trouble de la représentation',[30] a fissuring of the otherwise fixed certitudes of 'realistic' narrative. 'J'ai eu trop de foi aux proverbes' (V, 842) observes one of the characters of *Splendeurs et misères des courtisanes*, and one is strongly tempted to say the same about many of Balzac's most influential critics. Confronted with that dimension of the text which resists incorporation into stereotyped constructions of reality, they scornfully reject that element as 'exaggerated', 'improbable', 'melodramatic'. In short, it becomes what, borrowing a phrase from Georges Bataille, we might call 'la part maudite' of the text, existing in a strange, disturbing relation with the more 'respectable', conformist aspects of the text, putting into question and undermining the mere repetition of familiar, habitualized modes of representation and understanding. It is this interplay of conformity and subversion, repetition and transgression that I now want to look at in some more detail through the figure of Hulot in *La Cousine Bette*. †

† It will of course have been noticed—the absence is such a glaring one—that, in the account given here of the relationship between *vraisemblance* and the type, there has been no reference to what is perhaps the most fully developed theory of typicality in fiction,

namely Lukács's *Studies in European Realism*. Clearly, any adequate description of the problems of the fictional type must at some point encounter and seek to incorporate the ideas of Lukács. In terms of the present argument, Lukács's theory is in fact of quite exemplary value in that, among other things, it is a theory of typicality which not only explicitly confronts but also attempts to accommodate the principle of 'exaggeration'; and indeed, to make exaggeration a constitutive feature of Balzac's typification procedures which are themselves, in turn, identified as forming the heart of Balzac's 'realism'. Roughly stated, Lukács's argument is that Balzac was a writer struggling to represent the as yet unrepresented, unnamed forces of an emerging capitalist society, and that in order to achieve this, he had to create a literary convention within which the construction of the type (as representation of the essence of society) would entail, to borrow from the vocabulary of the Russian Formalists (although, sadly, Lukács would almost certainly have resisted being placed in such company), a certain de-formation or 'making strange' of established modes of social and historical understanding; in these terms, Balzac's typology, through its attempt to do something new, necessarily stands in a relation of opposition to the inherited typologies (both social and fictional) of the *doxa*, and was bound therefore to be received as 'exaggerated' by many of his contemporaries (such as Castille).   For Lukács, in short, Balzac—and it is this which makes him the archetypal 'realist' writer—invents a typology, creates a new level of *vraisemblance* that in some senses operates against the norms of the standardized *vraisemblance*; or, to use again a concept from the Russian Formalists, we find in Balzac's work a principle of 'back-grounding' and 'foregrounding', of competing levels of representation, out of which is born a new perception of society which the established models of representation in that society could not recognize or accept.

Lukács's account is a very powerful one. It is, however, an account developed solely in sociological terms, in terms of a specific theory of 'social realism', and it is these constraints which generate the difficulties and limitations of Lukács's position. In the first place, although Balzac's work was originally received as exaggerated in almost every respect, with the passage of time the specifically sociological correctness of Balzac's typology comes more and more to be taken for granted. Indeed the 'Balzacian' model increasingly comes to be seen as *the* model for the representation of history and society. It becomes absorbed into, as well as itself modifying, the nineteenth-century *doxa*, so deeply entrenched that one of the explicit tasks undertaken by Flaubert's *L'Education sentimentale* will be the ironic de-construction of that model (Fréderic Moreau approaches the world in terms of a set of expectations derived partly from his reading of *Le Père Goriot*, expectations that will of course be systematically disappointed). In itself this historical process of the 'recuperation' of Balzac in no way diminishes the force of Lukács's perception of the original link between type and exaggeration in Balzac. The difficulty arises when we set it alongside another phenomenon: the fact that, despite the massive 'doxalizing' of the Balzacian novel, there has nevertheless persisted, right up to the present day, a strong critical voice which still speaks of 'exaggeration' as central to the *Comedie humaine*. This is a fact in the history of reading and criticism that has to be explained. One could theoretically postulate that this ongoing voice is a kind of anachronism, somehow bypassed by history, which is still speaking on the basis of the same assumptions as Castille. But that is *prima facie* a somewhat implausible assumption. What is more likely is that, despite the historical promotion of Balzac to being the great Realist writer (in which Lukács's own argument has played a big role), there still remains a level of 'anomalous' matter in the writing to which Lukács's account is not adequate, and which a roughly contemporary criticism has been able to deal with only by returning to the vocabulary of Castille's day. Balzac, we might say, 'exaggerates' in directions other than those which can be formalized in Lukácsian terms, and for which another explanatory language is necessary (for example, that of psychoanalysis). This is not, however, to reject Lukács's reading, which still remains one of the best we have. On the contrary, I am directly following the example of Lukács in proposing and distinguishing different 'levels' at which the Balzacian text can be described, but also pushing the argument a stage beyond the terms of Lukács's own description. I am postulating a level of explanation which has only recently come fully into focus, which was unavailable to the early nineteenth

In the opening pages of *La Cousine Bette* Hulot is introduced to us in the following terms: 'monsieur le baron Hulot d'Ervy, commissaire ordonnateur sous la République, ancien-intendant général d'armée, et alors directeur d'une des plus importantes administrations du Ministère de la Guerre, Conseiller d'Etat, grand officier de la Légion d'Honneur, etc, etc' (VI, 136). A sequence of historical references and bureaucratic and honorific titles, this opening passage marks the various stages of an illustrious public career that spans almost half a century of French history. The passage is, however, more than a collection of various items of biographical information; through the phrase 'etc, etc', which indicates that the enumeration could be continued but that it is not necessary to do so, the writing here directs our attention not just to the individual items as isolated bits of information, but also to the fact that it is working within a known, a familiar code: the code of *Who's Who*, of the newspaper diary (the style of this opening passage will be directly and ironically echoed in the newspaper announcement giving the official 'reasons' for Hulot's resignation from high office), of any of those conventionalized texts, all the activity of which is to situate a given individual within the paradigm of the Eminent Person (in this particular case the distinguished public servant). In other words, through a gesture that we have already seen to be highly characteristic, the 'discours' of the novel seeks to establish Hulot as a 'realistic' fictional character by presenting him as a recognizable type, identifiable in terms of known social and historical patterns.

This procedure is indeed a more or less systematic one; in the first half of the novel a whole plethora of typifications is brought into play in the construction of Hulot's fictional presence. Thus, to stay within the code of historical knowledge, one of the major emphases of the 'discours' is on the importance of Hulot's past as a Napoleonic soldier; we are invited, for example, to 'read' Hulot's physical appearance as signifying

century, and which has been ignored or refused by much subsequent critical thought—a level which can be semi-formalized in terms of, say (to stay simply with the names cited in the body of the argument), the ideas of Freud and Bataille.

Naturally, the logic of such an argument dictates that this level of explanation is itself equally susceptible to 'recuperation'. For, as Todorov has remarked (*Poétique de la prose*, p. 99), however critically aware one becomes of the relative, context-bound nature of specific systems of *vraisemblance*, there is never any escaping the formal principle of *vraisemblance* as such, since this is a constitutive condition of any form of intelligible utterance. Every discourse, including the discourse which takes the *vraisemblable* as its object of critical inquiry, necessarily entails its own *vraisemblable*, which can in turn become the object of another discourse, and so on into that infinite regress of commentary and meta-commentary central to semiological theory. It is in this perspective that Todorov, referring to the relationship between 'truth' and *vraisemblance*, can speak of the former as nothing other than 'un vraisemblable distancé et différé'. Such an approach might provide a basis for writing a formal history of the novel as a dialectic of affirmations and negations, as a process in which a given *vraisemblable* is met (sometimes within the same text) by an *anti-vraisemblable*, which is subsequently absorbed into a new code of *vraisemblance* in turn generating its own opposite; our strongest sense of this process comes, of course, from those texts conventionally classified as 'anti-novels', such as *Don Quixote*, *Tristram Shandy*, *Jacques le fataliste*, *Bouvard et Pécuchet*.

his role as a representative figure of the military aristocracy of the Imperial period: 'Le baron Hector Hulot se montra dans une tenue parlementaire et napoléonnienne, car on distingue facilement les Impériaux (gens attachés à l'Empire), à leur cambrure militaire, à leurs habits bleus à boutons d'or (vi, 173); again, the crimes of fraud Hulot commits against the state, in order to finance his sexual adventures, are not seen simply as madly aberrant acts, but are explained by means of an explicit historical generalization, as characteristic or 'typical' of the values of the Napoleonic military caste in which he has been formed:

> Une des particularités du caractère bonapartiste, c'est la foi dans la puissance du sabre, la certitude de la prééminence du militaire sur le civil. Hulot se moquait du procureur du roi de l'Algérie, où règne le Ministère de la Guerre. L'homme reste ce qu'il a été. Comment les officiers de la Garde impériale peuvent-ils oublier d'avoir vu les Maires des bonnes villes de l'Empire, les Préfets de l'Empereur, ces empereurs au petit pied, venant recevoir la Garde impériale, la complimenter à la limite des départements qu'elle traversait, et lui rendre enfin des honneurs souverains? (374)

Similar typifying operations in the creation of Hulot's 'identity' as a character apply to the presentation of his private life as well as his public life. In an adaptation of the text of Biblical knowledge, the first part of the novel is subtitled *Le Père prodigue*, and hence Hulot is partly constituted in the socially familiar syndrome of the wayward father, whose sexual peccadilloes lead to the betrayal of familial obligations and responsibilities. Equally, in its initial descriptions of Hulot's *amours*, the rhetoric draws extensively on an endoxal text of psychological 'wisdom', on a body of psychological generalizations that society has accumulated around the type known and named as the libertine: 'Les libertins, ces gens que la nature a doués de la faculté précieuse d'aimer au-delà des limites que la nature a fixé à l'amour, n'ont presque jamais leur âge' (373); 'c'était bien là un de ces hommes dont les yeux s'animent à la vue d'une jolie femme' (173); le moraliste ne saurait nier que généralement les gens bien élevés et très vicieux ne soient beaucoup plus aimables que les gens vertueux' (175); 'Le libertin ressentit cette vive impression, passagère chez tous les Parisiens, quand ils rencontrent une jolie femme' (180); 'A cet âge, l'amour chez les vieux hommes se change en vice' (158). Finally, the 'discours' seeks to erect a bridge between the public and private domains of Hulot's experience, between history and psychology, by insisting that Hulot's libertinage is in many respects the inevitable product of specific historical circumstances, namely the downfall of the Napoleonic Empire: 'Inoccupé de 1818 à 1823, le baron Hulot s'était mis en service actif auprès des femmes. Mme Hulot faisait remonter les premières infidélités de son Hector au grand finale de l'Empire' (156).

By referring the reader to various interrelated areas of assumed 'knowledge' (historical, social, psychological), Balzac makes a serious and substantial attempt to elaborate Hulot's character and situation in terms of a number of 'typical' roles and contexts—as aristocrat, soldier, public servant, father, husband, libertine. In other words, the panoply of historical reference and psychological generalization constructed by the 'discours' of the novel serves, as it does with all the other characters in the book, to locate and define Hulot within a general, culturally based system of intelligibility, to render him intelligible ('readable') by inserting him into the diffuse text of the *vraisemblable*. As a novelistic creation, Hulot seems therefore to be securely ensconced within the established conventions of realistic 'representation'; he conforms unproblematically to what is generally received as 'reality' in terms both of the patterns of contemporary history and those of an enduring 'human nature'. Yet, as the narrative unfolds, culminating in Hulot's dismissal from public life and his disappearance into the Parisian lower depths, the assumption of that security increasingly comes under pressure until finally we reach the point where it simply cracks, where none of the cultural typifications, either individually or in combination, can contain what Hulot becomes. And it is, of course, at just this point that Hulot becomes problematical for a certain kind of literary criticism. At the moment of Hulot's exposure and disgrace, the Prince de Wissembourg remarks to him that he is 'plus un homme mais un tempérament' (421), echoed by the baron's brother, the Comte de Forzheim, 'cet homme est un monstre' (425). The remarks are interesting in a number of respects, but what specifically concerns us here is that the terms of the text itself have often been mobilized by criticism in the development of the argument against Balzac. The moral excess seen by the Prince as entailing a loss of humanity in Hulot has been construed by the critic as also, and in a radically disabling sense, a literary excess on the part of the author; the obsessional intensity of Hulot's transgression of the codes of sexual conduct is the author's transgression of the codes of psychological *vraisemblance*; a scandal not only on the ethical and social planes, but on the artistic plane, a scandal, that is, of literary 'representation'. In short, how can one 'believe' in Hulot as a fully realized, representative fictional creation?

Yet a criticism working within this framework of assumptions in fact misses what is most vital. It fails to see that, straining against the barriers of classic representation which otherwise contain so much of the Balzac text, and piercing through the thickly encrusted surface imposed by the naturalizing discourse of social knowledge, there is a significant move towards another, more radical mode of perception and writing, to which the 'common-sense' descriptions of 'exaggerated', 'unrealistic', 'melodramatic' are simply not adequate. The scale of Hulot's erotic adventures brings about a massive collapse, a disintegration at a number of levels that needs to be accounted for in terms quite different from those usually offered by traditional criticism. When Hulot withdraws from the scene of public life, Balzac describes him as 'cet homme quasi dissous' (VI, 425), and it is, precisely, a process of radical dissolution that we witness in the final stages of the book. At one level, it is a dissolution, under the pressure of erotic desire, of the different structures which throughout the narrative appeared to sustain Hulot's identity as a recognizable social being. In his book, *L'Erotisme*, Georges Bataille has connected the erotic experience with the experience of a certain kind of death, with the dissolution of the self constituted in and by the pragmatic world of everyday social relations and the instrumental categories of the discourse of reason:

> Toute la mise en oeuvre érotique a pour principe une destruction de la structure de l'être fermé qu'est à l'état normal un partenaire du jeu . . . Ce qui est en jeu dans l'érotisme est toujours une dissolution des formes constituées. . . de ces formes de vie sociale, regulière qui fondent l'ordre discontinu des individualités définies que nous sommes . . . Ce terme de dissolution répond à l'idée familière de vie dissolue, liée à l'activité érotique.[31]

In Bataille's suggestive conjunction of the ideas of 'dissolution' and 'dissoluteness' we may perhaps find a context for understanding and evaluating the real significance of Hulot's transgression. When, for instance, after abandoning his family, Hulot arrives at the home of the prostitute Josépha, he presents an image of total dispossession and exile that is significantly more than the rhetoric of self-pity: 'Je suis sans liard, sans espérance, sans pain, sans pension, sans femme, sans enfant, sans asile, sans honneur, sans courage, sans ami' (432). Profession, family, home, wealth, connections, power, prestige—all the social and cultural supports of Hulot's former existence have been swept away by the frenzy of desire; and a few chapters later, when we re-encounter Hulot living with the child-prostitute Atala in the Parisian slums, this motif of social collapse is further reinforced by the startling image of Hulot's physical dereliction:

> Un vieillard, qui paraissait âgé de quatre-vingts ans, aux cheveux entièrement blancs, le nez rougi par le froid dans une figure pâle et ridée comme celle d'une vieille femme, allant d'un pas traînant, les pieds dans des pantoufles de lisière, le dos voûté, vêtu d'une redingote d'alpaga chauve, ne portant pas de décoration, laissant passer à ses poignets les manches d'un gilet tricoté, et la chemise d'un jaune inquiétant, se montra timidement' (465).

Hulot's disappearance into squalid clandestinity is not to be read as a mere change in external social 'circumstance'; still less, despite the strong emphasis on outward decrepitude and decay, does it correspond to the stereotype of the exhausted, broken old man. For the outer signs of ruin and disintegration belie an inner blossoming, the release, in the very midst of squalor and ignominy, of an apparently invincible vigour and vitality, to which the surface forms of social life are utterly irrelevant except in so far as they threaten to impose constraints on what fundamentally animates Hulot. For the psychological mode in which Hulot relates to society is in fact essentially one of 'absence'. In an extremely perceptive article, Fredric Jameson has observed that, at both the opening and the close of the novel, Hulot is presented to us indirectly, through the comments and anecdotes of others, and that 'this formal absence corresponds to a profound reality in the character of Hulot.'[32] Hulot, indeed, is never really 'there'; when he disappears into the slums, he simply concretizes in action what has been inwardly a permanent condition. Society, in its organized forms, never, or only intermittently and weakly, takes hold of him. Thus, when Adeline finds her husband and offers him the possibility of a return to an ordered social life ('tu peux rentrer dans le monde, et tu trouveras d'abord chez ton fils une fortune'), Hulot's response is a curiously vacant and distracted one, expressed in the celebrated, and much criticized, line, 'Je le veux bien . . . mais pourrais-je emmener la petite?' (519). He will, of course, return 'to the fold', a return that is explicitly codified in the chapter heading 'le retour du père prodigue'; but the expectations of reconciliation and readaptation generated by that set of biblical allusions will be totally disappointed. Hulot's return is not a recuperation, and the temporary hold is soon followed by the familiar disruptive pattern of transgression, death (that of Adeline) and departure. No social or moral pressure, whether persuasive or coercive, can restrain Hulot. Mentally he withdraws into the asocial world of pure instinct, the mediations which sustain any 'normal' relation between self and social reality having been dissolved in the flux of pure libido. The final disintegration of Hulot's tenuous connection with established social roles and values, the spectacular collapse of the socially constituted personality, represents therefore the moment at which 'absence' is transformed into presence, the moment at which Hulot truly becomes one with himself. In the language of psychoanalysis, it is as if the energies of the id have joined forces with calculations of the ego to outplay and ultimately to shatter the authority of the superego.

Yet what really needs to be focused here is not so much the 'content', the psychological insights dramatized in Hulot's collapse, as the formal implications of those insights, their implications for Hulot's status as a fictional 'character'. Could it not be that the dissolution of the social persona, of the various transactions that maintain a more or less stable relationship between individual and society, is also the beginning of the dissolution of the solid 'realistic' character? We have seen that, elsewhere in the novel, Balzac works in the very opposite direction: the array of sociological and psychological typifications made available by the 'discours' of the text represents Balzac's attempt to establish Hulot as a substantial, 'realistic' individual, to situate and define him within the schemas of the *vraisemblable*. Yet, in the last analysis, none of these typifications or paradigms—wayward father, adulterous husband, licentious aristocrat—offers a frame of reference in which Hulot can be properly understood. Hulot not only disappears from organized society but, as the social persona evaporates, he also disappears from or transcends the controlling discourse of the novel. Its initial assumptions (Hulot *vraisemblable* because socially and historically known as the 'type' of the Imperial beau, libertine, etc.) can no longer accommodate or account for what he finally becomes, which is something much more impersonal, elemental and elusive than comfortable common-sense definitions can encompass.

Herein lies the deep tension or ambiguity over which the novel hovers. What is at first offered as functioning within the conventions of classic representation, becomes a questioning, a negation of representation, a critical interrogation of the very forms of intelligibility on which the *vraisemblable* is founded. Criticism has in fact been absolutely right to see Hulot as ultimately *invraisemblable*, but absolutely wrong in delivering that description in the form of a hostile value judgment. On the contrary, it is in just that transgression of the codes of *vraisemblance* that we can perceive the truly subversive energies of the text at work, bursting through the limits of the prevailing notions of narrative representation to arrive at the very threshold of 'modernity' ('modernisme, c'est-à-dire mépris des vraisemblances'[33]). In this respect, there is a passage in Nathalie Sarraute's *L'Ere du soupçon*, concerned with the destiny of the *personnage* in the transition from the nineteenth- to the twentieth-century novel, that might be considered relevant here:

> Il [le personnage] était très richement pourvu, comblé de biens de toute sorte, entouré de soins minutieux; rien ne lui manquait depuis les boucles d'argent de sa culotte jusqu'à la loupe veinée au bout de son nez. Il a, peu à peu, tout perdu: ses ancêtres, sa maison soigneusement bâtie, bourrée de la cave au grenier d'objets de toute espèce, jusqu'aux plus menus colifichets, ses propriétés et ses titres de rente, ses vêtements, son corps, son visage, et, surtout, ce bien précieux entre tous, son caractère qui n'appartenait qu'à lui, et souvent jusqu'à son nom.[34]

With but very few modifications, this description of the progressive collapse in the modern novel of the solidly constituted *personnage* of the nineteenth-century novel could be made to fit Hulot. Of particular interest is the last phrase 'et souvent jusqu'à son nom'. It will be recalled that Hulot's disappearance into clandestinity is accompanied by the adoption of pseudonyms: 'le baron Hulot d'Ervy', with all its connotations of social brilliance and distinction, gives way to the pseudonyms Thorec, Thoul, Vyder. 'What's in a name?'[35] asks Joyce's Stephen Dedalus and, from the point of view of the strategies of characterization in the classic novel, the answer, as Robbe-Grillet has pointed out,[36] is almost everything. The proper name is a verbal locus of social identity, an index of belonging to a known social world, and it is in just this respect that, as Proust (who was himself fascinated by the connotations of *le nom*) suggested in *Balzac et Sainte-Beuve*,[37] proper names often function in the *Comédie humaine*: the contemptuous play on the 'bourgeois' name of Goriot by the Duchesse de Langeais, Delphine de Nucingen addressing Clotilde de Grandlieu by her Christian name (Proust's example), the veritable galaxy of proper names habitually invoked at the typical Balzacian *soirée*, all these are instances of the weight of social meaning that can attach to the name in Balzac's work. Pseudonymity is not, of course, the same as anonymity, the absence of name so characteristic of modern fiction; furthermore, at one level, there is a perfectly straightforward 'naturalistic' explanation for Hulot's adoption of a series of pseudonyms. But, in the general context of Hulot's collapse as both social being and fictional character, the abandoning of the illustrious and evocative name and title of 'le baron Hector Hulot d'Ervy' for the neutral names of Thorec, Thoul and Vyder may perhaps be read as a tentative gesture towards that questioning of a socially grounded identity captured in the modern novel through the convention of anonymity. 'Il n'y a pas de nom pour moi' is the panic-stricken remark of the narrator of Beckett's *L'Innommable*;[38] similarly, one might pose the question, how, within the terms of the *vraisemblable*, can one name Hulot? Certainly, as we have seen, none of the typifications (not least that of simple libertine) offered by the text as the initial means of 'naming' Hulot is sufficient. Hulot at his most 'obsessional' is a phenomenon that tends to elude the verbal confidence of Balzac the author-magician, a phenomenon that is fundamentally unnamable, resistant to the mediations of representational language. A kind of 'gap' appears in the text (Hulot's literal disappearance is significantly accompanied by the virtual disappearance of the operations of the 'discours' where he is concerned), an absence or a blank which suggests, perhaps, a certain note of panic in the writing, an anxiety of representation induced by imaginative intuitions that run beyond the reassuring, because culturally stabilized, conventions of *vraisemblance*.

To speak here of 'anxiety' or 'panic' is of course to suggest something analogous to that 'trouble de la représentation' that Barthes, and before him Bataille, have perceived in *Sarrasine*. Yet, though legitimate up to a point, such a comparison needs qualification. For whereas in *Sarrasine* the sense of 'trouble' is linked to the symbolism of castration, that is, to a literal lack or void around which the text feverishly circulates, the partial dissolution of the constituted subject operated by *La Cousine Bette* is founded on the reverse, an exuberant, though disordered, plenitude of sexual being. Whereas in *Sarrasine* the representational economy of the text is troubled by the presence of the relation (much vaunted by contemporary psychoanalytic thought) between desire and a lack, in *La Cousine Bette* the opposite is the case: the problematic of representation issues rather from a narrowing of the gap between desire and its expression to a point where it has almost vanished; to the point where it has become almost imperceptible and unrepresentable, except by way of a certain hyperbolic straining at the text, a hyperbolic tension immediately converted by the language of orthodox criticism into the pejorative 'exaggeration'. Disorganized, certainly, but not dis-organ-ized[39] in the sense in which we may speak of *Sarrasine*, the essential mode of Hulot's apotheosis is less one of panic than of euphoria. In *La Part maudite*, Georges Bataille has written of a certain euphoric authenticity of being that resides in a commitment of energy, both economic and sexual, to the principles of excess and waste, the exhilarating freedom that springs from violently transgressing the pragmatic motive and utilitarian ethic on which social order is founded. Something of that kind of vision comes across in, for example, Josépha's description of Hulot's excesses as a 'brûlage général':

> Est-ce vrai, vieux . . . que tu as tué ton frère et ton oncle, ruiné ta famille, surhypothéqué la maison de tes enfants et mangé la grenouille du gouvernement en Afrique avec la Princesse?
>
> Le Baron inclina tristement la tête.
>
> —Eh bien! j'aime cela! s'écria Josépha qui se leva pleine d'enthousiasme. C'est un *brûlage* général! c'est sardanapale! c'est grand! c'est complet! On est une canaille, mais on a du coeur! Eh bien! j'aime mieux un mange-tout, passionné comme toi pour les femmes, que ces froids banquiers sans âme qu'on dit vertueux et qui ruinent des milliers de familles avec leurs rails qui sont de l'or pour eux et du fer pour les Gogos! (432–3)

It would be oversimple automatically to equate character with author here, especially in a novelist so committed to the autonomy of his creations as Balzac. In terms of Josépha, the flip cynicism of tone is characteristic of her role as a prostitute, a role which moreover hardly equips for the part of the unbiased witness: it is not surprising that she 'admires' Hulot since the 'sardanapale' type is evidently a more profitable sexual investment than the more prudential lecher. Yet, granted its psychological particularity, Josépha's speech does connect with the general euphoric tone of the novel. The description of Hulot as a 'mange-tout' and his activities as a 'brûlage général', in a context which evokes connotations of a certain grandeur, suggests a parallel with Bataille's notion of a liberating 'gaspillage'.[40] The operative contrast here is with the figure of Crevel. Crevel, the representative of the bourgeois social order, of an order bent on accumulation and regulated by calculating self-interest ('la haine de la dépense est la raison d'être et la justification de la bourgeoisie',[41] comments Bataille), is the individual whose pursuit of pleasure is never in excess of the limits imposed by the prudential ethic; for him, everything, including the erotic, is seen in function of the security of his investments; he will freely spend interest, but never, never bite into capital: 'Madame . . . un ancien négociant est et doit être grand

seigneur avec ordre, avec économie. . . . On ouvre un compte aux fre-
daines, on les crédite, on consacre à ce chapitre certains bénéfices; mais
entamer son capital . . . ce serait une folie!' (397). Measured against
Crevel's trivial, calculating lecheries, Hulot's luxuriant dissipations appear as almost epically gratuitous; in a perspective opened up by Bataille,
linking sexuality and primitive economic practice, we may perhaps see
Hulot's glorious 'gaspillage' as an erotic equivalent of the reckless
consumption of the *potlatch*.

The price of Hulot's recklessness (which the text in no way attempts
to conceal) is pure havoc; disorder and destruction are Hulot's natural
mode and, as such, he is roundly condemned by the conventional
morality of the 'discours'. But, unlike most of Balzac's other destroyers
(compare him, for example, with Lisbeth Fischer in the same novel), the
havoc created by Hulot does not spring from cruelty, hatred, frustration, neurosis, from some radical distortion or deprivation of the self.
Whereas the self-destructive obsessional behaviour of Balzac's other
'monomaniacs' is usually the manifestation of a neurotic displacement
of a primordial energy, Hulot's headlong flight into disintegration is
conducted in a state of almost unalloyed bliss; his plunging of self and
others into ruin brings the discovery not of anguish but of an expansive
'bonheur'. Thus, when he abandons Elodie for the next child-prostitute
Atala, and is thereby led even deeper into moral and physical squalor,
his own reaction is exclusively one of joy: 'Oh, je suis heureux, dit le
baron, dont la figure était éclairée par la joie d'un futur et tout nouveau
bonheur' (466–7). In a more conventional narrative one might perhaps have expected the 'moralist' in Balzac, the mind so strongly
committed to the ideology of 'order', to have linked the emphasis on
dispossession and dereliction to a principle of nemesis, a fate to be
experienced by Hulot as a deserved punishment for his transgressions.
Yet the exact opposite is the case: Hulot's hovel becomes not the inferno
of retribution, but the playground for the unalienated ego. His social
collapse, his triumphant release from the bondage of custom furnishes
the context for an experience of unconstrained rejuvenation and gratification. The social edifice is, of course, rebuilt on the ruins of Hulot's
wild adventure; Victorin restores the family fortunes; the social wheels
begin to turn again. But at the same time Hulot himself endures,
destructive and indestructible, menacing yet exhilarating. And in that
polarity of menace and exhilaration is to be found the coda to the whole
book. Through the ambivalent creation of Hulot, Balzac not only
organizes, intuitively and imaginatively, what Freud was to organize
abstractly and schematically; in his ability, so to speak, to wear two caps
at once, to sustain a deep ideological commitment to the values of social
order along with an equally deep imaginative engagement with the
dynamism of libido, he reaches out into an exploration of the ambiguities, antagonisms, contradictions between our sexuality and our
sociality—the contradiction between our submission to law and our
impulse to transgression.

Naturally, at the level of narrative form, such a creation cannot possibly be 'explained' in terms of the *vraisemblable*. Yet to describe Hulot as *invraisemblable* and then to dismiss him on these grounds, may well be simply an index of the repressions enacted in our own vision of 'life'. If we cannot see Hulot properly, it is precisely because our *vraisemblable* will not let us see, and this is exactly its cultural and ideological function—to protect us from danger;[42] it protects us by enabling us to reject as 'incredible', 'unrealistic', 'melodramatic' that which threatens its norms and its constraints. But if 'melodrama' is still a meaningful criterion here, then what we must speak of is the existence in *La Cousine Bette* of a powerful melodrama of subversion. In its feel for the euphoria of transgression, in its partial liquidation of the formal categories of the conventional 'character', *La Cousine Bette* is a text of negation, challenging and subverting, not the values of social order as such (which would be crude and banal in the extreme), but the assumption by that order of its own unmovable security, a challenge that includes the novel itself in terms of its role as instrument of naturalization. Paradoxically, it may well be that the beginnings of that dismantling of the 'Balzacian novel', so often adduced as the exemplary model of that naturalized *vraisemblable* which it is the self-appointed task of the modern novel to deconstruct,[43] are already to be found in the novels of Balzac.

III Conclusion

9 The official history and the secret history

Vous ne me paraissez pas fort en Histoire. Il y a deux Histoires:
l'Histoire officielle, menteuse qu'on enseigne, l'Histoire *ad usum
delphini*; puis l'Histoire secrète, où sont les véritables causes des
événements, une histoire honteuse.
(*Illusions perdues*, IV, 1020)

Despite ongoing controversy as to the ultimate quality of his work,
Balzac, at least in the French literary consciousness, has long since been
admitted to the pantheon of the 'classic'. In the present state of critical
affairs, that can of course be a dubious compliment, as current theoretical discussion in France (in particular that inspired by Barthes's theory
of the *texte classique*) has complicated the concept in new ways, and
effectively reduced it to being but the poor relation of the 'modern'. I
am using the notion of the 'classic' in the simpler, but still serviceable,
sense of a work that endures, though does not remain static in the ways
in which it is read, because sufficient people consider it to be of major
importance. This simplicity of usage can nevertheless disguise a great
deal. For, as Frank Kermode has shown,[1] the cultural processes and
critical choices which lie behind the establishing of a writer as a classic
constitute a remarkably complex, many sided and often contradictory
phenomenon; as his recent book amply demonstrates, the question
'what is a classic?' or rather, 'how does a work come to be seen as a
classic?' demands an extremely sophisticated set of answers. One such
process singled out by Kermode, although not endorsed by him, in
connection with the interpretation of a 'modern classic' (*Wuthering
Heights*), is the progressive discarding of what is assumed as the dead
matter of the text, to arrive at a sense of the living and enduring 'essence'
that guarantees its status as a classic. Representative of this form of
reasoning is Q.D. Leavis's essay 'A Fresh Approach to *Wuthering
Heights*'. For Mrs Leavis, *Wuthering Heights* is a great 'realistic novel',
but a serious account of its greatness requires a rigorous exclusion from
critical attention of all those aspects of the text which she classifies under
the heading of 'unregenerate writing'[2]—roughly, all the period
'Romantic' and 'Gothic' elements, entailing, among other things, a
relegation of the figure of Heathcliff to a position of virtual insig-
nificance, a mere product of self-indulgent Gothic fantasy.

Although the specific terms differ, the general process whereby
Balzac has been 'classicized' is strikingly similar. In his recent study of

the development of Balzac's critical reputation in the second half of the nineteenth century, David Bellos has shown how, largely under the influence of Faguet, Balzac became a 'classic'—an example of what Faguet called the tradition of 'réalisme classique'—by a systematic excommunication from the *oeuvre* of all those features which Faguet, using the term in its pejorative sense, bundles into the category of the 'romanesque'.[3] Balzac thus survives and travels but, under the surgical knife of Faguet, travels exceedingly light—Balzac without his belly, one might say. Yet, stripped of its excess weight, purged of its 'impurities', it may have less the aspect of a streamlined, robust classicism than a slightly anaemic air. Certainly, consecration of this kind is purchased at a high price. At the simplest level, it requires that we ignore what is after all there, in the text, and, while not every item is necessarily of equal value, and while in the act of reading the individual reader will pay more attention to some than to others, it would seem, minimally, *a priori* plausible that the greatness of a writer should not have to depend on dispensing with substantial parts of his text. This, in essence, is the difficulty located by Kermode in Mrs Leavis's hierarchical description of *Wuthering Heights* which, in order to bring out what she sees as its important qualities, consigns a great deal of the book to the critical waste paper basket. Kermode's view of the matter is more interesting and more convincing: he argues that we have no need, indeed no authority, to 'explain away' the outwardly embarrassing features of the novel, since it is one of the marks of the 'classic' that it is susceptible of plural readings, open to 'production' by the reader, and that consequently what Mrs Leavis feels compelled to jettison as 'unregenerate', as unreconstructed 'Gothic' or 'fairy tale', can, by virtue of the constitutive openness or indeterminacy of the text, be regenerated through active and creative forms of reading.[4]

Although this is not the place to get deeply embroiled in the theory of the plural text and its extensive 'rewritability', this broadly is the perspective in which the question of 'melodrama' in Balzac should, I think, be negotiated. Naturally, there are constraints on what can legitimately be done within this perspective; rudimentary conditions of the acceptability of a particular reading would be that it meet generally accepted criteria of intelligence and coherence (what Kermode, perhaps somewhat problematically, refers to as 'competence'). Equally, there are likely to be areas in the economy of the text with zero potential for 'productivity' by the reader. Doubtless there is some dead weight in the *Comédie humaine*, which no ingenuity of critical interpretation could possibly hope to revivify (to 'rewrite', as Barthes would put it) and, had the object of this study been a comprehensive survey of everything that could reasonably be described as 'melodramatic' in the *Comédie*, this limitation would have had to be taken more fully into account. Yet, although comprehensiveness has not been my aim, I believe I have touched, in one way or another, on all the major manifestations of 'melodrama' in Balzac's work. I have done so, because its presence is substantial and because, as a consequence, the critical argument that Balzac is great (is a 'classic'), despite the melodrama, seems inherently unsatisfactory. A more honest, or at least a more consistent, approach for a critic deeply troubled by the presence of melodrama in the *Comédie humaine* would be to argue that Balzac, for this reason, is not a novelist of the first rank, that he is not an eligible candidate for admission to the canon of the classic. Such a view can be plausibly developed (though sometimes with bizarre results: Martin Turnell manages the extraordinary feat of analysing and dismissing *Le Père Goriot* as immature melodrama without once mentioning, let alone discussing, the figure of Rastignac).

The view elaborated in this book has been quite different. It is unquestionably the case that melodrama in Balzac is heavily over-determined, and that, although crude period factors are part of the explanation of the melodramatic syndrome in the *Comédie humaine*, they are by no means the whole explanation. The youthful potboilers, contact with the general atmosphere of *le romantisme frénétique*, the commercial attractions of the *roman-feuilleton*, feelings of jealousy and rivalry vis-à-vis Eugène Sue, all these were undoubtedly determining circumstances in generating and keeping alive the melodramatic element in his work. But at the same time—as I hope I have succeeded in showing—other, more complex forces enter into both the making and the exploitation of the literary choices traditionally attributed to these unpromising circumstances, transforming the raw 'stuff' of melodrama in ways which not only transcend its customary functions, but which can also be said to contribute to some of the deepest artistic effects of the novels.

To understand the general significance of these transformations, it is necessary to return once more to the question of the function of melodrama. In chapter 1, following other commentators, I sketched a functional account of melodrama centred on the principle of fantasy: melodrama, both on the stage and in the popular fiction of the period, was essentially a form of mechanical entertainment providing an escape route from the repressions, boredom, deprivations of daily life; it offered a 'dream world' of vicarious excitements and wish-fulfilments, a series of gratifications of various kinds, but of which the most important was a fantasy of reassurance, a belief in the ultimate security and rightness of the moral order. Melodrama will characteristically present a catalogue of woe, disaster, misfortune, but in the end everything will come out right. Melodrama is thus profoundly conservative, and this in turn suggests—it has been implicit throughout the course of this book—another, related but deeper, function: that of confirmation, of confirming an existing order of meaning and reality, of complicity in the public, stereotyped meanings of what, adapting Aristotle, has been called the nineteenth-century *doxa*. Certainly, only the most ingénu of readers or spectators could have literally confused the 'dream world' of most nineteenth-century melodrama with the actual world he inhabited, but the point concerns less a relation of mimesis (although this in fact has some bearing on the question) than a confluence of symbolic orders. While it has been shown that, as a 'popular' form articulating certain needs and desires of a mass public, melodrama often contained a kind of 'protest' element, in particular an expression of class resentment (generally anti-aristocratic in the form of the upper class 'villain'), its essential structures and resolutions did not fundamentally trouble the implicit assumptions through which the nineteenth century represented its reality to itself; in the typical convention, 'villains', after all, were punished, the system cleansed of its malefactors, and order comfortably and comfortingly restored.

In their most significant manifestations, the operations of melodrama in Balzac are utterly different, paradoxically working above and against the self-confirming and self-reassuring images of nineteenth-century public versions of reality. As an example, let us briefly reconsider the role played by that primary strategy of melodramatic writing, mystery. In the conventional text, the posing of the mystery is initially a source of disturbance, even of menace, an invitation into zones of darkness and confusion, evil and transgression. It is, however, a specious invitation, titillation rather than exploration. For the unravelling of the mystery leads not to a worrying knowledge of a frightening or equivocal reality, but to the euphoric re-emergence of a stable moral universe; the moment of 'truth', the resolution of the enigma, coincides perfectly with the affirmation of order. As Peter Brooks puts it, 'Nous avons remarqué que les mélodrames commençaient souvent dans une atmosphère de mystère et d'énigme; le début de la pièce présente un certain nombre d'ambiguités morales apparentes. . . . Ces mystères se révèlent être le résultat d'une machination, d'une occultation maligne et délibérée; ils ne sont pas inhérents à la morale elle-même dont il sera demontré qu'elle peut et doit être sans ambiguité . . . De telle sort que la bravoure et la percée de la vertu ont pour but de nous assurer—encore et encore—qu'une lecture morale de l'univers est possible, que l'univers possède une identité et une signification morales.'[5] That this strategy stands in a direct relation to the taken for granted beliefs and attitudes of the official culture of the nineteenth century, is borne out by the fact that, over and over again, its specific content is that of the initial dispersal and eventual reunion of a family. I have already mentioned that the characteristic form of the mystery in melodrama is one of kinship, a continual ringing of the changes on the formula of abandoned children, lost fathers and the like. The theme of the dismembered family is, however, but a preamble to, a pretext for, its ideological superior, the theme of the reunited family, and the unfolding of the mystery becomes, precisely, the occasion for a happy family get-together, as well as a kind of moral (indeed often also a material) prize-giving. What is sundered is welded together again; loss gives way to discovery, wounds to healing; children cut off from parents by offending the parental codes are finally reincorporated through forgiveness; through highly mysterious concatenations of circumstance, 'orphans' learn that they are not in fact orphans, 'bastards' that they are not in fact illegitimate; around the corner of the fifth act or last chapter of countless melodramas there waits the lost and benevolent parent, usually the father—the forgiving father, the discovered father, two of the fundamental *topoi* of melodrama. We know of course the privileged place of the idea of the family in nineteenth-century ideology, and in particular the stress on the regulating and integrating authority of the father. Through its devices of recognition, rediscovery and reconciliation, the strategies of the 'hermeneutic code' in contemporary melodrama repeatedly endorse that privileged place (it is explicitly acknowledged in the remark by one of the characters in Pixerécourt's *La Femme à deux maris*: 'Un père offensé qui pardonne est la plus profonde image de la divinité'[6]).

In Balzac, however, the convention is, as it were, turned on its head; it is not a question of discovery or reconciliation, but of concealment and exploitation. In *Le Père Goriot* the kinship mystery is not one where deprived or wayward children are finally granted access to the haven of parental security but, on the contrary, is founded on the conscious suppression and expropriation of the father by his daughters. What is revealed is a scandal, a travesty of familial ideology, and the text organized around this revelation is written not in conformity with, but as radical questioning of, the endoxal text of nineteenth-century society. In other words, the mystery story provides a context for the realization of one of the deepest aims of the *Comédie humaine*—the rewriting of the official history of society in terms of the project of the secret history, that 'histoire honteuse', in the phrase form *Illusions perdues*, 'cette histoire secrète du genre humain', as Balzac formulates it in *Une Heure de ma vie*.[7] The mystery may have whetted the appetite of the readers of *Le Père Goriot* when it first appeared in instalments in the *Revue de deux mondes*, but its revelations were scarcely compatible with the cherished beliefs of many of those readers in the sacred family as part of the natural order of things (significantly, *Le Père Goriot* was generally considered to be both one of the most 'exaggerated' and one of the most 'immoral' of Balzac's novels). The extent to which Balzac's use of the mystery story works against the bulwark of nineteenth-century 'common opinion' may perhaps be gauged from a remark within the text itself. At one point early in the novel Madame Vauquer expresses complete disbelief at the suggestion that the rich and beautiful young women who visit Goriot at the Pension Vauquer are in fact his daughters:

> Quant aux femmes qu'il nommait ses filles, chacun partageait l'opinion de madame Vauquer, qui disait, avec la logique sévère que l'habitude de tout supposer donne aux vieilles femmes occupées à bavarder pendant leurs soirées: 'Si le père Goriot avait des filles aussi riches que paraissent l'être toutes les dames qui sont

venues le voir, il ne serait pas dans ma maison, au troisième, à quarante-cinq francs par mois, et n'irait pas vêtu comme un pauvre.' Rien ne pouvait démentir ces inductions. (II, 870-71).

On inherited, taken for granted models of familial relationships, Madame Vauquer's reasoning, her 'inductive' logic, is sound enough, and her 'opinion' may be taken as representative of general opinion ('chacun partageait l'opinion de madame Vauquer'), as deriving from the unquestioned stock of received ideas that constitutes the *doxa* ('Rien ne pouvait démentir ces inductions'). But the development of the plot is precisely the negation of those 'inductions' (they are in fact deductions, based on prior general ideas in the light of which the existing evidence is interpreted – which is, of course, the essential mode of the *doxa*); the assumptions of 'common sense', of the natural attitude, are reversed by a narrative which, working through the convention of the mystery tale, reveals the concealed horrors of society; to put it another way, the hermeneutic code, far from confirming, actually subverts the cultural code, the former exposing that which the latter seeks to conceal or of which it is ignorant.

This gives to Balzacian 'melodrama' a quite radical function. *Le Père Goriot* is, rightly, considered one of Balzac's masterpieces, indubitably a 'classic' of nineteenth century fiction (it has become one of the archetypal 'prescribed texts'). However, returning to my opening remarks, what needs to be recognized, is that its status as such is not to be established at the cost of discarding those elements which *prima facie* spring from a discredited genre, but rather by reincorporating and reinterpreting them through new strategies of reading. It is, moreover, of the utmost significance that the mystery of *Le Père Goriot* is built around the question of fatherhood, including here not only Goriot, but the other figure of 'mystery', Vautrin and his bid for the 'paternity' of Rastignac. We have noted the importance of the father in nineteenth-century social discourse, and the confirmatory role played by conventional melodrama in this respect. Yet, at the very moment in history when the institution of the 'bourgeois family' becomes so heavily naturalized, so firmly part of society's 'frame of unquestioned constructs',[8] certain key works of literature begin to raise fundamental doubts and queries. As always in these matters, it is difficult to set a precise date to the beginnings of this process, but a meaningful starting point could well be with Rousseau. In his brilliant essay on Rousseau's *La Nouvelle Héloïse*, Tony Tanner has argued that that much neglected book dramatizes a certain 'problematics of the family', speaks to us of an 'imminent crisis in the particular family structure on which Western society was based'.[9] Tanner goes on to locate the centre of that crisis in the text's implicit questioning of the 'Word of the father' ('We are entering a period in which the Word of the father and all that it implies . . . starts to come into question'[10]), and further suggests that this becomes increasingly the case in the development of the nineteenth-century

novel. The study of the displacement or subversion of the authority of
the father in nineteenth-century fiction remains to be written, but
Balzac will not only have a central place in it, it will be his melodramatic
texts that will attract the greatest attention. For it is here that we
encounter one of the most fundamental contradictions of Balzac's
work. As we all know, Balzac was not only ideologically committed to
the notion of the authoritarian father, he was also obsessed by what has
been called 'le mythe de la paternité',[11] a myth which, in various guises,
pervades the whole of the *Comédie humaine*. Is it therefore a mere
accident that in many of the texts I have discussed under the heading of
'melodrama', the theme of the father is central, but is articulated in a
way completely at odds with the ideological standpoints and the
imaginative fantasies? Frequently, they are stories of parental authority
and filial obedience falling apart, of absent fathers, rejected fathers,
renegade fathers: Hulot betrays his responsibilities and is both resisted
and finally usurped by his son; d'Aiglemont is defied by his daughter
Hélène; Goriot is humiliated and destroyed by Anastasie and Delphine;
Vautrin's quasi-paternal schemes for Lucien come crashing to the
ground. At its deepest level, this general spectacle of betrayal, disarray
and collapse includes that primary support of the traditional symbolic
and social order, the name of the father. Citing Lacan's famous remark,
'C'est dans le nom du père qu'il nous faut reconnaître le support de la
fonction symbolique qui, depuis l'orée des temps historiques, identifie
sa personne à la figure de la loi',[12] Tanner shows how in *La Nouvelle
Héloïse* the father's obsession with his name is crucial to the structure
of command and taboo of which he is the crowning figure. In some
of the Balzac novels we have been considering something like the
reverse occurs. In *La Cousine Bette*, 'le baron Hector Hulot d'Ervy' abandons his name at the moment he abandons his position in society. In
Le Père Goriot Rastignac unwittingly betrays a conspiracy of silence
when he mentions the name of 'père Goriot' in Anastasie's drawing
room:

> En prononçant le nom du père Goriot, Eugène avait donné un
> coup de baguette magique, mais dont l'effet était inverse de celui
> qu'avaient frappé ces mots: parent de madame de Beauséant. Il se
> trouvait dans la situation d'un homme introduit par faveur chez
> un amateur de curiosités, et qui, touchant par mégarde une
> armoire pleine de figures sculptées, fait tomber trois ou quatre
> têtes mal collées. (II, 898).

Here, in a complete reversal of the traditional function, the name of the
father becomes the object rather than the subject of taboo, the great
unmentionable, index of a repression which, on his death bed, Goriot
will describe as a 'parricide' ('c'est un parricide' (II, 1072)) and generalize
into an apocalyptic vision of total social disintegration: 'Je proteste. La
patrie périra si les pères sont foulés aux pieds. Cela est clair. La société, le

monde roulent sur la paternité, tout croule si les enfants n'aiment pas leurs pères' (1070).

The actual or incipient breakdown of the integrated and hierarchical family unit is thus seen as an undermining of the essential principles of the social contract itself. And in its place—and again within the 'melodramatic' fictions—new contracts, new 'families', bizarre and disconcerting leagues and associations, begin to arise, relationships and connections which the official history would of course seek to deny (to dismiss as 'implausible', 'melodramatic'), but which it is the duty of the secret history to uncover. The passage from *Histoire des Treize* with which I began this book would here acquire a new significance; the anonymous 'fraternity' of the Thirteen, with its codes of loyalty and dependence in a context of mutual collaboration in crime and violence, reads like an admittedly lurid but nevertheless meaningful symbol of just such social processes of displacement and transformation; similarly, we should recall the ironic play on the motif of *la parenté* in *La Fille aux yeux d'or*, society seen as a 'family' bound together only by a common competitive pursuit of money ('Il n'y a là de vrai parent que le billet de mille francs'), and also Victorin's pact with Vautrin and Madame Nourrisson, effectively signing a contract for the murder of his father-in-law in order to protect the family interests betrayed by his father; above all, there is the complex network of relations that, in a grotesque parody of the hierarchical family (the king at the top, the criminal at the bottom), 'unites' so many diverse personnages in *Splendeurs et misères des courtisanes*. All this can, of course, be interpreted in a variety of ways. In the case of Hélène's rebellion in *La Femme de trente ans* or Hulot's transgressions in *La Cousine Bette*, one could interpret the text as enacting the primordial contradiction between the repressive structures of the family and the force of desire, particularly sexual desire. Alternatively, one could propose a more historically orientated reading, which laid the main stress on the disruptive pressures on social order of a developing nineteenth-century individualism. The merits of particular interpretations are not, however, the main issue. What matters is our general awareness of a potential for interpretation in these works; that they are, in Kermode's phrase, 'patient of interpretation',[13] and above all the recognition that it is precisely what a certain critical tradition would classify as 'unregenerate writing' which makes this potential available.

But most important of all are the implications of this displacement or dismantling of the authority of the father for the system of formal conventions regulating the text or, more accurately, for certain disruptions of the system within which the *Comédie humaine* overtly situates itself. It has not gone unobserved that Balzac established a close connection between the figure of the father and the position of the artist, an analogy completed by the introduction of a third term, that of God. Father-God-Artist constitute a three-term analogy or homology that underlies the very conception of the *Comédie humaine* itself. Goriot the father compares himself to God: 'Un Père est avec ses enfants comme Dieu est avec nous' (II, 956); 'quand j'ai été père, j'ai compris Dieu' (957); Vautrin's expression of his feeling for his young protégés, Rastignac and Rubempré, brings together all three terms: 'Moi, je me charge du rôle de la Providence' (II, 940); 'Je veux aimer ma créature, la façonner, la pétrir à mon usage, comme un père aime son enfant' (IV, 1032); 'Je suis l'auteur, tu seras le drame' (V, 727)); finally, Balzac himself, who in his letters to Mme Hanska frequently speaks of his creations as if they were his 'children', and who, in the preface to *Histoire des Treize*, asks of the literary enterprise the evidently rhetorical question, 'n'est-ce pas usurper sur Dieu?' (XI, 191). This analogical triangle has been interpreted (notably by Gaëtan Picon)[14] as articulating basically a 'myth of fecundity', the dream of a vigorous, proliferating creativity in which the artist both replaces and rivals the father and God; this link comes out strongly in the correspondence with Mme Hanska in the last years of Balzac's life, where the fear of declining sexual potency is explictly related to a fear of declining artistic powers. An equally plausible view however would be to see these metaphorical exchanges as reflecting a fantasy of mastery. The master of the house, the master of the universe, the master of the text—three roles which combine in Balzac's imagination to evoke an ideal of transcendent and omnipotent control. Above all, they are different incarnations of the master of the word; the word of the father, the word of God, the word of the artist are so many forms of the dream of the paternal discourse ('Le père est alors celui qui sépare', writes Michel Foucault, 'c'est-à-dire qui protège quand, prononçant la Loi, il noue en une expérience majeure l'espace, la règle et le langage'[15]), of a discourse grasped not just as a social language of command and prohibition, but as source of nomination itself, origin of what is known and named as 'reality'. The artist, in this perspective, thus becomes the ruler over the empire of meaning (recall Balzac's famous comparison of his artistic project with Napoleon's imperial conquests); within the economy of meaning, he is the founder and proprietor of sense, the controller (the Comptroller—'je pèse mes phrases et mes mots comme un avare ses pièces d'or'[16]) of sense; lord and master of intelligibility, the artist is the figure who transacts nothing less than 'reality' itself to the reader.

Which is to say that the issue, in literary terms, is one of representation. Largely because of the long history of its association with positivist notions of 'realism', with the theory of a literal transcription of the world 'out there', the deeper roots of the idea of representation or mimesis have often been overlooked by literary criticism. These roots are in the profound psychic connection between the principle of mimesis and, precisely, the desire for mastery. Aristotle hinted at the relationship when, in the *Poetics*,[17] he traced the origin of mimesis to the child's use of imitation and its role in the process of the child's learning to control its environment. Freud made substantially the same point in his reflections on mimetic childhood play,[18] while the anthropologists' studies of 'primitive' magic and art have shown clearly how imitation is often experienced as a means of dominating and taming the natural world. In these terms, the vast Balzacian enterprise of a total representation of reality may be said to originate in a primal impulse to mastery, to be the expression of a sustained will to power and appropriation, and its supreme instrument is, as for Louis Lambert, the wielding of a master language:

> Est-ce à cet ancien Esprit que nous devons les mystères enfouis dans toute parole humaine? N'existe-t-il pas dans le mot VRAI une sorte de rectitude fantastique? Ne se trouve-t-il pas dans le son bref qu'il exige une vague image de la chaste nudité, de la simplicité du vrai en toute chose?... N'en est-il pas ainsi de chaque verbe? Tous sont empreints d'un vivant pouvoir qu'ils tiennent de l'âme, et qu'ils restituent par les mystères d'une action et d'une réaction merveilleuse entre la parole et la pensée (*Louis Lambert*, x, 356).

> On décomposera l'homme en entier, l'on trouvera peut-être les éléments de la Pensée et de la Volonté; mais on rencontrera toujours, sans pouvoir le résoudre, cet X contre lequel je me suis autrefois heurté. Cet X est la PAROLE, dont la communication brûle et dévore ceux qui ne sont pas préparés à la recevoir. Elle engendre incessamment la SUBSTANCE (449).[19]

This of course is heady stuff, and it may therefore come as no surprise that Louis Lambert in fact goes off his head (and, moreover, attempts to castrate himself). Lambert loses his sanity, as do the other compulsive questors of the absolute in the *Comédie humaine*. Similarly, Goriot casts himself in the role of God, but his offspring reject and destroy him; Vautrin's 'creation' (his 'child', his 'work of art') dissolves before his very eyes because, manipulator *extraordinaire* though he is, he is nevertheless unable to control all the circumstances around him. In short, the fantasy is a grand one indeed, but life on the ground does not, and cannot, accommodate it. This has bearing on my main theme in two fundamental respects. Imitative duplication may play a decisive role in the development of the child's sense of its ability to shape his world, but he also has to learn not only the limits on the actual power of imitation, but also that imitation is an historically and culturally rule-bound activity; in formal terms, his imitations are not his unique inventions, but are regulated by conventions inherited from tradition and society. In the same way, literature, however ambitious and innovative, to the extent that it wishes to be accepted as a convincing representation or imitation of reality has to submit to the terms of what we might call the mimetic 'contract', that body of socially shared agreements about the nature of 'reality', without which the very idea of an acceptable 'representation' is impossible. In other words, in the sphere of actual literary practice, the dream of the all-powerful paternal discourse, custodian and arbiter of sense and reality, becomes distinctly banalized, simply part of the social space of language that is the *doxa*. Louis Lambert strives for the ultimate utterance, the absolute *parole*, but ends up in the *nuit profonde*, the empty silence of complete incommunicability. Frenhofer the painter, in *Le Chef-d'oeuvre inconnu*, yearns to create the picture that will be the uniquely perfect and complete expression of reality, but produces instead an unintelligible chaos of colour, just as Gambara's grand musical ambitions yield but an incomprehensible cacophony of noise. Balzac, although he clearly identifies with his crazy geniuses, nonetheless avoids their fate, because he knows that the true ruler of the empire of meaning is not God, the father, the artist, but the *doxa* (the former are but the delegates of the latter), and that a condition of intelligibility is necessarily involvement in the *doxa*, accommodation, at some level, of the emphases and strategies of the official history. Balzac's creations may, in some sense, be his 'children', but if they are to be received and accepted as recognizable members of the species in general, they must conform to a text which does not originate in the individual artist and over which he has no ultimate authority.

We have seen some of the ways in which the Balzacian text moves through the forms of the *doxa* in the construction of a persuasively 'realistic' account of reality. The presence of the *doxa*, as a series of formal and rhetorical devices, in the *Comédie humaine* is deep and pervasive, for it is the only area in which the dream of the paternal discourse could, in any real, concrete sense, have found expression. It is, strangely, the place in which the artist can maintain the attitude of a confident, authoritative control over his material precisely through passive acquiescence in an order of representation of which he is not the unique source. Yet—and this is my second and concluding point—if the paternal and the endoxal go hand in hand in a relation of mutual reinforcement (the 'wisdom' imparted by the father in the socializing of the child is basically of this kind), there is a dimension of the Balzac text which not only sees this relation clearly, but also resists and subverts it. Just as Vautrin finally loses control of his creation, so in Balzac's novels there is often the threat of a similar loss of control, over which the paternal word and the endoxal text hold no sway. There appears a margin of excess, the element of the unexpected, the implausible, the inexplicable, dislodging the 'father', undermining the *doxa*, subverting the official history, challenging the conventions of representation and intelligibility silently or explicitly posited by the text itself. I have tried to describe something of this contradictory process, particularly in the last two chapters, but it has been, in one way or another, a central theme elsewhere in the book. It shows itself in a number of ways, but the area in which the process is most acutely felt is that of the text's relation to the *vraisemblable*, within the definition of the latter as the realization, at the level of cultural production, of the consensus knowledge which underlies and legitimates literary strategies of 'representation'.

My argument has been that the melodrama, in its exploitation of excess, exaggeration, implausibility, plays a decisive role in undermining the supremacy of the *vraisemblable*. There is however a considerable logical difficulty here (there are probably many). Normally, melodrama and realism are supposed to be opposites, the one committed to conventions of *vraisemblance*, the other showing complete disregard for them; as James Smith puts it, 'conventions of melodrama allow plausibility and common sense to be violated with impunity.'[20] That sounds reasonable enough and, on these terms, it would then presumably be simply a matter of claiming that, whereas low melodrama violates these canons in trivial ways and for trivial ends, Balzac's melodrama does so for different reasons and with different results. This indeed has been part of my case. I have, however, also argued, or implied, that 'melodrama' and 'realism' occupy a common space, in that both draw upon and confirm the forms and assumptions of the *doxa*, itself the foundation of the codes of *vraisemblance*. There is clearly a possible contradiction here, and it is implicitly brought into focus, though not examined, by Smith when elsewhere in his book he remarks that the characters of melodrama are the characters 'who can be guaranteed to think, speak and act exactly as you would expect'.[21] It is not clear what the precise meaning of 'expectation' is here, and it could be construed purely as generic expectation; in any given melodrama we expect characters to behave in the way they typically behave in the genre as such, but do not confuse this expectation with those we bring to bear upon our experience of the everyday world, and hence our general notions of what is *vraisemblable*. Obviously there are many melodramas which no one could possibly confuse with his knowledge of 'real life', but this is not necessarily the case with our reactions to all forms of melodrama. The point at issue here concerns the ambiguous status of the stereotype. I have suggested previously that stereotypes are fundamental to melodrama, and also that they enter directly into our social constructions of reality. And herein lies the ambiguity. To identify a character or an action as stereotypic is, at least implicitly, to move in the direction of labelling it 'melodramatic'; it is that in which we cannot believe because it embodies an unacceptably simplified reduction of experience. On the other hand, what some might see as stereotypic can be, and often is, uncritically received by others as 'realistic', and hence it is that which deviates from the stereotype that is likely to be described as 'implausible', as *invraisemblable* (this logical sliding between categories will have been apparent in my discussion of 'pastoral' in the chapter on *La Femme de trente ans* where, on one set of criteria, it was the fixed stereotype that is the sign of the melodrama of the text but, on other criteria, it is Hélène's departure from those norms which attracts the description 'melodramatic'). Evidently, the solution to the problem revolves around discriminating different levels of reading, different levels of consciousness and changing historical circumstances. The 'natural attitude' of the Victorian middle-class reader doubtless saw that level of Dickens's *Oliver Twist* which represents the criminal class (Fagin, Sikes) and the bourgeois class (Brownlow, Maylie) in terms of the good/wicked polarity as corresponding to 'reality' itself (which is of course not to say that this is the *only* operative level in Dickens's novel). The modern reader, on the other hand, is more likely to read this aspect of the text as embodying a naive moral fantasy, and for which the appropriate critical description would be stereotypic melodrama. Conversely, the transgression of a prevailing code of *vraisemblance* at a given historical moment, though often disturbing, even outraging opinion of the day, may be evaluated by later generations of readers as one of the major sources of strength in the works in question. The seventeenth century, as we have had occasion to note previously, provides several illustrious examples of just this phenomenon: what Bussy-Rabutin called the 'extravagance' of the Princesse de Clève's avowal to her husband is now seen by us as crucial to the meaning of that book; Chimène's marriage to Rodrigue, which played such a prominent part in the *Querelle du Cid*, viewed as a violation of what seventeenth-century opinion assumed as 'normal', is for us an act without which the play could easily be remembered as, precisely, a banal melodrama of 'honour', each character acting entirely within the constraints of seventeenth-century stereotyped constructions of reality (we should of course avoid the danger of complacency here; we, too, are surrounded by our own unquestioned stereotypes, and thus inhabit our own 'melodramatic' universe).

At its most radical, therefore—and it is this which makes it such a fascinating subject—Balzac's 'melodrama', in turning against the *doxa*, subverts both a certain practice of 'realism' and a certain practice of 'melodrama', at just that point where they converge in repeating and consolidating a ready-made system of meaning. That Balzac was perfectly aware of all this—and this does not entail running back into the intentional fallacy and removing the productive participations of the reader—seems to me clear from a remarkable passsage in *Le Père Goriot*, where the narrator explicitly raises the question of the 'exaggeration' (the improbability) of what he is about to narrate. Everyone is familiar with the celebrated statement on the first page of *Le Père Goriot*: 'ce drame n'est ni une fiction ni un roman. *All is true*' (II, 848). This is usually interpreted as a residue of the typical eighteenth century hostility to the idea of 'fiction' and the concomitant device of insisting that the novel is not a novel, but the record of a 'true story'. However, what is always overlooked here is the observation which precedes this famous statement: 'Après avoir lu les secrètes infortunes du père Goriot, vous dînerez avec appétit en mettant votre insensibilité sur le compte de l'auteur, en le taxant d'exagération, en l'accusant de poésie. Ah! sachez-le: ce drame n'est ni une fiction, ni un roman. *All is true*... '. Two points arise from this passage. One of the first gestures of the text is indeed to deny the fiction in the fiction, but as a kind of pre-emptive strike against the reader's putative accusation of 'exaggeration'. In other words, it is assumed that the revelations of the narrative ('les secrètes infortunes du père Goriot', the secret history of society) will not be granted credibility by the reader; the reader will protect himself against the impact of the story by retreating behind the walls of a stereotyped *vraisemblance*. Thus, the 'truth' of the novel is consciously, even aggressively, posited as a challenge to the *doxa*, as functioning outside, in opposition to the established conventions of the *vraisemblable*. The second, and related, point concerns the possible implications of the phrase 'vous dînerez avec appétit.' The placing of a remark about writing and reading in the context of a remark about eating lends itself to a wide range of interpretative comment. One level of meaning seems clear: the reader's appetite for his meal will not be blunted, and his digestion not troubled, by the narration of the misfortunes of Goriot, in so far as the 'unappetizing' story can be conveniently put on one side, the threat to the ease and comfort of the reader disposed of by classifying the story as 'exaggerated', the 'drame' as a *mélodrame*. Translating the food reference into metaphor, the implied suggestion seems to be—and for the period it is a startling insight—that the text which will satisfy the kind of reader in question is the text which can be consumed like a meal, that is, the *vraisemblable* text of instantly consumable meanings and representations (we know the importance of the metaphor of 'consumption' in Barthes's theory of the *texte lisible*; is there not therefore a certain irony in encountering that very emphasis in the work of a writer held up by Barthes, although of course with certain important qualifications, as a model of that sort of text?). The reader of *Le Père Goriot* is thus both attacked and forewarned. The novel cannot be painlessly absorbed (digested) into the corpus of pre-existing, ready-made significations; in terms of these consumer expectations, it will almost certainly appear exaggerated, but it is precisely the degree to which it rides rough-shod over those expectations that it commands our attention as a major work of literature.

And here, finally, is the ultimate justification for taking Balzacian 'melodrama' as a subject of serious concern. We have had to unlearn a great deal in order to learn how to read Balzac properly: in particular we have had to educate ourselves into seeing his books not as homogeneous, monolithic structures, but as housing contradictions and discontinuities of various kinds. Modern crictical theory has played an enormous part in teaching us how to perceive these things, although it is arguable that, by virute of a misleading historical definition of the 'classic', the most fertile contributors to such theoretical developments have set quite unjustifiably narrow limits to the scope of these disruptive movements in certain texts of the past[22] ('Balzac' has for too long been used as a device in polemical exchange). But, in any case, the terms 'gap', 'fissure', 'rupture', 'discontinuity' now have a firm place in the vocabulary of contemporaty critical discourse, notwithstanding the ongoing resistances and rearguard actions of the *ancienne critique*. In this context, melodrama, or what, in terms of the old criticism, I have called *la part maudite* of the text, the despised and rejected bits of the *Comédie humaine*, become charged with a new force and meaning. Alongside the staid, banal sanity of the discourse of common sense representations, it appears, at its most memorable, with an air of liberating madness. In a highly suggestive remark, Eric Bentley has written of melodrama that in it 'the writer enjoys a kind of *Narrenfreiheit*—the fool's exemption from common sense.'[23] As a metaphor in criticism, 'madness' can of course be misused, just as, in mere fashionable dalliance with the difficult work of some modern thinkers, it can be ideologically misused by persons very comfortably adapted to their social environment. Yet, in its transgressions of the limits and boundaries of the *doxa*, Balzacian melodrama is, I think, best defined in the spirit of Bentley's remark. It is a very different madness from that which overtakes Balzac's imperial dreamers, with their demiurgic fantasy of seizing and moulding the world in a single act of total mastery: the one derives from the frustration or obstruction of a drive towards absolute dominion of the realm of meaning, the other from the deep recognition of the gaps and inadequacies in a received system of sense—the difference, as it were, between the initial moments of the madness of Lear (of the usurped father) and the madness of the fool which, in its constant play with contradiction, inversion, paradox, tells us of things which the legislating orthodoxies repress and the text of official knowledge ignores.

Notes

Notes to chapter 1

1 Ralph Waldo Emerson, *Letters and Social Aims* (London 1885), p. 254.
2 Marcel Proust, *'Balzac et Sainte-Beuve'* in *Contre Sainte-Beuve* (Collection Idées) (Paris 1954), p. 205.
3 'It was in fact one of the signal achievements of romantic idealism that it took precisely these elements of the popular novel and drama and made them yield unsuspected potentiaties.' Donald Fanger, *Dostoyevsky and Romantic Realism* (Harvard University Press 1965), p. 17. Fanger's book is unquestionably the best and most sustained study so far of the relations between serious fiction and popular writing in the nineteenth century. Some of my arguments inevitably overlap with his, in particular the impor- tant connection he makes between melodrama and the vision of the modern city developed in the work of Dickens, Balzac and Dostoyevsky. Most of the questions and problems I deal with, however, are ones with which Fanger's book is not concerned.
4 James Smith, *Melodrama* (London 1973), p. 3. For a study of Pixerécourt and his times, see Paul Ginisty, *Le Mélodrame* (Paris 1910) and Willie G. Harthog, *Guilbert de Pixerécourt: sa vie, son mélodrame, sa technique et son influence* (Paris 1912).
5 See Maurice Bardèche, *Balzac romancier* (Paris 1943), pp. 86 ff.
6 For a general discussion of the relations between 'Gothic' and 'melodrama', see Richard Chase, *The American Novel and its Tradition* (New York 1958), p. 37.
7 In his study of the relation of Dostoyevsky's novels to sources of nineteenth-century popular writing, George Steiner uses the terms 'Gothic' and 'melodrama' virtually as synonyms, without any damaging imprecision as to the general argument; *Tolstoy or Dostoyevsky* (London 1959) p. 193.
8 Michael Booth, *English Melodrama* (London 1965), p. 14.
9 Eric Bentley, *The Life of the Drama* (London 1965), p. 205.
10 *ibid.*, p. 210.
11 Robert B. Heilman, *Tragedy and Melodrama, Versions of Experience* (University of Washington Press 1968), pp. 65–86.
12 See Peter Brooks, 'Une ésthétique de l'étonnement: le mélodrame', *Poétique* XIX (1974), p. 354: 'la fonction primordiale du mélodrame est de redécouvrir et de réexprimer clairement les sentiments moraux les plus fondamentaux et de rendre hommage au signe du bien.'
13 Joyce's young hero in 'An Encounter' provides a good example of this kind of excitement in the reading of popular romances and pulp literature: 'But when the restraining influence of school was at a distance, I began to hunger again for the escape which those chronicles of disorder alone seemed to offer me.' James Joyce, *Dubliners* (London 1946), p. 19.
14 Brooks, 'Une ésthétique', p. 348.

15 Ann Radcliffe, *The Itálian* (London 1797) I, p. 124.
16 Eugène Sue, *Les Mystères de Paris* (4 vols, Brussels 1844) III, p. 250.
17 Keith Hollingsworth, *The Newgate Novel* (Detroit 1963), p. 4.
18 Sainte-Beuve, *Correspondance* (Paris 1935) II, p. 608.
19 Thackeray, 'Solitude in September', *National Standard* 14 September 1833.
20 Sainte-Beuve, 'Vérités sur la situation en littérature' in *Portraits contemporains* (Paris 1855), I p. 330.
21 John Bayley, 'Oliver Twist' in *Dickens and the Twentieth Century*, edited by J. Gross and G. Pearson (London 1962), p. 50.
22 Dickens, *Oliver Twist* (Oxford illustrated edition 1942), p. 363.
23 Northrop Frye, *Anatomy of Criticism* (Princeton University Press 1957), p. 47.
24 A. O. J. Cockshut, *The Imagination of Charles Dickens* (London 1961), p. 70.
25 Smith, *Melodrama*, pp. 50–55.
26 Bentley, *Life of the Drama*, p. 217.
27 Balzac, *Correspondance*, edited by R. Pierrot (Garnier, Paris 1960–69), I, p. 158.
28 Albert Prioult, *Balzac avant la Comédie humaine* (Paris 1936). Bardèche, *Balzac romancier*.
29 Sainte-Beuve, *Mes Poisons* (Paris 1926), p. 111.
30 André Le Breton, *Balzac, l'homme et l'oeuvre* (Paris 1905), pp. 71–3.
31 Gustave Lanson, *Histoire de la littérature française* (Paris 1906), p. 988.
32 Emile Faguet, *Balzac* (Paris 1913), p. 129.
33 Martin Turnell, *The Novel in France* (London 1962), pp. 223–4.
34 Steiner, *Tolstoy or Dostoyevsky*, p. 205.
35 See Leo B. Levy, *Versions of Melodrama: a Study of the Fiction and Drama of Henry James, 1865–1897* (University of California Press 1957).
36 Quoted in Bentley, *Life of the Drama*, Bentley does not give a source.
37 F. R. Leavis, *The Great Tradition* (London 1962), p. 231.
38 Dickens, *Oliver Twist*, p. 389. This irony has been stressed by Bayley, 'Oliver Twist', p. 68.

Notes to chapter 2

1 Sainte-Beuve, 'De la littérature industrielle' in *Portraits contemporains* (Paris 1863) I, p. 491.
2 Sylvestre de Sacy, *Rapport sur le progrès des lettres* (Paris 1867), pp. ii, 26.
3 *ibid.*, p. 4.
4 Amédée Duquesnel, *Du travail intellectuel en France* (Paris 1839), p. 157.
5 Alfred Nettement, *Histoire de la littérature française sous le gouvernement de juillet* (Paris 1854) II, p. 237.
6 Edmond Werdet, *De la librairie francaise* (Paris 1860). p. 118.
7 cf. Nicole Robine, 'La Lecture' in *Le littéraire et le social*, edited by Robert Escarpit (Paris 1970), p. 234.
8 cf. Norah Atkinson, *E. Sue et le roman-feuilleton* (Paris 1929); René Guise, 'Balzac et le roman-feuilleton', *L'Année balzacienne*, 1964.
9 René Bazin, *Questions littéraires et sociales* (Paris 1906), p. 78.
10 cf. Alan W. Raitt, *Life and Letters in France: the Nineteenth Century* (London 1965), p. 31.
11 cf. Louis Reybaud, *Jérôme Paturôt à la recherche d'une position sociale* (Paris 1846), p. 55: 'Que l'on songe ensuite aux femmes si avides de tout ce qui est imaginaire, et le succès de la littérature romanesque sera expliqué.'
12 The instructive figures here are undoubtedly those of the rising newspaper circulation: in the late 1820s the combined circulation for both Paris and the provinces totalled around 76,000; by 1830, the Paris figure alone was 60,000, and by 1846 nearly 200,000. The actual readership must, of course, have been much larger, since a newspaper was generally read by more than one person (cf. Balzac's *Les Paysans*: 'Après avoir roulé du Café de la Paix chez tous les fonctionnaires, le *Constitutionnel*, principal organe du libéralisme, revenait à Rigou le septième jour; car l'abonnement, pris au nom du Père Socquard, le limonadier, était supporté par vingt personnes. Rigou passait la feuille à Langlume, le meunier, qui la donnait en lambeaux à tous ceux

qui savaient lire.') The newspaper figures are important because their spectacular growth was due in large part to the invention of the *roman-feuilleton*, which in turn is the most significant context for a discussion of Balzac's relations with the general reading public. For the figures, see Charles Ledré, *Histoire de la presse* (Paris 1958).
13 Pedro Salinas, 'Les pouvoir de l'écrivain' in *Hommage à Balzac* (Unesco, Paris 1950), p. 370.
14 cf. Gilbert Mury, 'Sociologie du public littéraire' in *Le littéraire et le social*, pp. 205–21.
15 Pierre Barbéris, 'Balzac et la critique', *L'Année balzacienne*, 1968, p. 194.
16 Charles de Mazade, 'Romans d'hier et d'aujourd'hui', *Revue de deux mondes*, 1858, p. 238.
17 *ibid.*, p. 239.
18 Reybaud, *Jérôme Paturôt*, p. 58.
19 Raymond Williams, *Culture and Society, 1780-1950* (London 1968), p. 289.
20 cf. Raymond Giraud, *The Unheroic Hero* (New Brunswick 1957), p. 39.
21 Paul Féval, *Rapport sur le progrès des lettres*, p. 39.
22 Raymond Williams, *The Long Revolution* (London 1968), p. 169.
23 Quoted in André Maurois, *Les Trois Dumas* (Paris 1951), p. 172.
24 Reybaud, *Jérôme Paturôt*, p. 55.
25 Sainte-Beuve, 'Vérités sur la situation en littérature' in *Portraits contemporains* II, p. 332.
26 Philarète Chasles, *Chronique de Paris*, 9 April 1837.
27 Louis Reybaud, *Moeurs et portraits du temps* (Paris 1853) II, p. 158.
28 Charles de Mazade, 'De la démocratie en littérature', *Revue des deux mondes*, 1 March 1850, p. 916.
29 Leconte de Lisle, preface to *Poèmes antiques* (Paris 1928), p. 207.
30 Alfred de Vigny, *Discours à l'Académie française* (Larousse, Paris 1922), p. 189.
31 Raitt, *Life and Letters in France*, p. xx.
32 Stendhal, *Correspondance* (Pléiade, Paris 1962), III, p. 395.
33 Sainte-Beuve, 'Notes et pensées' in *Causeries du lundi* (Paris 1868–70) XI, p. 499.
34 Vigny, *Journal d'un poete* (Larousse, Paris 1922), pp. 64, 62, 60, 42, 102, 103.
35 Baudelaire, *L'Art romantique* (Garnier, Paris 1962), p. 687.
36 Flaubert, *Préface à la vie d'écrivain ou extraits de la correspondance*, edited by Geneviève Bollème (Paris 1963), p. 128.
37 *ibid.*, p. 20.
38 Goncourt, *Journal* (Paris 1935) II, p. 253.
39 Balzac, *Correspondance*, edited by Roger Pierrot (Garnier, Paris 1960–69).
40 Félix Davin, *Études de moeurs aux XIXe siècle* (Pléiade, Paris 1965) XI, p. 228.
41 *Correspondance* I, p. 449.
42 Balzac, *Lettres à Mme Hanska*, edited by Roger Pierrot (Delta, Paris 1967–9) III, p. 225.
43 *ibid.* I, p. 99.
44 Quoted *ibid.* II, p. 420.
45 Sainte-Beuve, *Causeries du lundi* XI, p. 497.
46 *Correspondance*, I, pp. 36, 108.
47 *Lettres à Mme Hanska* I, p. 623.
48 *Correspondance* I, p. 98.
49 *ibid.*, p. 543.
50 *ibid.*, p. 417.
51 Salinas, *Hommage à Balzac*, p. 390.
52 *Avertissement quasi-littéraire*, *Le Cousin Pons*, Pléiade Vol. CI. p. 421.
53 *Correspondance* III, p. 591.
54 *ibid.* I, p. 113.
55 *Préfaces*, Pléiade. Vol. XI. p. 393.
56 *ibid.*, p. 302.
57 *ibid.*, p. 284.
58 *ibid.*, p 336.
59 *ibid.*, p. 138.
60 *Lettres à Mme Hanska* I, p. 40.
61 *Correspondance* I, p. 463.

62 *Préfaces*, p. 426.
63 René Guise, 'Balzac et le roman-feuilleton', *L'Année balzacienne*, 1964.
64 *Correspondance* II, p. 167.
65 *ibid.*, p. 192.
66 Quoted in Maurice Regard, *Introduction, Béatrix* (Garnier, Paris 1962), p. xiv.
67 *Lettres à Mme Hanska* I, p. 645.
68 *Correspondance* IV, p. 23.
69 Reybaud, *Jérôme Paturôt*, p. 60.
70 *Correspondance* IV, p. 752.
71 *ibid.* V, p. 108.
72 *Lettres à Mme Hanska* I, p. 517.
73 *Correspondance* IV, p. 683.
74 *Lettres à Mme Hanska* II, p. 467.
75 *Préfaces*, p. 387.
76 *ibid.*, p. 370.
77 *Oeuvres diverses* (Conard, Paris. 1940) III, p. 272.
78 *Lettres à Mme Hanska* II, p. 158.
79 *Oeuvres diverses* I, p. 142.
80 *Ibid.* II, p. 39.
81. *Préfaces*, p. 375.
82 *ibid.*, pp. 254–5.
83 *ibid.*, p. 276.
84 *ibid.*, p. 171.
85 *ibid.*, p. 166.
86 *ibid.*, pp. 396–7.
87 *Oeuvres diverses* II, pp. 372, 274.
88 *Préfaces*, p. 418–19.
89 *Lettres à Mme Hanska* III, pp. 317, 428, 444, 477.
90 *ibid.* I, p. 553.
91 Guise, 'Balzac et le roman-feuilleton', p. 309.
92 Geneviève Delattre, *Les Opinions littéraires de Balzac* (Paris 1961), p. 338.
93 *Lettres à Mme Hanska* II, p. 535.
94 *ibid.*, p. 509.
95 *ibid.*, p. 229.
96 *ibid.*, p. 511.
97 *ibid.* III, p. 216.
98 *Préfaces*, p. 419.

Notes to chapter 3

1 T. S. Eliot, *Selected Essays* (London 1932), p. 415.
2 cf. James Smith, *Melodrama* p. 65.
3 André Gide, *Les Faux-Monnayeurs* (Paris 1925), p. 236.
4 Eugène Sue, *Les Mystères de Paris* III, p. 339.
5 Marcel Proust, *A la recherche du temps perdu* (Pléiade, Paris 1954) I, p. 44.
6 Boris Pasternak, *Dr Zhivago* (London 1967), p. 485.
7 *ibid.*, p. 21
8 Ralph Maitlaw, 'A Visit with Pasternak', *The Nation*, 12 September 1959, cited in W. J. Harvey, *Character and the Novel* (London 1965), pp. 138–9.
9 *Oeuvres diverses* II, p. 109.
10 *ibid.* I, p. 622.
11 *ibid.* III, p. 277.
12 In *La Cousine Bette* Balzac himself explicitly draws the analogy between the structure of tragedy and the structure of his own novel: 'Ici se termine en quelque sorte l'introduction de cette histoire. Ce récit est au drame qui le complète... ce qu'est toute exposition à toute tragédie classique' (VI, 264).
13 Antoine Allemand, *Unité et structure de l'univers balzacien* (Paris 1965), p. 85.
14 Quoted in Pierre Laubriet, *L'Intelligence de l'art chez Balzac* (Paris 1961), p. 34.

15 Karl Marx, *The Manifesto of the Communist Party* in *Selected Works* (London 1970), p. 38.
16 Thomas Carlyle, *Past and Present* (London 1872), p. 214.
17 *Journal des feuilletons politiques* in *Oeuvres complètes* (Conard, Paris 1912–40) XXXVII, p. 284.
18 *Scènes de la vie privée et publique des animaux* (Paris 1941–2) in *Oeuvres diverses* III, p. 436.
19 Carlyle, *Past and Present*, p. 126.
20 Lionel Trilling, 'Manners, Morals and the Novel' in *Forms of Modern Fiction*, edited by William Van O'Connor (Minneapolis 1948), p. 148.
21 cf. Lucienne Frappier-Mazur, 'Les Métaphores du jeu dans la *Comédie humaine*', *L'Année balzacienne*, 1969.
22 Dostoyevsky, *The Gambler* (London 1916), p. 154. See John Carroll, *Break-Out from the Crystal Palace, the Anarcho-Psychological Critique: Stirner, Nietzsche, Dostoyevsky* (London 1974), p. 158: 'The vision of the Midas touch, that everything can be had suddenly and for nothing . . . holds for the capitalist and the gambler alike.' Carroll pursues this analogy at some length, construing Gambler as a kind of 'ideal-type' embodying a 'vital psychological undercurrent' in the development of capitalism. Since he takes Dostoyevsky's story as his central literary text, it is somewhat surprising that he does not cite the passage we have quoted, since it is the only one in which the analogy is actually made explicit.
23 Trollope, *The Prime Minister* (2 vols, Oxford 1952) I, p. 29.
24 Carlyle, *Past and Present*, p. 232.
25 Ruskin, 'The Roots of Honour' in *The Genius of John Ruskin*, edited by John Rosenberg (Boston 1963), p. 238.
26 Eugène Buret, *De la misère et des classes laborieuses en Angleterre et en France 1840*, I, p. 236.
27 *Le Constitutionnel*, 25 March 1838.
28 Louis Reybaud, *Moeurs et portraits du temps*, pp. 23–4.
29 Walter Benjamin, commenting on the motif of the gambler in Baudelaire's poetry, has stressed how the nineteenth-century consciousness typically perceives its reality in terms of 'chance', but evaluates this as an index of its moral bad faith, as a way of evading responsibility for the socio-economic reality it has created by seeing itself purely as the passive victim of the random and uncontrollable forces of the 'market'; *Charles Baudelaire, a Lyric Poet in the Era of High Capitalism* (London 1973) p. 136. Clearly, the idea of 'chance' can have this ideological function, and it is therefore of the utmost importance that in *La Maison Nucingen*, as in other Balzac texts, the emphasis falls as much on the swindle as on the gamble; that is, the financier's actitivies are seen as much in moral terms as in circumstantial ones.
30 Jean-Louis Bory, *Vautrin* (Paris 1948), p. 51.
31 cf. Spoelborch de Lovenjoul, *Histoire des oeuvres de Balzac* (Paris 1886), p. 82.
32 *Lettres à Madame Hanska* II, p. 370.
33 *ibid.*, p. 423.
34 *ibid.*, p. 475.
35 *ibid.*, p. 229.
36 *ibid.*, p. 223
37 *ibid.*, p. 373.
38 Donald Fanger, *Dostoyevsky and Romantic Realism*, p. 19.
39 Quoted *ibid.*, p. 125.
40 Lionel Trilling, *The Liberal Imagination* (Peregrine Books, London 1970), p. 73.
41 *Westminster Review* 1866 in K. Graham, *English Criticism of the Novel* (Oxford 1965), p. 45.
42 Aristotle, *Poetics*, translated by S. H. Butcher (London 1951), p. 51.
43 Virginia Woolf, *Collected Essays* (London 1966) II, p. 101.
44 Quoted in Gérard Genette, *Figures II* (Paris 1966), p. 72.
45 Roman Jakobson, 'Du réalisme artistique' in *Théorie de la littérature*, edited by T. Todorov (Paris 1965).
46 *ibid.*, p. 100.

47 Roland Barthes, *S/Z* (Paris 1970).
48 Dostoyevsky, *Correspondence*, edited by N. Gourfinkel (Paris) IV, p. 120.

Notes to chapter 4

1 Tolstoy, letter to N. N. Strakhov (April 1876), quoted in R. F. Christiansen, *Tolstoy, a Critical Introduction* (Cambridge University Press 1969), p. 130.
2 Roland Barthes, 'Structure du fait divers', *Essais critiques* (Paris 1964), p. 191.
3 Dorothy Van Ghent, *The English Novel: Form and Function* (New York 1953), p. 163.
4 John Forster, *The Life of Charles Dickens* (2 vols, Everyman, London 1927)
5 Quoted *ibid.* II, p. 182.
6 cf. Peter Brooks, 'Une esthétique de l'étonnement: le mélodrame', p. 353: 'les mélodrames commençaient souvent dans une atmosphère de mystère et d'énigme.'
7 Albert Béguin, 'Balzac visionnaire' in *Balzac lu et relu* (Paris 1965), p. 81.
8 The idea of the 'limit-text' was first suggested by Georges Bataille, *Avant-propos* to *Le Bleu du ciel* (Paris 1957), p. 7. It is taken up by Roland Barthes in *S/Z* where Barthes argues that the transgression of the sexual divide (masculine/feminine) and, more generally, the subversion of the securities of classification and representation founded by the figure of antithesis is one of the more radical moments of *Sarrasine*.
9 André Rouveyre, 'Préface', *La Fille aux yeux d'or* in *L'Oeuvre de Balzac*, edited by A. Béguin and J. Ducourneau (16 vols, Paris 1950–53) I, p. 787.
10 The 'specularity' of this episode has been noted by Leyla Perrone-Moises, although she rather spoils her point by drawing a quite meaningless analogy with Lacan's theory of the 'stade du miroir'. 'Le récit euphémique', *Poétique* XVII (1974), p. 37.
11 cf. Gaëtan Picon, *Balzac par lui-même* (Paris 1956), p. 110.
12 Mario Praz, *The Romantic Agony* (Fontana Library, London 1962), pp. 131–2.
13 Marcel Proust, *Contre Sainte-Beuve*, p. 265.
14 See Béguin, 'Balzac visionnaire', pp. 81–7; Michel Gueude, 'La vision colorée dans *La Fille aux yeux d'or*', *Synthèses*, July-August 1970. There is also the (to me) quite unintelligible article by Maurice Laugga, 'L'Effet *Fille aux yeux d'or*', *Littérature*, December 1975, pp. 62–81.
15 I. A. Richards, *The Philosophy of Rhetoric* (New York 1936) p. 94.
16 Walter Benjamin, *Charles Baudelaire*, pp. 40–44.
17 George Orwell, 'Dickens' in *Collected Essays* (London 1961), p. 65.
18 Dickens, *Bleak House* (Oxford University Press 1948), p. 219.
19 Raymond Williams, *Modern Tragedy* (London 1966), p. 139. See also *The Long Revolution* (London 1961), p. 278, where 'the realist tradition in fiction' is defined as 'the kind of novel which creates and judges the quality of a whole way of life in terms of the qualities of persons. . . . Every aspect of the personal life is radically affected by the quality of the general life, yet the general life is seen at its most important in completely person terms.'
20 The terms 'totalizing' and 'totalization' are used with reference to the nineteenth-century novel by Terry Eagleton, *Exiles and Emigrés* (London 1970), p. 10.
21 Preface to *Une Fille d'Eve*, Pléiade, Vol XI, p. 374.
22 Georg Lukács, *Studies in European Realism* (New York 1964), pp. 6–8.
23 Martin Turnell, *The Novel in France*, p. 240.
24 Roland Barthes, *S/Z* (Paris 1970), p. 26.
25 Peter Brooks, 'Balzac: Melodrama and Metaphor', *The Hudson Review* XXII, no. 2 (1969), p. 214.
26 Peter Brooks, 'Balzac: Melodrama and Metaphor', *The Hudson Review* XXII, no. 2 (1969), p. 214.
26 *ibid.*, p. 215.
27 It is on this point that I would differ from Peter Brooks's fine analysis of *Le Père Goriot*. Citing Richards's definition of metaphor as a 'transaction between contexts'. Brooks argues that the juxtaposition and interpenetration of social worlds in *Le Père Goriot* is regulated by the figure of metaphor. It would seem however more appropriate to see the rhetorical logic articulating the structure of the novel as being of an essentially metonymic or synecdochic order. The Pension Vauquer and the Faubourg Saint

Germain relate to each other on the principle of contiguity; they occupy a common context (Paris), in the literal sense of physical contiguity and in the figurative sense of a pervasive moral squalor systematically conveyed throughout the novel by variations on the image of 'bourbier', etc. Hence, just as each unit of the description of the Pension Vauquer functions metonymically as an evocation of the whole, the whole of the description of Pension Vauquer may be said to express metonymically the totality of Parisian social reality, from top to bottom.

28 See the interesting description by Louis Chevalier of the physical and social topo- graphy of nineteenth-century Paris: 'les quartiers du centre eux-mêmes, où la crois- sance complexe et désordonnée de la capitale, enchevêtrant ruelles, passages, cours et culs de sac, a juxtaposé en un paysage que nous avons du mal à lire, les zones d'ombres et de lumière, les vues ensoleillées et les cloaques, les maisons bourgeoises et les taudis.' *Classes laborieuses et classes dangereuses* (Paris 1958), p. iv.

29 Maurice Bardèche, *Une Lecture de Balzac* (Paris 1964), p. 150.

30 François Mauriac, 'Actualité de Balzac' in *Hommage à Balzac*, p. 333.

31 See Donald Fanger, *Dostoyevsky and Romantic Realism*, p. 63.

Notes to chapter 5

1 Gérard Genette, *Figures I* (Paris 1966), p. 159.
2 Robert Heilman, *Tragedy and Melodrama*, pp. 84–5.
3 *ibid.*, p. 78.
4 François Mauriac, 'Actualité de Balzac', p. 332.
5 Maurice Allem, Introduction to *'La Cousine Bette'* (Garnier, Paris 1962), p. 1.
6 cf. Leo Bersani, *Balzac to Beckett* (New York 1970), p. 47.
7 Philippe Bertault, *Balzac* (Paris 1962), pp. 187–8.
8 Jean Hytier, 'Un chef-d'oeuvre improvisé', *Romanic Review*, April 1949, p. 91.
9 Maurice Bardèche, *Une Lecture de Balzac*, p. 162.
10 *La Démocratie pacifique*, 12 December 1846, quoted in André Lorant, *Les Parents pauvres* (Geneva 1967), p. 338.
11 Georges Poulet, 'La Distance intérieure' in *Etudes sur le temps humain* II (Paris 1952), pp. 122 ff.
12 It is on this point that I would disagree with Fredric Jameson's interpretation in *'La Cousine Bette* and Allegorical Realism', P.M.L.A. LXXXVI, April 1971, pp. 241–54.
13 *ibid.*, p. 249.
14 Bersani, *Balzac to Beckett*, pp. 41 ff.
15 Hippolyte Taine, *Essais de critique et d'histoire* (Paris 1858), p. 196.
16 *Lettres à l'Etrangère*, III, p. 541.
17 Quoted in F.W.J. Hemmings, *Balzac: an Interpretation of 'La Comédie humaine'* (New York 1967), p. 101.
18 For a discussion of the question of 'exaggeration' in Balzac, see below, chapter 8.
19 *Lettres à l'Etrangère* III, p. 216.
20 Michel Butor, 'Les parents pauvres' in *Répertoire II* (Paris 1964), p. 195.
21 The view of Maurice Allem may be taken as fairly representative: 'Lisbeth Fischer . . . n'est ni maltraitée par ses riches cousins, comme Pierrette, ni chassée de chez eux, comme Pons. . . . Ils ne se conduisent pas en mauvais parents; la mauvaise parente, c'est elle.'
22 Lorant, *Les Parents pauvres* II, pp. 37–8.
23 Percy Lubbock, *The Craft of Fiction* (London 1968), p. 204.

Notes to chapter 6

1 'One after another, the rarer, obscurer effects of fiction are all found in Balzac, behind his blatant front.' Percy Lubbock *The Craft of Fiction*, p. 204.
2 cf. Robert Baldick, *The Life and Times of Frédérick Lemaître* (London 1959).
3 James Smith, *Melodrama*, p. 43.
4 Leo B. Lévy, *Versions of Melodrama*, p. 15.
5 *ibid.*, p. 22
6 John Bayley, 'Balzac Possessed', *The New York Review of Books*, 4 October 1973, p. 25.

7 Lubbock, *Craft of Fiction*, p. 48
8 Roland Barthes, *S/Z*, p. 222.
9 F. W. J. Hemmings, *Balzac: An Interpretation of the Comédie humaine* (New York 1967), p. 58.
10 cf. Maurice Bardèche, *Balzac romancier*, p. 600: 'Sur toute une vie ou un fragment de vie, il laisse des zones de ténèbres, impénétrables au créateur lui-même, il tâtonne dans ces ténèbres, et par des signes, par des indices, il jette quelques lueurs malgré lui.'
11 Hugo von Hofmannsthal, 'L'Univers de la *Comédie humaine*', *Etudes balzaciennes* I (1951), p. 23.
12 Henry James, 'The Art of Fiction' in *The House of Fiction* (London 1962), p. 32.
13 Roger Kempf, *Sur le corps romanesque* (Paris 1968), p. 70.
14 Marcel Proust, *Contre Sainte-Beuve*, p. 257.
15 *Lettres à l'Etrangère* I, p. 665.
16 Maurice Bardèche, *Une Lecture de Balzac*, p. 226.
17 H. J. Hunt, *Balzac's Comédie humaine* (London 1964), pp. 228, 229, 231.
18 Bardèche, *Une Lecture de Balzac*, p. 226.
19 Joachim Merlant, 'Le manuscrit de Béatrix', *Revue d'histoire littéraire de la France*, July 1913, p. 633.
20 cf. Alain Robbe-Grillet, *Pour un nouveau roman* (Paris 1963), p. 115.
21 Marcel Proust, *A la recherche du temps perdu* I, pp. 125–6.
22 Letter to Réne Micha, quoted in R. Micha, *Nathalie Sarraute* (Paris 1966), p. 66.
23 Nathalie Sarraute, *Portrait d'un inconnu* (Paris 1956), p. 215.
24 Stephen Heath, *The Nouveau Roman, a Study in the Practice of Writing* (London 1972), p. 499.
25 Michel Butor, *Répertoire I* (Paris 1960), pp. 79–80.

Notes to chapter 7

1 John Bayley, *Tolstoy and the Novel* (London 1968), pp. 147, 149-50.
2 *ibid.*, p. 149.
3 *ibid.*, p. 150.
4 James Smith, *Melodrama*, p. 18.
5 Ramon Fernandez. 'La Méthode de Balzac' in *Messages* (Paris 1926), pp. 67, 71.
6 Samuel Rogers, *Balzac and the Novel* (University of Wisconsin Press 1953), pp. 103-116.
7 Emile Faguet, *Balzac*, p. 135.
8 For the genesis of *La Femme de trente ans*, see Pierre Citron's introduction to the Garnier-Flammarion edition (Paris 1965).
9 Maurice Bardèche, *Balzac romancier*, p. 262.
10 See Balzac's note in his private papers: 'Un livre intitulé *Même histoire*, composé de fragments détachés sans queue ni tête en apparence, mais ayant un sens logique et secret'. Quoted in Citron, p. 31.
11 cf. Richard Bolster, *Stendhal, Balzac et le féminisme romantique* (Paris 1970).
12 Bayley's phrase, in connection with Eugénie Grandet, *Tolstoy and the Novel*; p. 150.
13 *Lettres à l'Etrangère* II, p. 170.
14 *ibid.*, I, p. 295.
15 André Gide, *Journal* II (Paris 1954), p. 1218.
16 For a sustained discussion of this isssue, see Wolfgang Holdheim, *Theory and Practice of the Novel, a Study on André Gide* (Geneva 1968).
17 Ramon Fernandez, *Balzac* (Paris 1943), p. 167.
18 Stendhal, *Mélanges d'art, Oeuvres complètes* (Paris 1927–37), p. 42.
19 Michael Wood, *Stendhal* (London 1971), p. 12.
20 Stendhal, *Journal* in *Oeuvres intimes* (Pléiade, Paris 1955), p. 419.
21 Bayley, *Tolstoy and the Novel*, p. 156.
22 The phrase 'internalized probability system' is used by Leonard Meyer in connection with music; *Music, the Arts and Ideas* (Chicago 1967), p. 47. In the context of literary criticism it has been taken up by Frank Kermode, *The Classic* (London 1975), p. 119.
23 Jules Janin, *Journal des débats*, December 1830, quoted in Bolster, p. 43.

24 Simone de Beauvoir, *Le Deuxième sexe* (Paris 1949) I, pp. 364 ff.
25 Martin Kanes, 'Balzac and the Problem of Expression' in *Symposium*, fall-winter 1969, pp. 290–91.
26 Bardèche, *Balzac romancier*, p. 267.
27 Wood, *Stendhal*, p. 85.
28 'Etudes sur M. Beyle' in *Oeuvres diverses* III, p. 402.
29 Emile Faguet, *Politiques et moralistes du XIXe siècle* (Paris 1903), III, p. 51.

Notes to chapter 8

1 Philippe Sollers, *Logiques* (Paris 1968), p. 228.
2 Georges Bataille, 'La notion de dépense' in *La Part maudite* (Paris 1967), p. 44.
3 Quoted in the Oxford English Dictionary
4 Herbert J. Hunt, *Balzac's Comédie humaine*, p. 445; André Bellessort, *Balzac et son oeuvre* (Paris 1946), p. 338; Ferdinand de Brunetière, *Balzac, l'homme et l'oeuvre* (Paris 1906), p. 130; André Le Breton, *Balzac, l'homme et l'oeuvre* (Paris 1905), pp. 209, 222, 225.
5 Hunt, *Comédie humaine*, p. 57.
6 Hippolyte Castille, 'Monsieur Honoré de Balzac', *La Semaine*, October 4 1846, quoted in Spoelborch de Lovenjoul, *Histoire des oeuvres de Balzac*, p. 367.
7 Peter Berger and Thomas Luckmann, *The Social Construction of Reality* (Penguin, London 1971), pp. 69, 76–7.
8 *ibid.*, pp. 56, 82.
9 *ibid.*, p. 83.
10 Kenneth Burke, 'Literature as Equipment for Living' in *The Philosophy of Literary Form* (New York 1957), p. 256.
11 Gérard Genette, 'Vraisemblance et motivation' in *Figures II* (Paris 1969), p. 74.
12 See the comment of Berger and Luckmann on 'deviance': 'Since this knowledge is socially objectivated *as* knowledge, that is, as a body of generally valid truths about reality, any radical deviance from the institutional order appears as a departure from reality.' *Social Construction of Reality*, p. 83.
13 Tzvetan Todorov, 'Poétique' in *Qu'est-ce que le structuralisme?* edited by F. Wahl (Paris 1968), p. 149.
14 It is in fact far from 'clear' that Aristotle offered the kind of connection suggested by Todorov and others. As so often in matters of Aristotelian exegesis many of the problems arise at the level of the ambiguities created by translation across languages. The French *vraisemblable* is itself ambiguous. If we translate it as English 'probable', the generally accepted corresponding word for that in Aristotle's text is *eikos*. This of course is the key term of the discussion in *Poetics* about 'probability' or 'verisimilitude' in literature. But here there is no significant attempt to construct an argument linking *eikos* with *endoxon* or *doxa* ('common opinion'), Aristotle's main interest in *Poetics* being with the distinction between *eikos* and *anagkaion* ('necessary'). If, however, we translate *vraisemblable* as 'plausible' or 'persuasive', the Greek for that is *pithanon*. There is some discussion of the relations between *pithanon* and *endoxon* in *Rhetoric*, especially chapters 1–2 (cf., for example, 1355 a 17ff and 1356 b 26 ff), and in *Poetics* the notion of the poetic *eikos* is explicitly linked to *pithanon* ('For the purposes of poetry a convincing impossibility (*pithanon adunation*) is preferable to an unconvincing possibility (*apithanon dunaton*)'). Crudely reconstructed, one might therefore be able to represent Aristotle's argument as follows: the persuasive force of *pithanon* is articulated through a general order of discourse (the *eikos*) whose characteristic forms and arguments (such as the enthymeme) are manifested concretely in the stock of opinions that constitutes the *doxa*. In this network of relations, the system of literary verisimilitude which Aristotle discusses in *Poetics* would, to some degree at least, depend upon the moulding pressures of the *doxa*. What is evident, however, is that while it may perhaps be legitimate to infer a connection between *eikos* and *endoxon*, the strictly textual grounds for doing so are, to say the least, somewhat tenuous; it is simply quite misleading for Todorov to claim that 'Aristotle a clairement dit' that such a connection exists. Not surprisingly

perhaps, in citing the authority of Aristotle, Todorov does not in fact refer us to any actual source in Aristotle's own writings.

15 Rapin, *Réflexions sur la poétique*, quoted in Genette, *Figures II*, p. 73.
16 Scudéry, *Observations sur le Cid*, quoted in Genette, *ibid.*, p. 71.
17 *Lettres sur la littérature* in *Oeuvres diverses* II, p. 320.
18 *ibid.*, p. 320 (my italics).
19 *ibid.*, p. 278.
20 *Feuilleton des journaux politiques* in *Oeuvres complètes* XXXVIII, p. 244.
21 *Lettres à l'Etrangère* II, p.125.
22 Berger and Luckmann, *Social Construction of Reality*, p. 37.
23 *Lettres sur la littérature*, p. 278 (my italics). See Pierre Laubriet, *L'Intelligence de l'art chez Balzac* (Paris 1961), p. 37: 'Le vraisemblable semble devoir pour une bonne part être ce que reçoit l'opinion commune.'
24 Émile Benveniste, *Problèmes de linguistique générale* (Paris 1966), pp. 239, 242.
25 *ibid.*, p. 240.
26 Genette, *Figures II*, p. 66.
27 Berger and Luckmann, *Social Construction of Reality*, pp. 46, 53, 58.
28 Burke, 'Literature as Equipment', pp. 253, 256.
29 *Oeuvres diverses* III, p. 278.
30 Roland Barthes, *S/Z*, p. 222.
31 Georges Bataille, *L'Erotisme* (Paris 1957), p. 22.
32 Fredric Jameson, '*La Cousine Bette* and Allegorical Realism', p. 250.
33 Genette, *Figures II*, p. 78.
34 Nathalie Sarraute, *L'Ere du soupçon* (Paris 1956), p. 71.
35 James Joyce, *Ulysses* (Penguin, London 1969), p. 211.
36 Alain Robbe-Grillet, *Pour un nouveau roman*, p. 27.
37 Marcel Proust, *Contre Sainte-Beuve*, pp. 239, 264.
38 Samuel Beckett, *L'Innommable* (Paris 1953), p. 240.
39 The pun is borrowed from Jacques Derrida's essay on Artaud, 'La Parole soufflée' in *L'Ecriture et la différence* (Paris 1967), p. 281.
40 Georges Bataille, *La Part maudite*, p. 60.
41 *ibid.*, p. 38.
42 cf. Roland Barthes, *Critique et vérité* (Paris 1964), p. 16: 'Par un procédé de renversement habituel, l'incroyable procède du défendu, c'est-à-dire du dangereux.'
43 cf. Stephen Heath, *The Nouveau Roman, a Study in the Practice of Writing.*

Notes to chapter 9

1 Frank Kermode, *The Classic* (London 1975).
2 Q. D. Leavis, 'A Fresh Approach to *Wuthering Heights*' in F. R. Leavis and Q. D. Leavis, *Lectures in America* (New York 1969), pp. 83–152, quoted in Kermode, *The Classic*, pp. 131–4.
3 David Bellos, *Balzac Criticism in France, 1850—1900* (Oxford 1976), pp. 154–6.
4 Kermode, *The Classic*, p. 133.
5 Peter Brooks, 'Une esthétique de l'étonnement: le mélodrame', pp. 353–4.
6 Guilbert de Pixerécourt, *La Femme à deux maris*, *Théâtre choisi* (4 vols, Geneva 1971) I, p. 336.
7 *Une heure de ma vie* in *La Femme auteur et autres fragments inédits*, edited by Maurice Bardèche (Paris 1950), p. 243.
8 The phrase is taken from the sociologist Alfred Shutz, *Collected Papers: 1 The problem of Social Reality* (The Hague 1967), p. 33.
9 Tony Tanner, 'Julie and "La Maison Paternelle": another look at Rousseau's *La Nouvelle Héloise*', *Daedalus*, winter 1976, p. 23.
10 Tanner, 'Julie', p. 35.
11 Gaëtan Picon, *Balzac par lui-même* (Paris 1956), p. 114.
12 Jacques Lacan, *Ecrits I* (Points, Paris 1966), pp. 157–8.
13 Kermode, *The Classic*, p. 134.
14 Picon, *Balzac par lui-même*, p. 121.

15 Michel Foucault, 'Le "Non" du père', *Critique*, March 1972, p. 205, quoted in Tanner, 'Julie', p. 45.
16 *Lettres à l'Etrangère* I, p. 8.
17 Aristotle, *The Poetics* (1448b), p. 15. There is also a reference to children's imitative activities in *Politics*; *The Politics of Aristotle*, edited by W. L. Newman (Oxford 1902) III, p. 486.
18 Sigmund Freud, *Beyond the Pleasure Principle* (London 1922), pp. 14–16. On the connection between imitation and mastery in the writings of both Aristotle and Freud I am indebted to Leslie Hill of Selwyn College, Cambridge.
19 For a discussion of some of the similarities between Louis Lambert and Balzac around the issue of language, see Charles Affron, *Patterns of Failure in 'La Comédie humaine'* (Yale University Press 1966), pp. 114ff.
20 James Smith, *Melodrama*, p. 24.
21 *ibid.*, p. 18.
22 For a discussion of some of the problems arising out of Barthes's definition of the *texte classique/texte lisible*, see Frank Kermode, 'The Use of the Codes' in *Approaches to Poetics*, edited by Seymour Chapman (Columbia University Press 1973).
23 Eric Bentley, *The Life of the Drama*, p. 203.

Select bibliography

Allemand, Antoine, *Unité et structure de l'univers balzacien*. Paris, 1965.
Atkinson, Norah, *Eugène Sue et le roman-feuilleton*. Paris, 1929.
Bardèche, Maurice, *Balzac romancier*. Paris, 1943.
  Une Lecture de Balzac. Paris, 1964.
Barthes, Roland, *S/Z*. Paris, 1970.
Bataille, Georges, *L'Erotisme*. Paris, 1957.
  La Part maudite. Paris, 1967.
Bayley, John, *Tolstoy and the Novel*. London, 1968.
Béguin, Albert, *Balzac lu et relu*. Paris, 1965.
Bellos, David, *Balzac Criticism in France, 1850—1900*. London, 1976.
Benjamin, Walter, *Charles Baudelaire: a Lyric Poet in the Era of High Capitalism*. London, 1973.
Bentley, Eric, *The Life of the Drama*. London, 1965.
Benveniste, Emile, *Problèmes de linguistique générale*. Paris, 1966.
Berger, Peter (and Luckmann, Thomas), *The Social Construction of Reality*. London, 1971.
Bersani, Leo, *From Balzac to Beckett*. New York, 1970.
Booth, Michael, *English Melodrama*. London, 1965.
Bory, Jean-Louis, *Eugène Sue, le roi du roman-feuilleton*. Paris, 1962.
Brooks, Peter, 'Une esthétique de l'étonnement: le mélodrame'. *Poétique* XIX (1974).
  'Balzac: Melodrama and Metaphor'. *Hudson Review* XXII (1969).
Burke, Kenneth, *The Philosophy of Literary Form*. New York, 1957.
Butor, Michel, *Répertoire II*. Paris, 1964.
Delattre, Geneviève, *Les Opinions littéraires de Balzac*. Paris, 1961.
Eliot, Thomas Stearns, *Selected Essays*. London, 1932.
Escarpit, Robert, *Sociologie de la littérature*. Paris, 1964.
  editor, *Le littéraire et le social*. Paris, 1970.
Fanger, Donald, *Dostoyevky and Romantic Realism*. Cambridge, Mass., 1965.
Fernandez, Ramon, *Messages*. Paris, 1926.
Frye, Northrop, *Anatomy of Criticism*. Princeton, N. J., 1957.

Genette, Gérard, *Figures I, II*. Paris, 1966, 1969.

Heath, Stephen, *The Nouveau Roman: a Study in the Practice of Writing*. London, 1972.

Heilman, Robert, *Tragedy and Melodrama, Versions of Experience*. Seattle, 1968.

Jameson, Fredric, *La Cousine Bette* and Allegorical Realism'. *PMLA* 86 (1971).

Kempf, Roger, *Sur le corps romanesque*. Paris, 1968.

Kermode, Frank, *The Classic*. London, 1975.

Laubriet, Pierre, *L'Intelligence de l'art chez Balzac*. Paris, 1961.

Lévy, Leo, *Versions of Melodrama: a Study of the Fiction and Drama of Henry James*. Berkeley, 1957.

Lorant, André, *Les Parents pauvres*. Geneva, 1967.

Lubbock, Percy, *The Craft of Fiction*. London, 1968.

Lukács, Georg, *Studies in European Realism*. New York, 1964.

Picon, Gaëtan, *Balzac par lui-même*, Paris, 1956.

Praz, Mario, *The Romantic Agony*. London, 1962.

Prioult, Albert, *Balzac avant la Comédie humaine*. Paris, 1936.

Proust, Marcel, *Contre Sainte-Beuve*. Paris, 1954.

Rogers, Samuel, *Balzac and the Novel*. Madison, Wis., 1953.

Smith, James, *Melodrama*. London, 1973.

Steiner, George, *Tolstoy or Dostoyevsky*. London, 1973.

Todorov, Tzvetan, 'Poétique'. In *Qu'est-ce que le structuralisme?*, edited by F. Wahl, Paris, 1968.

Trilling, Lionel, *The Liberal Imagination*. London, 1970.

Turnell, Martin, *The Novel in France*. London, 1962.

Williams, Raymond, *Culture and Society*. London, 1968.
    The Long Revolution. London, 1968.

Index